MAN'S MEASURE

MAN'S MEASURE

A Study of the Greek Image of Man
from Homer to Sophocles

by Laszlo Versényi

Albany

State University of New York Press

1974

Published by
State University of New York Press,
99 Washington Avenue, Albany, New York 12210

First Edition

© 1974 State University of New York. All rights reserved.
Printed in the United States of America.

Library of Congress Cataloging in Publication Data
Versényi, Laszlo.
Man's measure: a study of the Greek image of man
from Homer to Sophocles.
Bibliography: p.
1. Greek literature—History and criticism. I. Title.
PA3052.V4   880'.9'35   73-17420
ISBN 0-87395-254-5
ISBN 0-87395-255-3 (microfiche)

For Adam and Andrea

Contents

Acknowledgments

I am indebted to the National Endowment for the Humanities for its award of a Senior Fellowship and to Williams College for granting me extended leave from teaching duties so that I would be able to complete this study.

Thanks are due to Margaret Mirabelli, copyeditor and friend, who helped eliminate from the manuscript my worst offenses against the English language.

Introduction

This is a study of the development of the Greek image of man from Homer to Sophocles. Its aim is to present the pre-Socratic views that formed the background and prepared the ground for the emergence of the first truly philosophical reflection on human nature in Socratic thought.

This is not a complete, all-inclusive historical account. It concentrates on significant and critical turning points in the history of early Greek thought and discusses only a few representative works and trends in an attempt to highlight that history.

Although this study emphasizes the close relationship between form and content in early Greek thought and attempts to delineate the parallel development of the Greek image of man and of the form in which it is presented, its aim is primarily philosophical. Since different forms of communication allow for different modes of thought and are appropriate to the expression of different views of the nature of man, a study of form is at the same time a study of content and is undertaken here for the sake of the latter.

Chapter 1 inquires into the nature of myth and oral poetry and discusses Homer's notions of man, gods, fate, and time in order to show the correspondence between the structure of oral poetry and the structure of Homer's world. Oral poetry is paratactic, has a loose unity, strives for full visibility, and emphasizes what is present. The same loose parataxis, orientation toward full visibility, and concentration on the present are characteristic of Homeric morality, temporality, and world. The necessities of oral composition have shaped the content of oral poetry and limited what the oral poet could say and think. At the same time the *Iliad* was an end as well as a beginning, a turning point between oral and written literature, and the chapter ends by contrasting the two and forecasting what the introduction and use of writing would enable man to think and do.

Chapters 2–4 deal with the transformations of the Greek image of man from Hesiod to Solon. They show not only how conceptions of human nature and morality have changed in this period, but also how the use of writing, and the gradual realization of the possibilities inherent in this use, influenced and helped to bring about this change. Writing, with its fixity and permanence, made possible a new type of thought: one demanding coherence, unity, organic wholeness, and logical connection and fostering the development of abstract universal concepts that connote an underlying rather than immediately visible pattern, order, law. How and to what extent these demands were fulfilled and these new possibilities realized in the archaic period is the subject of these chapters.

Chapter 5 discusses Dionysian religion as a contrast to and partial reaction against this rationalization of Greek religion and morality. It shows what forms of expression and conduct are appropriate to a nonrational striving for mystical-emotional communion with the Divine, and how the Greeks came to terms with ecstatic religion by institutionalizing and taming it.

Chapter 6 focusses on some of the achievements and shortcomings of early philosophical speculation about man and his world.

Chapter 7 turns to tragedy. It contrasts the form and content of the first two plays of the *Oresteia* with those of the third and attempts to elucidate why the tragic view of life took the form of drama in fifth-century Athens and was presented in a theater with actors and chorus enacting scenes from Homeric myth before a communal audience.

Chapter 8 deals with Sophocles' *Oedipus Tyrannus*. A discussion of *Oedipus Tyrannus* provides a fitting conclusion to this study for two reasons. This greatest of Greek tragedies embodies the highest and most profound image of man in pre-Socratic thought. At the same time the *Oedipus Tyrannus* dramatizes the subject of this study—the development of the Greeks' self-discovery from Homer to Sophocles—by putting it on the stage as the growth and development of one paradigmatic individual's self-discovery. Sophocles not only crystallizes in Oedipus' person and life the history of a whole culture, but he also shows the ideal of that culture to be nothing but human culture: the self-cultivation of man.

1. *The* Iliad

"Sing, Goddess, the ruinous wrath of Achilles . . . " so the singer begins his song. The song tells a tale, a story, a myth. *Mythos,* in Homer's time, did not mean fable in our sense of the word; the tale was not something mythical, fabulous, fictional, and therefore untrue. Myth meant simply word of mouth, a story told rather than written down, winged words not fixed in an enduring medium but orally related and transmitted from generation to generation.

Such myth has a life of its own. The unwritten tale cannot be preserved totally unchanged; it changes imperceptibly in the telling. Each singer unavoidably recreates and transforms it in accordance with his own ability and dominant interest, each generation unknowingly projects itself—its own character and aspirations—into it. The story changes organically in line with the changes that take place in changing generations. Thus at all times myth mirrors the present and gives expression to the singer's—and hearer's—own experience of the world.

That is why living myth is always true; true, that is, to the experience, ideals, and aspirations of each generation. The myth of ten generations ago might clash with the present image of man and his world—if it had been preserved intact. But it never is, in an oral tradition. Precisely those elements which now might be felt to be alien and untrue—had they survived—have been eliminated in the gradual process of modification that living myth undergoes. Thus there is never any distance between living myth and its bearers; and since no distance, no critical reflection. The image a people gives itself in myth is an image in which it is reflected, not one on which it reflects. *Mythos* and *logos,* imagination and thought, are not yet distinct.

Living myth is true, furthermore, indeed it is the very instrument of truth, in the original sense of the Greek word *aletheia.*[1] For in its saying myth lays open to sight what without it would be utterly concealed; it reveals, lifts out of a primordial hiddenness and brings to light a whole world; it brings all things forth and gives them form: a visible palpable presence. Like Plato's Good, living myth is the source of all knowledge (*idein:* sight, vision, as well as *eidos, idea:* visible form and image), all truth (*aletheia:* disclosure, revelation), and all being (in the sense of appearing and shining forth rather than remaining in darkness and oblivion).

The world of myth is, in its own way, fully as timeless and unhistorical as are Plato's forms. Although myth is invariably a story of the past, it really knows neither past nor future. For the past presented in myth is only the present projected backwards, and the projection itself serves not to reveal a dead past but to hallow the living present. Situating it in a time long gone, and deriving it from a distant past, myth shows the present to be forever living and lends it weight and substance. It follows that myth knows no future. For if nothing truly past—and no longer living—is ever preserved (i. e., present as past), nothing can point to a time to which today's present would have to be a dead past for that future to be real future. Radical novelty is a category totally alien to myth; the very thought of it would appall mythical man. Since tradition hallows and justifies all, the utterly novel would be utterly ungrounded and without substance: the mere shadow of a shade. When the man of myth contemplates the future and wants to be remembered by generations of men to come, it is just such radical change that he wants to avoid: he wants to live on, beyond death, in the forever living present of the song.

All this does not mean that the people living in an age of myth are not conscious of the passage of time. As individuals, they witness others' birth and death, they grow old, and they know that they have to die, just as we do today. It is as a people that they are historically unconscious of another generation that lived, felt, and died in a way significantly different from theirs, of a generation that believed and valued, with the same assurance, something quite different from, something even opposed to, what they now believe and value. For they know no image, no experience, other than their own. This is what gives living myth its force: the unshaken authority of a tradition that has always been, the tremendous weight of a time without end that passes but does not change.

Once the story is written down, history begins. But this is the beginning of the end of myth. The singer, stilled, yields his place to the rhapsode who repeats rather than recreates. The song grows old, the fossilized story becomes archaic, the image no longer mirrors the present. But since the image is there in the written work it can no longer be changed; the present can no longer be presented in the guise of the past. The disparity between the two becomes more and more difficult to gloss over as the distance between them grows, and so, instead of myth being immediately present, it is presented by reflective thought as something past. Men thus acquire a real past whose image is substantially different from that of the present, but in the process they lose the authority of an unchanging tradition and communal belief which were the strongest supports of myth. The spell of the song is broken. What is new is seen as new, and therefore in need of a new justification. No longer can men claim—as the singers did—to be mere transmitters of an ageless truth. Unhallowed by tradition, the new word lacks authority and imposes the burden of critical reflection and appropriation on each man. Critical freedom and responsibility of thought are born together.

As a last step signifying the death of myth, the very meaning of the word *mythos* is changed to "fabulous, fictional, factually untrue tale." We pass thereby from image to concept, from communal immediacy to individual reflection (reflection on what separates generations as well as on what is common to all), from mere individual consciousness of temporality to a more embracing consciousness of historical change and underlying unity. We pass from *mythos* to *logos*.

* * * * * *

One might question the appropriateness of these remarks on living myth to a discussion of the *Iliad,* a poem which, by virtue of the mode of its preservation, seems to belong to a literate, rather than oral, mythical, tradition. After all, the one fact that is beyond controversy in the whole field of the Homeric problem is that the *Iliad,* in the form in which it is extant, was written down, and so its poet—the man who did the writing or dictated the text—undoubtedly lived in a—however limited—literate culture. Whether or not he himself knew how to read and write, some others did. Some form of literature, in the literal sense of the word, did exist at the time, and he had to be at least minimally acquainted with it or else the writing down of the *Iliad* would never have taken place.[2]

Nevertheless, the last fifty years of Homeric scholarship have firmly established the *Iliad* as the mature outcome of some five centuries of continuous oral tradition. To be sure, Homer lived at the end of that tradition and was its last great representative. It is also true that the poem in its monumental form could not have come into being, and certainly would not have remained in being, but for the availability of a highly developed art of writing, and that some of its elements, at least, bear the marks of a written rather than purely oral culture. But this makes Homer, at the most, an end and a beginning, a transitional figure, whose poem to some extent combines elements of both cultures. It does not change the fact that the poem is, on the whole, a predominantly oral composition, exhibiting all the traits of living myth. This is what I shall try to show in what follows: that Homer's epic is characterized, both in its form and its content, by the timelessness, unhistoricity, and full disclosedness that are characteristic of living myth.

The first important stylistic characteristic of oral composition that is fully exemplified in the *Iliad* is the use of stock phrases, epithets, characters, scenes, themes, and stories. The oral poet does not invent his poem out of whole cloth, but, having a rich store of fixed, formalized elements at his disposal, constructs it largely out of these building blocks. He may show originality in their arrangement, but it is only by retaining them that he is capable of practicing his craft. Improvised recitation depends for its very being on the skillful use of ready-made elements, without which the singer would have to be silent—except on very rare occasions. But the Greek *aoidos* had to be ready to perform frequently and whenever he was called upon. If he wanted to live, he could not wait for the rare and occasional inspiration of the modern poet—for the muse to move him. His Muse, as it is often pointed out, was Mnemosyne: his ability to remember, and his basic and absolutely necessary material: the memorable phrase, theme, and story.

Such material is necessarily the fruit of a long tradition. Fixed formulas are the result of centuries of slow organic development during which whatever is unmemorable, unfunctional, and uneconomical is gradually eliminated and the store of crystallized, stylized, compressed, formal expressions grows. If so, it is not false to say that a poem like the *Iliad* had been "many centuries in the making,"[3] before it reached its Homeric form: it simply had the organic life that is characteristic of all living myth.

This does not mean that the oral poet was in no way original, and had, as it were, nothing to do with the creation of the poem. Although he utilized traditional language and material in the composition of his poem and constructed it piecemeal, the way one constructs a collage or a mosaic, arranging the parts one has at one's disposal in an artistic pattern, this composition and arrangement was entirely his own work. As so was the selection: from the immense storehouse of traditional material Homer had to select the pieces that suited his purpose and design and build them into a unitary structure. The elements may have existed prior to his work, but the poem did not; the fragments—fixed, discrete, and unconnected—were there, but the poem as a whole was not. It was created at the moment of the recital, and there it also died as a fixed form, so that it had to be recreated each time the "same" poem was sung again. Even the larger themes and stories were available only in skeletal outline: as bare bones that had to be fleshed and clothed and given concrete life by the individual singer on the occasion of his song. And here the singer reigned supreme: it was his talents and interests that shaped the poem in its—momentarily—final form. The poem was at the same time traditional and constantly changing, long-lasting and ephemeral, the work of generations and that of a single man. It was nourished by tradition and it kept tradition fluid and therefore alive. In other words, it was living myth.

The oral character of the *Iliad* is especially noticeable when we consider the kind of unity that this poem has. Written composition enables the writer to produce monumental works in which long lines of argument are pursued without break from beginning to end, obvious repetitions as well as long-winded detours and deviations from the main theme are avoided, and all contradiction and inconsistency is eliminated. At its best, the written work is an indivisible organic whole from which nothing can be subtracted and to which nothing can be added without weakening or even destroying the essential unity of the thing.

But Homer's poem, though monumental enough, does not have this type of unity. It is, rather, a loose arrangement of not absolutely interdependent pieces, artfully conjoined, but for the most part not necessarily connected, beautifully stitched together, but not at all inseparably knit. It is true that the poem as a whole does have an overarching theme: the wrath of Achilles. But the majority of the episodes in the *Iliad* do not directly—and at times not even indirectly—

advance the Achilles story.[4] The overall story serves more in the manner of a pair of loose brackets that hold the diverse parts of the poem together without giving them organic unity.

It is the nature of oral recital that accounts for this structural peculiarity of the epic. The whole of the *Iliad* would take some twenty-five to thirty hours of continuous singing to perform,[5] and obviously no singer is capable of such performance, and no audience of listening to it. The capacity and leisure of singer and audience set natural limits to oral recitation and make the epic episodic: a collection of smaller parts that stand in a loose relation to each other, neither sharply separated, nor closely connected. If the monumental poem had an unbroken unity it could never be performed, which is to say that as an oral poem it could not exist. The longer the epic is, the more the singer must be able to begin it almost anywhere [6] and to interrupt and continue it at a great many points without either making the audience keenly aware of what it had missed or leaving it with a sense of incompleteness, unfulfilled expectation, and a disappointing letdown after suspense. Since the episode, and not the monumental poem, is the largest organic unit of the oral epic, it is in its composition, and not in that of the epic as a whole, that the singer has to excel. For if he fails here, he has failed altogether as an oral poet. The episode must be brilliant in itself, it must be a complete, self-contained whole that grips the audience instantly, transports it immediately *in medias res,* and never lets it go till the recital ends.

This tremendous concentration on the present moment, dictated by the necessities of the singer's art, affects the very nature of time in the epic poem. Since long lines of argument are precluded, and a careful preparation for what is to take place much later in the poem is unessential, all that matters is the present event. It must be presented vividly, firmly, directly, and laid fully open to sight so that it shines forth with a dazzling flash of light that leaves no shadows and allows nothing to remain hidden and undisclosed. *Aletheia,* the shining disclosure of the moment, being the essential virtue of the episode, pure presence, the pure Present, is the temporal category of the epic as it is of all living myth.

Even when the poet refers to the past—though not necessarily to something that had taken place in the poem itself—or forecasts the future—though not necessarily one to come within the poem— in an episode, such references serve only to reveal and enhance the present, to show what is now taking place. (A real revelation of past and future events would in any case be unnecessary, for the Greek audience already knows the story, e. g., the facts connected with the fate of Achilles, to a greater extent than ever related in the *Iliad*). Episodic epic is not concerned with past and future, it "knows no before and after, but only the pure preseence of what has been and what is to come."[7] "Homeric style knows only a fore-ground, only a uniformly illuminated, uniformly objective present."[8] There are no unexpressed, yet to be externalized, half-illuminated symbolic elements in the episode which point toward something other than what is immediately visible. All content being fully disclosed and present, suspense, a state involving hidden background and temporal tension, is completely alien to the epic.

Epic time is not a continuum, an unbroken line defined by two limits—the beginning and end of a process of organic change and growth; it is not pure duration,[9] nor a temporal tension between past and future. It is a loose succession of atomic nows without an overarching principle, an aggregation of discrete events succeeding rather than presupposing and implying each other. Epic time is symbolized by Zeno's moving arrow that stays still at every moment of its flight. It is a paratactic time whose elements are lined up next to each other without necessary sub- or superordination and without a fixed framework within which they are unequivocally located. They are contiguous rather than connected. For continuity and connection depth is necessary: the present latent in the past and pregnant with the future. But episodic epic is pure visible surface; it has no hidden layers and no depth. Its only dimension is the eternal present of living myth.

And this present, like Zeno's arrow, stands still. Not only is there no organic development in the epic as a whole, but, for all the glittering succession of dazzling events, in a sense nothing has really taken place in the *Iliad,* no significant changes have occurred, and everything is, at the end, pretty much as it was at the beginning. A number of people have died but the fight goes on, supposedly, much as it did before. Although the audience knows, from other poems, that the end is near, in the poem itself everything is just about the same at the end as it was at the beginning. Historically speaking, the whole *Iliad* is one—very long—moment.

That this moment is not unbearably long even to the present-day reader, who is not restricted to piecemeal performances of the poem but can read the whole *Iliad* from beginning to end, is due to the extraordinary vividness, variability, and richness of the individual episodes. It is interesting to note that the poetic device that contributes most to making even the ever-recurring moment varied and vivid is in its nature as paratactic, atomistic, and present-oriented as is Homeric time. Unlike the metaphor that fuses the dissimilar, the Homeric simile keeps the compared terms strictly separate and lets them touch at one or more points of similarity without merging. And while the metaphor always implies more than it can clearly and directly say, the simile does not; it brings to light and makes immediately present what it presents without leaving shadows and pointing to deeper, more obscure, and not directly disclosable truths.

It has long been noted that in the *Iliad* metaphors are few, conventional, and almost perfunctory, while similes are plentiful, fresh, live, and masterly as well as carefully elaborated, at times almost to the point of becoming independent episodes themselves. The reason for Homer's preference for the simile is not far to seek. The creation and large-scale use of metaphors presuppose a prior fixation of terms, a clear separation in previous usage of the individual symbols that the metaphor is to combine and fuse.[10] But in oral poetry, as Stanford pointed out, "language is just beginning to be formalized," [11] the precise meaning of words is just beginning to be fixed, and exact connotations are still being established rather than loosened and widened through metaphoric expansion. ". . . because words lacked precise definitions in Homer's time, Homer could not, even if he had so wished, have used daring metaphors." [12] "He had to use every means in his power to stereotype, to define, to achieve clarity; hence in syntax he chose the paratactic not the hypotactic style . . . [and] tautology and analogy by simile, but never metaphors, for metaphor fuses and confuses meaaning" [13] and destroys immediate clarity by bursting the bonds of prior definition. It is this symbolic fixation, naming and graphically defining, that the simile accomplishes so well.

The Homeric simile is clear, limited, and precise; it lets things be seen in their exact identity and brings them immediately before our eyes. Its function is pure presentation: to make the unfamiliar familiar, the hidden—emotions, psychological states—perceptually evident, and the inexperienced and unknown sensuously vivid and present. The simile is not a metaphysical device that points to abstract resemblances and structural similarities that only the intellect can grasp; even when it does not illustrate actual perceptual characteristics, it concretizes and brings all to the surface, engaging the senses rather than the deeply probing mind.

As such a concrete presentational device the simile is ideally suited not only to the necessities of oral poetry—immediate presentation and symbolic fixation—but also to the capacities of the oral audience which would find it very difficult to distinguish clearly between perception and thought, inner and outer movement. And it is equally well suited to the subject of the oral poem, the Homeric hero as presented in the *Iliad*.

* * * * * *

Homer's men are as directly visualized and as perception-oriented as is the Homeric simile. They are not yet subjects in the

literal sense of the later Greek *hypokeimenon:* they have no underlying center uniting the different aspects of their personality. All
they are at any particular moment is visible at that moment. They
have no secrets, no unvoiced motives, no concealed emotions; at
every moment the epic hero lays open his heart, and what he, or the
poet in his behalf, does not in fact say he does not even imply.

Fully disclosed at all times, the Homeric self has the same paratactic structure as do Homeric style and time. It consists of discrete,
separate organs that are not yet fused into an organism. A man's
"body is a mere construct of independent parts variously put together"[14] and so is his soul; indeed, as Snell has shown, it is misleading to use such terms as "body" and "soul" with reference to
Homer. For to us they imply precisely that unity which Homeric
man does not yet have. When the epic hero speaks of his body he
does not refer to his *soma*—in the *Iliad* the word means only corpse
—but to his skin, limbs, hands, feet, head, chest, teeth, etc., as the
context of the action may demand. Similarly, his *psyche* is only the
living breath or soul that departs from the body at the moment of
death, while his "soul"—in our sense of the word—consists in a
collection of organs like *phren, thymos, noos,* or even particular
emotions like hate, love, anger, sorrow, etc., depending on what
overriding impulse or appetite happens to motivate the hero's action
at the moment. What we would describe as internal tension, division, or conflict in the depths of a man's heart, appears in Homer
as a surface conflict between diverse parts of the psychic make-up of
man. The hero is disturbed in, deliberates with, understands through
his various organs (e. g., *kata phrena kai kata thymon, Iliad* 3.671,
8.179, 11.411, 17.106, 18.15, 20.264—an especially well-worn formula),
he expresses regret by wishing that the "anger which incites the
great mind and makes it violent . . . smoldering like smoke in the
breast of man" (18.107–110) would vanish from among gods and
men. He is or is not urged on by his fierceness (*menos*) and spirit
(*thymos*) (e. g., 20.174, 22.346, 24.198), and he is infused with
courage not as a whole but when "the spirit inside my breast drives

me on . . . and my feet underneath and my hands above are eager
. . . and the invincible hands are eager and fierceness is growing
and both feet beneath are driving me on so that I long to fight"
(13.73–79).

It is not that the self in Homer has absolutely no unity. To begin with it has the same kind of loose unity that the episodic epic
as a whole has: one that barely holds the separate and discrete
aspects of a man's personality together. Having no depth, the self is
not so much the cause and ground of a man's acts as it is their sum.
Fully disclosed, man consists of his discrete doings and sufferings,
rather than in an inner unitary being. That is why even while the
hero speaks in the first person, his "ego" may be addressing "his
own great-hearted spirit," or any other one of his many correlated
parts, as if he were conversing with someone else. In this dialogue [15]
—which it would be anachronistic to call "internal"—all the forces
"inside him" may be participants. What is all important is that they
be expressed: the hero talks to make himself—all his parts relevant
to the moment's act—fully visible (to himself as well as to others),
almost as if, but for his visibility, he would not really be "there,"
(i. e., fully present). Homer "objectifies the internal states of his
characters into visible objects, other persons, gods," [16] because without such objectification the "subject itself" would not exist.

Since the subject has no inner, hidden essence which could be
gradually revealed through his action in the course of the poem, it is
on the whole incapable of functional change and growth. Growth
implies the realization of something present though not yet actual,
the development of a hidden potential. But Homeric man, being
fully externalized, has no latent potential and thus no history. He is
as unhistorical as the oral epic itself, and as nontemporal as epic
time. He is of a fixed age, and, for the most part, of a completely
fixed character. This is what gives him identity and—for all parataxis
—a kind of unity: not that all changes in his personality are reduci-
ble to and explicable as the results of the organic growth of the same
person, but that there are no significant changes here. His identity

is not that of a unity underlying temporal change, but an unhistorical sameness. It is only because he is static, because all his acts manifest the same unchanging character, that he remains visibly the same in all his diverse appearances. Repetition, not growth, insures epic unity and identity.[17]

Aias is always steadfast, reliable, a tower of strength; Odysseus always the embodiment of bravery tempered by common sense and the will to live; Hector always the loyal son, husband, father, the support of the city, its women and innocent children. The Homeric hero acts so much in character, responds to all diverse situations in so much the same way, that he becomes a "character" himself: a role, mask, or *persona* rather than a person, the representative of a certain pattern of behavior rather than a unique individual in his own right. While conventional epithets may be occasionally inappropriate to the hero's actual action, it is very seldom that his actions are inappropriate to his role. For the most part the action is typical of the hero as a pure type. ("Pure type" is not a derogatory term here; it does not mean that the hero becomes a lifeless abstraction or cliche. On the contrary, Homer's extraordinarily vivid characters make the type live by making it immediately and concretely visible.)

There are exceptions to this. A minor hero's character is seldom sufficiently developed to make him a distinguishable type, and occasionally even the major protagonists act dangerously alike. In such cases the scene is more typical than the individual protagonist; the latter acts not so much in his own role—qua this particular character —as he acts out and brings to life the typical scene.[18] It is the pattern of the stock scene rather than the pattern of behavior of the stock character that carries on, as if by itself, the action.

Still as a rule the major hero's character colors the action sufficiently to make it representative of his rather than the stock scene's constitution. In fact, he acts so much in character that any deviation from his normal pattern of behavior is automatically attributed to external, mostly divine, influence and interference. And even here, what is affected from without is usually consistent with what we would expect from the hero himself: it is an access of power, a strengthening of courage and insight, an excess of the norm—along the lines of the normal pattern; something more, rather than something other than what is typical.

Only seldom does the hero do something totally unexpected and inexplicable—such as Achilles not killing Agamemnon at the beginning of Book One—something that seems out of character even to the poet and thus has to be accounted for by bringing in a god. In general a person is apt to blame on the gods any action of his that has turned sour, regardless of the fact that to singer and audience alike that action appears totally consistent with the fixed character of the actor. And even such disclaimers are very much what we would expect: the present (ruinous) result of a past act is abhorrent to the hero now, therefore he is unable to understand how he could ever have wanted it; it seems totally alien to him, and so he naturally disowns it. We have seen that Homeric man is all surface; he is to himself what he is visible to himself as being in the present. And so is the act: it is (now) present result rather than past intention. Since the two are not at all identical, there is no reason for the hero to identify himself with the act. While he remained visibly the same—he still wants what he has always wanted: respect, honor, glory—the act has changed, it has lost its identity—as something desirable—and so it is not something he can conceive of himself as having ever desired and done.

The disclaimer is facilitated by the epic self's paratactic view of itself and reinforces it at the same time. Since a man's anger has never been more to him than a loose component of his being, now that it has become undesirable—in its results—he can easily slough it off without suffering any noticeable loss of identity. And since it is so easy to disown any—undesirable—part of one's make-up, the epic hero is quick to do so; and this practice necessarily fragments his being to the point where even the gods become, as it were, constituent parts of it. The transition from one's own act to that of a god is, in any case, easy and smooth. Not only because, as we shall see, there are not many hard and fast dividing lines in Homer between men and gods, but also because there are not any between what is internal and what is external to the paratactic self. With the loose coordination of the many organs and emotions of the self the distinction between an act one no longer understands, and therefore disowns, and an act brought about by heaven-sent blindness is at best one of degree (of distance) rather than one of kind. The transition from one to the other involves no *metabasis eis allo genos.*

The attribution by Homeric man of what we would call his own action to divine interference does not legally exculpate him. For it is not volition and intention that make him liable to punishment but the act itself. It is the visible result rather than the hidden intent that matters. In the absence of a distinction between inner core and outer behavior, a distinction between will and act cannot be made, and, as it is often pointed out, "Homeric man does not possess the concept of will." [19] Thus there is no inconsistency in Agamemnon's offering to pay huge damages for what he did, while at the same time insisting on his innocence—since his transgression was caused by *ate,* divine interference. Nor is it puzzling that the Achaians find such retribution perfectly just and accept Agamemnon's guilt—in the etymological sense of the word—without morally condemning Agamemnon himself, as he is now. With the emphasis on the present, and the paratactic view of the self, the (past) act—and the blame—is simply detached from the (present) man; he is innocent, i. e., harmless, now, even while the act is guilty (liable to damages).

This emphasis on the present, the visible surface, pervades and shapes the whole of Homeric morality. We have seen that the epic does not describe or analyze the hidden substance of a man but presents him as he appears at the moment to himself and to others. The "subject" is objectified, becomes public image, and so does his morality: it is outer- and other- rather than inner-directed. Since the hero recognizes himself, as it were, by externals—not the least of these being the others' recognition of him—he evaluates and judges his action in terms of its external results and the others' approval or disapproval. He has, strictly speaking, no conscience: his "conscience" is entirely in the others' keeping. He has an almost fanatic sense of honor, but honor to him means being honored, and his self-respect depends completely on the respect others have for him. His moral feeling is *aidos:* a sense of (public) shame, a fear of (public) loss of face, and his overriding ambition: the desire for public recognition, admiration, and status.[20]

That is why *timē,* honor, is often literally equivalent to honors and honoraria: material prizes, possessions, public gifts, compensation, and recompense. It is not that the hero wants to be paid for his virtue; the payment is part of his virtue, a visible sign of its recognition by others (without which it would not be visible to the hero himself) as well as a lasting source of future recognition and thus honor. That is also why the Homeric hero is so agonistic and competitive: he wants to surpass others—in rank, status, possessions, power—rather than himself, because it is only in relation to others that he can measure his own excellence. Of course, the *Iliad* is a story of war, in which scenes of combat and thus warlike characteristics naturally predominate. But, apart from the fact that the *Iliad's* protagonists are often more combative in the assembly than on the field of battle, the choice of subject for the most monumental poem of an era is hardly uncharacteristic of the mentality of that era itself.

Homeric morality bears the same marks that we have already found characteristic for the language and content of the oral epic. It emphasizes publicity, surface visibility, and disclosure, the outer image rather than a hidden substance. And it is as paratactic as are Homeric language, style, time, and men: it is not simply located in the individual but fragmented and divided among all the members of his society, who are its keepers. Curiously, the fragmentation destroys its unity as little as the loose organization of the individual's feelings and acts destroyed the unity of his character. Precisely because this morality is completely public, it is completely uniform.

Since "everything in the world is regularly presented as all men (all men within the poem, that is) commonly perceive it," and the accepted attitude toward each thing is constantly emphasized, "moral standards and the values of life are essentially agreed on by everyone in the *Iliad*." "Men say the same things about the same things, and so the world to them . . . is one." [21] Homeric morality is an expression and product of the same unity of experience that characterizes all living myth.

This more than anything else provides the overall unity of the *Iliad*. I have remarked earlier that the Achilles story, to which a great many episodes fail to make a direct contribution, serves only as a loose framework that is insufficient to unify the poem organically. But if we look upon the telling of that story not so much as the central purpose of the *Iliad* but rather as a convenient device— together with all the other stories of individual *aristeiai*—to present something else, i. e., the heroic image and the heroic conception of life,[22] then we can see the real organizing principle of the whole poem. It is not the slowly developing story but the unchanging, almost completely uniform and agreed-upon ideal of humanity that is the central theme of the poem, and to this central theme just about every episode directly contributes.

It is not the way of the epic to give abstract definitions and formulate general laws. Instead, the epic concretizes the universal and makes it appear through an endless series of instances which repeat and make immediately visible the same theme. They are paratactically arranged rather than organically fit into a gradually unfolding story. Yet as they merely "rehearse the same fundamental keynote which rings most powerfully in the central action," [23] re-enact the same essential scene, and embody the selfsame ideal, they do not break the unity of the poem. But this unity, just like that of the individual characters, is one of unchanging identity rather than organic growth.

Whitman's analogy between the principles of composition in geometric pottery and those in oral poetry seems to me basically mistaken.[24] But if we thought of geometric composition not in terms of a total design in which "the basic ceramic shape is felt as a controlling rhythm to which all the painted parts are subordinated so that the whole emerges as an organic unity," [25] i. e., not vertically as Whitman does but horizontally, then the analogy would become more apt. For as on some pieces of geometric pottery each horizontal band repeats the same motif interminably and with little or no variation, so the same pattern is endlessly repeated in the monumental oral epic from beginning to end.

* * * * * *

Homer's gods fit into this geometric design of the poem all too well inasmuch as they too merely repeat the basic theme and exemplify the selfsame ideal on another level—a parallel band, as it were, to the human one—but without significant variation. The paratactic structure of the poem and of time and men in the poem, the unity given by surface sameness rather than hidden substance or principle of growth, the emphasis on visibility and the consequent lack of depth that we have dealt with in the preceding are just as characteristic of the nature and functioning of the Olympians as they were of their mortal subjects.

The most obvious, though perhaps not the most significant, aspect of the paratactic nature and lack of unity of the Homeric concept of divinity is its polytheism. The divine is fragmented here into many parts and divided among many representatives who are only loosely conjoined into a not-too-well defined hierarchy and associated as a group under the not-too-often exercised leadership of Zeus. What ties the group as a whole together in a common cause is a further fragmentation, namely, that the gods are, to some extent at least, set apart from men and insist on this separation and difference. Yet this is at best a very loose bond and a very tenuous difference. Most gods prefer, at one time or another, some human beings to some of their fellow divinities and adopt the former's cause with the result that the whole of Olympus often rocks with dissension. And the character and morality of the gods is little, if at all, different from, let alone higher than, that of men, so that it is justly said that the Olympians exhibit both the virtues and the vices, the aspirations and the aversions of their human subjects to an even greater extent than they do themselves. Once again we see substantial sameness in spite of surface diversity (between men and gods).

That this should be so is understandable. Revelation, clear visibility, being the essence of the epic, the function of the gods is to a large extent simply to make visible the forces that govern men's lives, to make transparent what would otherwise be hidden to us in our own nature. Therefore the gods necessarily become "men writ large," anthropomorphic, outsize images of what is best and worst in us. They are but a splendid mirror the epic holds up to ourselves. This also accounts for their fragmentation. Since human action has little underlying unity and man is driven in diverse directions by a diversity of forces, the representatives of these forces will be equally diverse. It takes four goddesses—Hera, Athene, Artemis, Aphrodite—to "signalize the four aspects of womanhood, . . . to bring out the spiritual peculiarities of the female sex" and thus to make "the notion of femininity intelligible." [26] And it takes a number of gods to make visible what it means to be a man—warrior, healer, singer, lover, craftsman, etc. "In their persons the Olympians give clear expression to all that is great and vital in this world. Nothing is concealed; all the forces operating in body and mind are drawn into the portrait of the gods." [27] Conceptual abstraction as such is alien to myth, but not so the brilliant instance, the splendid embodiment of the universal. The exhibition of the shining particular is, however, as far as the epic can go, and so we encounter diversity, fragmentation, coordination of forces rather than connecting and underlying unity, in the realm of gods just as much as in the realm of men.

What then separates the gods from men, what makes this all-too-human gathering of Olympians divine? The answer to this is simple: power, strength, might are the essence of divinity. "Divine nature is power and power is the essential attribute of the gods."[28]

The words *theos, dios, theios* in the *Iliad* are not synonymous with our word divine; they mean powerful, mighty, excellent, awful, marvelous. This is why not only gods but also men and even animals and inanimate objects can be "divine" insofar as they exhibit a more-than-usual excellence in their particular function. The difference between gods and men, and everything else, with respect to divinity, is by no means absolute. It is merely a difference in degree. The gods are more powerful than men, and the more powerful, the more divine. But, in the absence of an absolute difference, it is not inconsistent for Homer to call almost all the greater heroes in the *Iliad,* at one time or another, divine. They all have their great moments, and in these moments they are truly god-like, i.e., excellent and strong.

That *theos* should have this meaning in Homer is not surprising if we consider that the conception of personal gods itself evolved from an earlier conception of impersonal powers and forces.[29] What made the elements "awful" was precisely their more-than-human destructive force against which man's power was of no avail. Although in the development of myth the nature-functions of the gods gradually eroded and the gods came to be distinguished by personal character rather than impersonal sphere of operations,[30] divinity continued to consist of surpassing power and irresistible might.

Excellence and power seem to imply a field of action in which one excels, yet it is not by a difference of functions that the gods and men are kept apart in Homer, but merely by a difference in the degree of excellence. The most depised of gods, Ares, is no less divine for all the scorn the gods and men heap on him, inasmuch as he "excels" in insatiate, bloodthirsty, dreadful warmaking. If he is less divine than others, it is because his power and competence are more limited, because even in battle he is less powerful than Zeus,

Athene, or Apollo. All her failings do not make Aphrodite ungod-
like, because they do not affect her excellence and power in matters
of love. Yet on the whole she is less godlike, because less powerful,
than Athene and Apollo.

There is some complaint about the amorality of the gods in
Homer in our days, often exaggerated to the point where it seems
that Homer merely parodies the Olympians [31] and uses their "divine
burlesque" [32] mainly as a comic relief heightening the pathos of the
human struggle. But these objections largely result from applying
our notions of morality and divinity to the *Iliad*. In terms of
Homer's concept of divinity, the morality of the Olympians is easily
understood.

If the essential nature of the gods is power, then, to the extent
that they can be said to have any rules of conduct, any moral code
at all, whatever enhances their power will be right and just and
whatever curbs it wrong and unjust. It is beside the point to say
that "even the highest conception of deity in Homer does not ex-
clude the element of fraud" [33] (though it is true enough), and it is
misleading to assert that the measure of these gods is greatness as
opposed to justice, unless one uses these terms anachronistically.
For justice—the way, the appropriate way for a god to act—is
simply what affirms and increases the god's greatness and majesty,
and these are measured exclusively in terms of power. It is not that
the gods have no morality. Rather, their morality is one of self-
assertion, and their actions, if they are to be understood at all, must
be understood on this basis. What is just for these gods is what
makes them more essentially what they are, what helps them fulfill
their function (of being awful and powerful), what makes them
gods. And this is power, power, and more power. That is why it is
just that they should assert and jealously guard their position and
strength and honor, that they should mercilessly crush all transgression against them and show their greatness even in revenge. If
they do not, they lose face, honor, strength: their divinity.

If Zeus vaunts his power and threatens to throw all the Olym-

pians from heaven, this is just, for he can make the threat good.
If Apollo smites the Achaian camp with the plague and kills
(though not the offender Agamemnon) until he gets satisfaction
(though not directly from Agamemnon), this is just. It rees-
tablishes his honor and manifests his power for all the Greeks to
see. To kill Agamemnon himself would not serve the purpose as
well, since allowing him to live brings ruin to the Achaians and
honor to the Trojans, the favorites of Apollo, which further increases the god's honor. And this is just. The gods do no harm
without cause, though they may seem to do so, for offense on the
part of men is not the only cause. It may affirm their power to kill
the unoffending too.[34]

If these gods insist on honors, sacrifices, offerings from men,
they insist merely on what is due to them as powerful rulers. The
gifts they receive are not a dishonorable bribe; on the contrary, they
are the visible embodiment of the honor due to power. It is
anachronistic to say that "the gods in the *Iliad* are primarily concerned with their honor" and not with "justice as such."[35] What is
just is precisely what increases their honor; honor means to be honored visibly and tangibly, and the most visible and tangible evidence
is the gifts the less powerful bring to the mighty. As among men
"honor" almost equals gifts, portions received,[36] so it does among
gods and in the intercourse of gods and men. The man who fails to
pay, fails to honor the gods. Even to fail to turn to the gods on any
important occasion is transgression, for it means to withhold recognition—of their power—to withhold honor. This is hybris.

The natural delight of all deities in war is due to the same
thing. War is a contest for power, i.e., for honor, and how could an
honor- and power-bent deity refrain from this contest? It is the test-
ing ground of his divinity. Divine power, like its human counterpart, is not a latent underlying force but overt might displayed in
action and recognized by all. With the epic emphasis on publicity
and visibility, divinity, like anything else, is not real unless publicly
demonstrated, exhibited for all to see. That is why the gods, just

like their human subjects, constantly boast of and verbally boost
their power: to make it visible to themselves as well as to others,
to make it visible to themselves through (having it accepted and
recognized by) the others, and thus to make it real.[37] In the epic
world where being equals appearing and shining forth, the gods
have to be as other-directed as the men. Hence to be a god means to
be agonistic: to be engaged in a never-ending struggle for status,
recognition, honor.

Once again we see that the fragmentation of the epic world
does not destroy its unity. The "separate" realms of gods and men
have the same standards and values; they agree on and in what is
essential. This is what makes the intercourse between gods and men
easy, in spite of the discontinuity that parataxis seems to imply.
When Apollo insists on an absolute difference between divinity
and humanity in his warning to Diomedes—"Beware, son of
Tydeus, and give way, nor seek to match your spirit with gods, for
in no way alike are the race of immortal gods and that of men who
walk the earth" (5. 440)—he is overstating the case with the boast-
fulness proper to power. The likeness is only too evident. Indeed
the very words of Apollo might have been spoken by any king of
men to his own subjects.[38] *Gnothi sauton:* know your place and
do not seek to quarrel with your betters. Apart from immortality
—a subject to be dealt with later—the difference between gods and
men is simply one of power. The gods are more powerful and men
are conscious of this, or at least they had better be if they know
what is good for them. But this is a quantitative, not qualitative,
difference, which makes the dividing line between men and gods
fluid, and at the same time provides a *raison d'être* for communication as well as a common language which they both understand.

The gods' interference in the human realm is motivated by the
same aspiration as the men's turning to the gods: the quest for
power and honor. Since the gods are only quantitatively different
from men, it is all the more important for them to insist on this
difference and make it manifest at every turn of events. Their

power must be felt by men to be real to gods and men alike. And it is felt, for in critical moments mortal heroes do turn to the gods. Conscious of the fact that more than ordinary greatness is an evidence of divine interference in human affairs, they pray for the surpassing strength that is a semblance of the substance of divinity.

Since the intercourse between gods and men is just about exclusively conducted in the common language, one might almost say the common currency, of manifest power, it is not surprising that the heroes' formulaic prayers often sound like commercial notes, bills presented for past delivery of goods: "If I ever did such and such for you . . . now remember. . . . " Honor rendered deserves honor returned.

Men's acknowledgment of the nature of divine-human transactions pays dividends to them in defeat just as much as in victory. For while no warrior is too eager to ascribe his successes to gods—this would hardly increase his honor—all are quick to blame their failures on divine interference. This is the way to avoid what they most fear: loss of face, honor, fame. To be thwarted by a god is not so shameful, it does not demonstrate one's weakness as patently as to be defeated by mortal man. The gods, on their part, cheerfully condone this practice. Regardless of the facts of the case—i.e., whether they were indeed involved in the particular matter—the practice itself is an open acknowledgment of their power, and as such most pleasing to their ears. It is a public admission of the incommensurability of gods and men, which is what they have been insisting on all along.

The manner in which Homer's heroes blame the gods throws a curious light on the Homeric association of power and knowledge. The gods send *ate,* a temporary clouding of the faculty of understanding. They do not rob man of his will or spirit but take his insight. Thus blinded, he will trespass but is scarcely responsible for his failure. The trespass is a kind of error in judgment, a mistake, a temporary insanity, as it were. Of course, lack of "responsibility" or absence of "bad intention" will not avert the gods' wrath, for what they punish is the actual transgression and not "sinful will."

Indeed, the attempt itself is almost admirable—at least to men—
since it demonstrates a proud spirit, which, in an agonistic society,
is something to respect. The agent himself only learns of the "bad-
ness" of his act from the fact that it failed.[39] And since it failed, it
must have been the outcome of lack of insight, *ate,* sent by some
god.

The gods send *ate,* but they also give insight. By prophecy,
signs, and epiphanies, they advise, enlighten, counsel—if it suits
their purposes. Whether such counsel actually helps men is almost
beside the point. If it helps, it is a proof of the gods' superior wisdom; if it does not, it only shows how inferior men are in their understanding, how almost beyond assistance they wallow in their
weakness where even good counsel is of no avail.

What is curious about the Homeric association of wisdom and
power is that it is taken for granted without too much evidence or
actual demonstration. To be sure, Odysseus's cleverness may have
something to do with his being a doughty warrior, but Nestor is
even more revered for his wisdom in spite of the fact that he rarely
gives very useful advice. And while the most powerful gods—Zeus,
Apollo, Athene—are also the ones called most wise, it is by no
means evident that their power is in any way connected with, let
alone the result of, their wisdom. Men, conscious that their insight
and power were limited, simply invested their gods with an excessive amount of both. That they did not even feel the need to account for this association is typical of the epic mentality. The uniformity of belief, characteristic of an age of living myth, does not
give rise to critical reflection, and the paratactic view of the world
requires, and can provide, only conjunction (in this case of knowledge and power) and not connection or underlying rationale.

* * * * * *

Although great power and insight are the marks of divinity,
divine power is by no means unlimited. Beside the not-too-dissimilar
realms of the human and the divine there is a third force in the

Homeric world against which men, and sometimes even the gods, are powerless. This is the power of fate.

Insofar as the Homeric words for fate, *moira, aisa, moros, ker, pepromene, daimon, nemesis,* have a common meaning, it is "lot," "share," "portion." With the exception of *aisa* and *ker* they all derive from verbs (*meiro, daio, nemo, poro*) connoting "allot," "apportion," "distribute," "give" (in middle voice: to receive as share), while *aisa* contains the root of *isos,* referring to an equal share (*isomoros*) in the sacrificial offering. What makes these almost innocuous words—share, lot, portion—so fateful is that the Greeks conceive them in the past perfect, as it were (metaphorically rather than literally speaking, except for *heimarmene* and *pepromene*). The lot has already been allotted, the share fixed, the portion given. There is an irrevocability about this allotment that colors its meaning, an irreversibility that binds and turns the portion received into a bond that is bondage. Who it is that allots the portions is seldom questioned. *Moira* is almost exclusively impersonal in Homer. Even when personalized or given quasi-personal agents, such as the Erinyes, it lacks real personality. The Erinyes have only a function, that of enforcing *moira,* and they are devoid of personal traits. The same is true of *daimon* in the sense of allotter. The word connotes a function and not a distinct personality. It is this lack of personality that lends *daimon* the occasional connotation of a dark, fearsome, unknown force.

Though the portions and functions allotted are particular and individual rather than universal, they are intertwined to such a degree that it is not false to say that Homeric *moira* contains an idea of an as-yet-unarticulated, regulative principle governing all things. It stands for the way of things, the order inherent in all, the law, persistence, and necessity of the whole of that growth and flow which the later Greeks called *physis.*

What is most inevitable in man's life, the portion none of us can escape, the lot we all share, is death. *Moira, moros, ker, aisa,* all acquire different shades of this meaning. This does not *eo ipso* explain why *moira,* as lot or fate, should be so predominantly negative, privative, and limitative for Homeric man. *Prima facie,* receiving a share is more of an enrichment than a deprivation, so why is it not regarded as a gift to be used? The reason is that men become aware of their portion when they are trying to go beyond it. As long as one is content to remain within the limits of one's allotted share or function, the necessity of doing so, and thus the limit qua limit, is not apparent. Only he who desires more than or other than his share will become conscious of it as "his own," and the frustration that makes him conscious will color *moira* negatively.[40] What is decreed is seldom evident except in terms of what is not allowed. What is given as one's portion appears only in terms of what is not, and even one's share of life allotted—one's positive portion—becomes one's lot only in face of its opposite: death. Thus *moira* acquires the privative, limitative, and predominantly negative connotation of a "dark" fate.

Things, animate and inanimate, also have their allotted shares and functions, but as they scarcely ever go against them (as do, for example, the horses of Achilles) these rarely become apparent in the negative way in which man's fate does. Nor do they need to be enforced by the Erinyes. Nevertheless, the Erinyes are not guardians of a specifically human, "moral" order. They represent order as such and rectify transgressions. Oaths are in their domain not because they have something to do with morality, but because by an oath one binds oneself, imposes on oneself a kind of *moira,* or bondage. Even in human relations, what is against *moira* is, as it were, against nature, be this the nature or portion of a thing or man.

It is interesting to note, too, that volition plays as little part in the enforcement of *moira* by the Erinyes as in its violation by men. Men violate *moira,* try to transcend the limits of their portion and trespass on alien territory, from lack of insight. Retribution follows transgression even more blindly. It is enough for the Erinyes that *moira* is violated. They do not inquire into motivation; nor can they, for, in spite of their superficial personalization, they are hardly more than the immovable weight of the rule of fate. Totally volitionless, they represent order versus disorder and put an end to infractions against the way of things. They not only lack volition, but they cannot even be called a conscious agency. The act of transgression does not arouse them, as if from outside, to a pitch of fury and to vengeance but is, rather, merely one link in the process of an automatic restoration of the balance of *moira*. The process itself—*ate-hybris-nemesis*—is rather like what we today call a natural process taking place in accordance with its own inexorable law.

What is the role of the gods in this process? How are they related to fate?

On the one hand, the gods—especially the older ones—also have their portions and shares allotted to them,[41] and, to the extent that a god bears traces of an allotted function, he is more powerful and awful, i.e., godlike, within its limits but less, or not at all so, without. (This is what makes it hard for Zeus, lord of the air, to decide his controversy with Poseidon, a lord of the sea, through mere force). Death is not their portion but lies altogether outside their province. They have no control over it and want to have nothing to do with the dead. Much as it hurts them, they abandon those that are to die (Zeus, Sarpedon; Apollo, Hector), and, while they may weep over their favorites' fate, they cannot change it. (It is interesting that death, so eminently associated with *moira* as to be often synonymous with it, marks the only clear-cut difference between the portion of gods and men. While this may be taken simply as a consequence of the gods' *moira*—it is not their lot to die—it may also be considered an indication that to this extent at least the gods are not subject to fate).

On the other hand, it is significant that it is the old and weak gods who have a portion or elemental function, while the newer ones almost completely lack it, and even where they exhibit traces of one, their power does not seem to be either derived from their particular portion or completely bound by it. (Zeus as lord of the air does not seem to derive his power from this function, nor is he completely limited by it, for he could, with some labor, defeat Poseidon in spite of the original difference in portions and spheres of operation). Not only is their power not *moira*-bound, but, if anything, the gods seem bent on interfering with the usual order and course of things to such an extent that if anything untoward or out of the ordinary happens it is usually ascribed to them. It is they who send *ate* [42] that leads to *hybris,* a transgression and violation of *moira,* so that it is not altogether without cause that Menelaus accuses Zeus of favoring those who transgress (13. 631). It is they who give men insight, strength, and valor beyond men's portion, and while they cannot avert death, they may well punish a man *hyper moron,* beyond what is decreed.

The most one can say is that at times and to some extent the gods seem to be subject to fate in Homer, while at other times they seem to be, or at least to feel, above it. At times they appear to be like executors, at other times like originators, again at others like opponents of fate. Since the relation between the gods and *moira* is by no means clearly and consistently defined by Homer, it would be foolish to try to draw clear-cut distinctions between their respective functions in the *Iliad.*

One can do this abstractly, of course. But such an attempt only underlines and helps to explain the fact that within the epic all indications as to the relations between these forces must necessarily be confused, conflicting, and inconsistent. For fate and the gods are not only two different principles of power; they are radically opposed principles. [43]

Moira is impersonal—the gods have personality. *Moira* lacks volition and purpose—the gods are aim-directed, conscious agents. *Moira* stands for order and regularity—the gods for what is willful, arbitrary, unusual, and extraordinary. *Moira* is the way of things— the gods: whimsical interference with the way. *Moira* is immovable —the gods can be swayed. It is true that the gods qua "functions"— having their allotted portions—are within *moira,* but to that extent they lack the personal nature and individuality of gods and are nothing but the remains of an older conception of nature-powers much more easily reconciled with the power of fate. The more anthropomorphic and personally active they become, i.e., the more the function-conception pales, the more they are outside, above, and even opposed to law.

Were the gods as personal agencies not other than, and often opposed to, the impersonal and unswayable force of fate, they would be of little use to Homeric man. In the first place, they would not reveal human nature—conscious, teleological—as opposed to impersonal fate. In the second, their presence would not serve to account for all that is extraordinary and unexpected, all that happens without rhyme or reason in the world. Nor could they be prevailed upon by prayer and sacrifice to alleviate man's insecurity in a dark and hostile world by helping him within, without, and even against the unknown order of things.

If the gods were not set over against fate but became a mere embodiment of and guarantee for the reality and fulfilment of law —as they do gradually become in the development of Greek thought subsequent to Homer—they would lose their function and could be dispensed with as personal agencies. They would be a mere standby for *moira* and we would have a completely *moira*-bound world in which ad-hoc personal power has no role to play. If law reigns absolutely and without qualification, man is not dependent on the gods, while to the extent that it does not, he depends on the favor of gods beyond law.[44]

However, the reasoning that establishes such clear-cut opposition between the gods and fate is alien to myth. It belongs to a higher stage of reflection, a stage made possible precisely by the presentation—conceptually unclear and inconsistent as it is—of the contrasting powers in the epic. It is the function of myth to present, make visible, reveal. This explains not only why the epic cannot reflect upon and critically harmonize what it presents, but also why personal gods as opposed to *moira* appear in the epic in the first place.

The epic has to bring to light; it insists on surface visibility. But the encompassing order and unitary connection, the general lawfulness of things that is without doubt dimly felt in the *Iliad,* cannot be made immediately visible. It is always an *underlying* principle, at best manifested by but never visibly embodied in the phenomena, i.e., in what literally appears. So the epic attempt to make it visible—make it a phenomenon—goes against its very nature. To the extent that this attempt succeeds it necessarily shatters the unity of law and breaks it up into so many fragments; not universal, all-encompassing fate, but individual fates and portions. Automatically the (universal) force of law *appears* as particular, personal power and action, as a diversity of unconnected forces operating side by side. Epic truth—*aletheia,* surface disclosure—once again leads to parataxis rather than organic interconnectedness.

But once the underlying law, which transcends the particular and is therefore alien to the epic that deals only with the particular (the brilliant instance, the dazzling moment), is shattered through the very attempt to make it visible, it loses not only its unity but also much of its lawfulness. The diverse ad-hoc powers—gods—that were supposed to make it visible begin to serve not only as its embodiments but also, at the same time, as powers opposed to it. Since no obvious connecting principle unifies and governs the gods' action, their shining presence can be used to explain not only what happens in accordance with the hidden, invisible, unknown law, but also whatever cannot otherwise be explained, i.e., whatever is unexpected, irregular, and extra-ordinary, whatever happens contrary to the nature of things. The gods' role becomes more and more ambiguous, and their relation to fate—still dimly felt as an impersonal, invisible, universal force—is not one that the epic is in any way capable of clarifying. For it implies a tension—of universal and particular, hidden and visible, darkness and light—a tension between surface and depth, which is alien to myth; so to the extent that it appears at all—as the conflict between gods and fate—it appears confused, unclear, and inconsistent, precisely as it does in the *Iliad.*

This inconsistency, and even the contradiction between the two principles—gods and fate—which it masks, is, of course, not too disturbing to the hearers of the oral epic. The fragmentation of the song prevents them from getting too much of an overview and thus from becoming too aware of internal conflicts and contradictions in the fabric of the myth. The formal parataxis of the epic leads to and allows for a material parataxis: the peaceful existence of contradictory elements side by side.

* * * * * *

The preceding account of the nature of men and gods stressed the similarity between the divine and the human spheres to the point where differences between the two almost disappeared and it seemed that there were only two, rather than three coordinate realms—men and gods vs. fate, rather than men, gods, and fate—in the *Iliad*. This view is not wholly correct, for there is one clear-cut, qualitative rather than quantitative, distinction between men and gods in the *Iliad*: the immortality of the gods. It is the fate of men to die—and so conscious are they of this that fate in the *Iliad* is almost synonymous with death—while the gods live forever. In this particular respect they are not subject to fate.

At first sight even this qualitative difference seems to bring with it little real distinction. Homeric man is unable to conceive a transcendent life significantly different from his own, and so his gods simply live the immanent, earthly life of mortals—forever. They are still the shining expression, if not of the actual nature of men, at least of their most fervent aspiration: to live on, without end, in the forever living present.

Nevertheless, the sheer fact of their deathlessness makes the gods incapable of wholly representing men. Since they are never confronted with an utter, unsurpassable limit, they are never utterly committed to and essentially involved in what they do. Since they face nothing ultimate—literally the last thing—nothing ultimately serious and irremediable ever happens to them. Since it is not their fate to die, life itself loses its urgency; no issue, no single moment of it is of fateful importance. Life itself is simply not fatal to them. In contrast to men, for all their passing sorrows and afflictions, the gods live without true seriousness. Zeus weeps over the loss of Sarpedon, and Apollo is not happy when abandoning Hector, but neither god is essentially moved by the events. When it comes right down to it, they simply cannot empathize with the dying, not even in the angry, contemptuous manner of Achilles deriding Lykaion; they simply cannot put themselves in the place of mortals because it is clearly not their place. With respect to death, men and gods have no common language because they have nothing in common.

This difference heightens the pathos of the human struggle and gives men a tragic dignity that the gods, for all their power and brilliance, do not possess.[45] Abandoned by the gods in the face of their last extremity, men dwell in a region and develop a sense of life which is truly, exclusively their own. This realm and this life the gods illuminate only by providing contrast, by emitting the light that enables us to see the shadows. But since such shadowed, shadowy, doomed existence is men's inevitable portion, to appreciate what it is like we have to turn our eyes away from the dazzling brilliance of the gods and take a closer look at the mortal heroes of the *Iliad*.

The shadow of death darkens the life of Achilles, the traditional hero of the *Iliad,* more than it does that of any other man. While his choice between glorious death and long uneventful life is one that to some extent all warriors face as a possibility, Achilles' certain knowledge of the alternatives sharpens his dilemma and makes it extreme.[46] Others may hope for glory and long life, Achilles has to give up one or the other.

There is never much doubt about the outcome of Achilles' deliberations. Not just because the audience of the song already knows the outcome, but because the choice clearly follows from the character of Achilles in Homer. Given his warlike spirit, his general disregard, almost blindness, for all but honor and glory, his choice is predetermined. There is a kind of innocence to Achilles' action even at its cruelest; he is simply ignorant of and insensitive to aims, ends, and goods other than his own, other than the ones which—as his allotted portion—determine his fate. The simplicity of his character is such that he has but one role to play.

⋃ This role, however, is a truly epic one; given the alternatives Achilles is facing, his character and the choice that follows from it are an almost pure expression of the nature and functioning of man in the age of oral poetry. This man is mortal and, deeply conscious of his own doom, desires the everlasting life that the gods, representatives of his deepest aspiration, possess. But there is only one way to immortality open to mortal men: acquiring such outstanding honor, fame, and glory as will live forever in the memory of men.[47] The hero remembered does not altogether escape death, yet he does not sink completely into oblivion either: his spirit lives on as long as the song is heard. As the song is handed down and kept alive from generation to generation, so is the hero kept alive. Dying gloriously he has become immortal here and now rather than in some transcendent afterlife.[48]

In the preceding we emphasized that for the man of myth visibility and shining presence almost equals being and life; conversely, oblivion and obscurity are almost equivalent to not living at all. Now all this comes together interrelated; the epic hero is caught in a hermeneutic circle: with the epic emphasis on visibility, visibility equals life; everlasting life becomes everlasting visibility, and the Homeric mortals' wish for immortality is a wish for such everlasting visibility as only the song provides. Thus the song enhances man's need for the song while enhancing epic behavior: to enter the song one must be splendidly visible to begin with, one must have one's dazzling moment of glory, one must adopt the course of Achilles.

In this light Achilles' choice can be understood not only as the best of two evils, a compensation, as it were—immortality in the song compensating for actual, swift death—but as the only possible choice. For living on in obscurity, the other alternative open to him, could hardly be called life, so that Achilles' choice, now simply one between life and death, is simply the epic choice, the one that any other epic hero would have made in his stead.

However, others in the *Iliad* are not quite in Achilles' position; they are not faced with such clear-cut alternatives—glorious death or long undistinguished life—and this separates Achilles from all the others even while he is their typical representative. Once his choice is made—and it is made, implicitly, as soon as he learns of the alternatives—death, although it does not lose its sting, is no longer a factor influencing his behavior. All that remains for him to consider is glory. And this is what makes Achilles' action in the *Iliad* so different from all other men's that it becomes almost in-human: more and less than human at the same time.

"It is the universal limitation of death which causes human beings to restrain their passions, and Achilles' disregard of that limitation is what allows him to carry his passion so far and become more like a god than a man." [49] The gods are not kept in bound by the fear of death, and, with his death certain and imminent, Achilles is not either. Even while he broods over his impending end, bitter resentment rather than prudence and moderation color his thought and action. The only fear he knows is the fear of not attaining the one thing that still matters to him: immortal fame. This fear, the fear of any measure of glory escaping him, is one that he shares with the gods. This, more than his having an immortal mother, divine armor, and deathless horses and partaking of divine nourishment, makes him godlike. Not unmindful yet uncaring of death, he is half immortal even while he races toward his doom.

And this makes him inhuman in the literal sense of being less than human too. For unrestrained passion is bestial. Achilles invincible, spattered with gore, wishing to eat the heart of his enemies and their flesh raw; Achilles wrathful, out of his mind, relentlessly raging, cruel, and merciless, is at times more like a rabid dog than a man. He is almost incapable of feeling pity. Pity is for beings like oneself, and Achilles and other men hardly even belong to the same species.[50]

Lonely, self-centered, semidivine, semibestial, Achilles is almost completely cut off from human contact. Even in the few relationships he sustains—to Briseis, Patroclus—he seems more concerned with his own honor than with the life of beloved and friend. Aias' pleading, "stubborn man that cares not for his comrades' love . . . have *aidos* for your house, for we are all, all of us Danaans, under the same roof" (9.630, 640-1), is in vain. The mutual respect and love that unites men and saves lives in battle (15.561-3) is an all-too-human virtue—or necessity; what has Achilles to do with that? He fights his own battle and would even rejoice if all others perished, for this would increase his fame. His one obsession blots out all other claims and makes him deaf to others' cries. Unhearing, unseeing, almost untouchable, he lives alone in the midst of the Greek host, in his own private world.

The contrast between Achilles and Hector could not be greater. While Achilles, beastly and godlike, is lonely, self-centered, isolated almost to the point of being a stranger to the rest of humanity, Hector is the embodiment of a humane ideal of civic and family virtue. Father, brother, husband, son, guardian of the city, beloved by all, caring for all, he is as involved with others as Achilles is detached from them.

It is not of himself he thinks when bidding his mother sacrifice to Athene "so that she will have pity on the city and the wives of the Trojans and their helpless children" (6.275-6); when chiding his brother—"the people are perishing around the city . . . let us go lest the city be burnt with terrible fire" (6.327, 331); when refusing Helen's entreaty to rest—"already my heart is impelling me to come to the aid of the Trojans who miss me sorely in my absence" (6.361-2). It is not just for himself that he fights; his motto, the "one omen" he believes in is "to defend one's country" (12.240).

While Aias vainly urges uncaring Achilles to "have *aidos*" for his own country and friends, Hector needs no urging: "I would feel shame (*aideomai*) before the men and women of Troy" (6.441-2) if I shrank from battle, "nor would my own spirit let me" (444). Where Achilles is pitiless, merciless, hard, Hector feels pity for all and is gentle even to those that brought disaster on the city.

Achilles, jealous of his own honor, warns even the man closest to his heart: "obey me, so you can win great honor and glory *for me*," but do not go too far "without me, for you would then diminish *my honor*" (16.80-90). Hector wishes to be surpassed by the one he loves best: "may it be said of him, far greater is he than his own father" (6.479).

Achilles broods about his death and looks beyond it to immortality; Hector refuses to dwell on it and looks to life. Death is certain, but "do not grieve overmuch in your heart" (6.486), he consoles Andromache. We shall die when it is fated; in the meantime let us attend to living and doing our allotted tasks (6.487-9). Of course, Hector has something to live for, while Achilles can achieve what he wants only through death. That is why Hector is "a great joy to the city and all the people" (24.276) and Achilles a bane for friends and enemies alike.

Hector is a pure type. The formulaic epithet "guardian of the city, the wives, and innocent children" almost exhausts his character. But he is a new, humane type. Unlike fearless Achilles, Hector is often cowardly; but in the end he exhibits a courage Achilles cannot even dream of: overcoming his fear he faces hopeless odds with dignity and resolution. To be sure, he too fights for honor. But unlike Achilles and the wilder gods to whom warlike power and insensate slaughter are almost ends in themselves, Hector conceives even of honor in terms of civil ends, in terms of love, duty, reverence for others. "He has no dishonor who dies for his country, for then his wife shall be safe and his children thereafter, and his house and land unharmed" (15.496-8). This is other-directed honor at its best.

So great is the contrast between Achilles and Hector, and, for the most part, so onesided is Homer's sympathy for the latter, that some scholars came to regard the person of Hector in the *Iliad* as Homer's own creation rather than a traditional figure. In view of the nature of oral composition, and the continuous transformation of the poem in each successive retelling, this contention cannot be substantiated. Since the *Iliad* is our earliest source of the epic, how is one to determine what exactly is its last poet's contribution, and what changes have taken place through the mythopoetic work of previous singers in the generations just preceding? What is important for us is that Hector, as he appears in our *Iliad,* is undoubtedly the expression of a new ideal of man while Achilles bears traces of an older, Mycenean tradition.[51] Whether Homer's exclusive creation or the end product of centuries of gradual change, Hector certainly embodies a new emphasis and a trend toward a new morality. Ares, the god of the *arete* of the *aristoi,* yields to newer, gentler deities not only on the Olympus but on the human level too. The shift from Achilles to Hector signalizes the end of an era—warlike, agonistic, Mycenean—and the beginning of another—civic, civilized, communal, and humane.

Myth is the preserver of tradition, and Achilles was the traditional hero of the Trojan war. There was little Homer, or other poets, could do about that. But only facts are tenacious and unyielding in the life of the story; not so the spirit in which they are retold. Facts are more or less fixed past, but their presentation and interpretation is fluid and always expressive of the spirit of the living present. This is evident in the *Iliad* not only through Homer's loving portrayal of Hector's character and his relative lack of sympathy for Achilles. Even apart from this opposition of "hero and villain"—as Graves regards the two, not altogether unjustly— Achilles' own character and behavior, taken by itself and on its own terms, implies a subtle, perhaps not even conscious criticism of the older heroic ideal. For Achilles is, of course, not just a villain. There is a point where his efforts become so self-defeating that he acquires a pathos all his own and becomes the first paradoxical hero in Western literature.

We have touched upon the fact that Achilles' singleminded pursuit of glorious death isolates him and makes him almost a stranger to humanity. What we have not pointed out is that the degree of his alienation is almost sufficient to frustrate his own purpose and deprive him altogether of the fruits of any possible victory. For in the end Achilles not only refuses the visible signs of honor —as offered by Agamemnon—for the sake of which he began his lonely battle. In his excessive disregard and even contempt for others he just about gives away, physically and spiritually, those who alone can give him the honor he wants: the community. In an other-directed society honor means being honored by others. But if these others count for nothing—as they do more and more in Achilles' eyes—of what worth is their respect and that of all succeeding human generations? Without *mutual* recognition—the beginning of a communal spirit—and that means recognition by Achilles of the others' worth and of the common nature he shares with them, no recognition by the others can weigh much in the balance. Thus Achilles achieves immortality in the song. But his pursuit of this goal makes meaningless the achievement. Even while winning the prize he has lost its substance.

Is this an indication that Achilles, while unable to rise above the epic ideal, in the end still negated it? That he was disillusioned with, yet incapable of surpassing the Mycenean heroic standard? That in Achilles' person Homer strained the epic ideal to its breaking point where it revealed its own futility? Certainly Parry's closing remarks seem appropriate: "Achilles' tragedy, his final isolation, is that he can in no sense, including that of language, . . . leave the society which has become alien to him. And Homer uses the epic speech a long poetic tradition gave him to transcend the limits of that speech" [52] and of that tradition.

One might object that Achilles' excessive isolation was the result of his uncommon situation and not one inherent in the heroic ideal as such. But this is not quite so. To be sure, Achilles' character as well as his situation is exaggerated; an excessive expression

of an ideal stretched to its limit. Yet an expression of this ideal it is
nonetheless. For as long as the ultimate mark of excellence is honor,
and the way to achieve honor, the visible sign of excellence, is "to
overcome all others" (6.208) by brute force or cunning, the men of
this society will always be set against each other in their individual
struggle for recognition. Such a society will necessarily break up
into rival power centers—individual heroes or gods—existing side
by side. It will be paratactic rather than organically structured, and
the unconnected ad-hoc powers of which it must be composed will
be not only antagonistic but even anarchic by nature. Their drive
for self-assertion and their unlimited struggle for recognition will
prevent them from recognizing each other unless forced to do so,
and the man victorious in this struggle will come out of it least constrained to recognize anyone. So he, above all, will be recognized
only by those to whom he accords no recognition. Thus his struggle
is necessarily self-defeating[53] for the honors he wins can never be
anything but meaningless to him.

Homer may have exaggerated so as to reveal, but he did not
misrepresent the contradiction inherent in the ancient heroic standard. And having revealed it, he helped to put an end to the epic
ideal of warlike excellence and took the first step toward replacing
it with a less self-defeating and more humanly achievable norm. In
the following we shall follow the development of this new ideal
from Hesiod's *Erga*[54] to the Aeschylean *Eumenides*. It is important
to note, however, that the growth of this more humane and civilized
notion of man that Hector already embodied in the *Iliad* represents
only one strand of the post-Homeric development of the Homeric
ideal. For the Achillean image of the paradoxical hero was also developed in post-Homeric times. To be sure, the purely other-directed
heroism of the epic hero gradually gave way to a deeper and more
inner-directed ideal of human excellence. But it was only its exclusive surface-orientation and paratactic morality that died with
the epic. The vision of man implicit in the highest types of epic
humanity proved stronger than the poetic form in which it was

first presented. The lonely hero whose highest act of heroism seals his fate, since he can attain what he most values only at the cost of his life, is not just an epic ideal. In the person of Achilles, and in the persons of so many of the *Iliad's* fragile yet courageously struggling mortals who come up against an unconquerable limit in the very act of supreme self-assertion, Homer created the image of the tragic hero that was to survive the death of the oral tradition.

Thus what made the *Iliad* an end and a beginning, a radical turning point in the development of the Greek spirit, was not just the passing of an ideal. Even the type of unconscious criticism we have just dealt with, which injects a new spirit into a traditional idea and refutes it while still presenting it in a skeletal form, is a possible device of oral poetry. What really put an end to the epic is the simple fact that it was written down. The art of writing killed the song, for it made a gradual, imperceptible, organic, and historically unconscious development of the story impossible, and thus brought about the end of living myth. With the passing of generations and the concomitant change in social structure, the customs and ways of thinking, the moral, intellectual and emotional demands of the Greeks changed, but the *Iliad,* the written poem, remained the same. As the temporal distance grew, the difference between the old and new spirits became more and more noticeable, and critical reflection on the past became not only possible but inevitable. With the quiet, unconscious unfolding of the myth arrested, the age of historical consciousness began.

It is not just that the conflict between the old and new ways of living became apparent with the passing of time. More than that, the inner conflicts within the myth, the conflict between the disparate elements paratactically brought together in the poem, could now be clearly seen for the first time. With epic parataxis no longer the dominant form of thought, its shortcomings became visible and unacceptable. And writing made this possible.

Writing, with its fixity and permanence, allows the reader to range back and forth over the text, to compare its parts and become aware of inconsistencies, to follow a long line of gradual development and growth, to see general patterns slowly emerging through particular incidents, to see, synoptically, the whole of what is revealed through the parts. As such, writing brings with it a wholly new type of thought: one demanding coherence, unity, harmony, organic wholeness, and logical connection in all diversity. This type of thought is fully aware of the tension between surface and depth, potentiality and actuality, and it can conceive of a hidden order, a not immediately apparent connection, an underlying law. It fosters a new sense of time: real differences between past, present, and future become visible, as well as the overarching, unchanging pattern. It asks for a new truth: not surface visibility (*aletheia*), but the vision of something not immediately visible, the form or idea that transcends the particular and is yet immanent in it. It has a new concept of reality: the real is not what appears to sight but precisely that which does not and cannot be seen except by the reflective intellect. And it brings with itself a new responsibility. To the individual who is no longer spellbound by his own unconscious absorption of the oral tradition, an explicit deviation from that tradition is no longer an anathema. But the possibility of deliberate innovation lays the burden of justifying what tradition no longer hallows on the innovator himself. Critical thinking, unsupported by tradition, must henceforth provide its own justification and be its own primary foundation and support.

Of course, this new type of thought did not spring ready-made into the world. As a long tradition of oral poetry preceded and made possible its perfect form, so it took several centuries of literacy to develop fully its potential. But once the process began, a return to the mode of thought the oral epic fostered was impossible. And once the process was completed, in the fifth and fourth centuries, the basic modes of thinking for Western man were fixed for millenia.

2. *The* Erga

Unlike the anonymous singers of living myth, Hesiod proudly confronts us in the first person at the very beginning of his poems. "One day (the Muses) taught Hesiod fair song while he was herding his sheep under holy Helicon, and this was the first word the goddesses said to me . . . 'we know how to speak much falsehood resembling the truth, but we know how to tell the truth too, when we so please.'" (*Theogony* 22–28) There is a radically new note here. If the Muses can lie just as easily as they can tell the truth, then the poets of the past too may have sung truthfully or only seemingly truthfully, i.e., falsely. If so, one can no longer rely blindly on what has been handed down for generations and accept even long-held beliefs as the gods' own truth. Rather the poet, and each individual who is capable of it, must think for himself. This is in fact what Hesiod advocates. "That man is best of all who thinks for himself" (*Erga* 293) and, failing that, "he too is good who listens to a good advisor" (*Erga* 295). And such an autonomous thinker and truthful advisor Hesiod claims to be as he addresses his audience: others may lie, but I will tell the truth (*Erga* 10), others may mislead you but I will speak good sense (*Erga* 286). Gone is the quasi-unconscious and uncritical mythopoeia of the oral poet, and the unbreakable hold of tradition is broken. Homo-

43

geneity of belief is a matter of the past. In Hesiod's poems, for the first time in Greek history, it is the self-conscious individual who speaks: an individual conscious of the difference between his beliefs and those of others and at the same time deeply aware of his role as educator and improver of mankind.

This individual is also historically conscious. The oral poet sung of the unchanging past that was the myth's forever living present, but Hesiod, who wants to "celebrate what shall be as well as what has gone before" (*Theogony* 32), conceives of a past, present, and future that encompass essential development and genuine change. His *Theogony* already told a story of the rise and fall of generations of gods, a story of the development of the divine essence from chaos and conflict to intellectual order and harmony. But historical as well as critical consciousness is even more implicit in the *Erga,* the work in which Hesiod's break with the past and his awareness of this break strike the reader at every step.

Hardly has the *Erga* got under way and we find Hesiod doing something novel. "Verily the gods keep hidden from men the means of life" (*Erga* 42) he notes. But instead of just stating that life is hard and leaving it there as the way of things, the only conceivable way perhaps, he immediately envisages an alternative possibility (*Erga* 43-44) and proceeds to give an account of why things are as they are. It is true that the accounts Hesiod gives are "mythical" in the modern sense of the word; still the enterprise of giving them at all is utterly unmythical in the sense of being quite alien to the oral epic. For living myth's implicit assumption is that things have always been essentially what they are now and therefore need only to be presented not explained. Stories of the past are brought into the epic only to illuminate the present. Even if the need for an explanation could arise, which is unlikely in an oral context, explanations providing connections between altogether dissimilar states of affairs are alien to the paratactic mentality. But Hesiod's approach is historical and etiological. He not only envisages a different state of affairs as possible but presents it as having actually existed in the past, and, confronted with the problem of historical change, he raises and attempts to answer the causal question: how has it come about that things are so different now from what they once used to be? With the first appearance of historical novelty the need for justification and explanation is also immediately felt.

And Hesiod's way of explaining things is also strange. He is not content with merely telling a tale of how things have come about; he tells not one but two totally different stories to explain our present misery. Now the presence of several explanations for the same phenomenon is a commonplace in Herodotus, who usually adds for our information which of them he thinks most credible and why. But for Hesiod to connect the two stories with a casual "or, if you will, I will highlight for you another account" (*Erga* 106) is revolutionary. It is also profoundly disturbing to an audience brought up in the oral tradition, for once you have conflicting alternatives you cannot remain a passive receiver of what is transmitted. You cannot accept what you are told uncritically but it is up to you as an individual to reflect and choose. And the choice is complicated by the fact that the presence of two conflicting stories is bound to discredit each to some extent, and to that extent it also discredits or at least weakens the unquestioned authority of tradition that was the strongest support of living myth. Not only is it impossible for both stories to be true, but they may both be false; or if not altogether false—for Hesiod promised to tell the truth —they may be true in a new nonliteral sense, i.e., they may be mere fables of the kind that immediately follows them in the *Erga* (202–212): likely accounts to be taken as heuristic tales rather than literal truth, stories told for the sake of a moral rather than to reveal something that actually happened. If so, we have an entirely new category of "myth" here. These stories are allegorical rather than tautegorical: they mean something other than what they actually say. If there is any truth to them at all, this must be a new type, a hidden, underlying truth rather than the immediate surface revelation of the Homeric epic. Seeming and being, the phenomenal and the real, the mythical and the nonmythical are beginning to be separated in the *Erga*.

Still the actual separation of fact from fiction is something that the thoughtful reader has to perform himself; the poet does not do the job for him in any obvious way. For the stories Hesiod tells are neither altogether mythical—in the sense of being nonfactual— nor entirely historical—in our sense of the word. They are rather a mixture of the fabulous and the factual, and this is something important for us to note if we are to gauge the extent of the poet's consciousness of history.

The second story Hesiod tells in his attempt to account for our present misery is especially interesting in this connection. It is a tale of the five ages of mankind spanning the distance from the first generation of man to the present. It is a story of overall decline, but, against all our expectations and unlike its Near Eastern predecessors, this tale does not relate the continuous degeneration of man from the good, carefree, and happy creatures of the golden age to the evil and wretched race of iron now living. There is no such continuity here. The fourth generation breaks the line of unbroken descent; it is definitely nobler and better than the one preceding it. This break in the story caused by the interpolation of a heroic age can be explained only by the assumption that Hesiod was trying to accommodate historical facts within his ideal scheme. Because the Homeric epics existed the heroic age could not be simply ignored. Nor could it be modified and absorbed into the story as one of the ages, for the Homeric heroes' character did not fit any of the generations of the model scheme, and the writing down of the Homeric epic [1] made a gradual modification impossible. Therefore a past, different from the present, had to be accounted for even though it fit neither the framework of the story nor the didactic purposes of the storyteller too well.

The necessity of interpolating the heroic age turned Hesiod's story of the five ages at least partially into real history. But this history was of a peculiar kind. To begin with, it was not a history of individual men or tribes. As Rosenmeyer points out,[2] even when

Hesiod deals with the heroic age he introduces names and places more to identify the race than for their own sake, and for the rest the generations he tells of are completely nameless. Individual names, individual representatives of a race, do not seem to matter; it is the general characterization of the ages that concern Hesiod. Now this in itself is a very unepic note. In the epic general characterization is achieved by singling out a particular individual and making him a pure type, a prototype of the kind of man to be described. But here the type is directly described and discussed as such rather than by way of an individual example. Abstraction and generalization rather than particularization in the shining image are at work.

Furthermore, Hesiod's "genera" are not human generations confined to a life-span each,[3] nor are they connected biologically, one giving rise to the other in the course of nature. They are cultural rather than genealogical divisions, so that even while including a "historical" age Hesiod is giving us a cultural rather than factual history. In myth, individuals die and generations pass, but families, tribes, and nations remain, and certainly no cultural change is consciously recorded. But here even whole races, i.e., types of man, perish and others, entirely different in morality and nature, take their place. Such an explicit consciousness of a possible change in the make-up of man is the final blow to the authority of tradition. If things have ever been so profoundly different, then what is is no longer necessary simply because it is. And if things can change so greatly, then they are still subject to change, and thus instead of obeying tradition one might be justified even in bringing about its fall, especially if one is as dissatisfied with the status quo as the author of the *Erga* seems to be (174-5). Hesiod's historically conscious account of the ages of man opens the way and provides the impetus for conscious and deliberate moral reform.

Such moral reform is in fact the central undertaking of the *Erga*. It is the purpose that unifies the diverse parts of the poem and determines its line of thought.

In the poem Hesiod announces his intention to sing of Zeus,

guardian of justice, "through whom mortal men are famed or un-
famed, sung or unsung alike. . . . For easily he makes strong and
easily he brings the strong man low; easily he humbles the proud
and raises the obscure, easily he straightens the crooked and blasts
the proud" (*Erga* 3–7). Although the poet does not explicitly say
that the proud man he wishes to be brought low is the warrior-
ruler of the Homeric song, there is little doubt left about this as
the poem proceeds. The description of the two strifes that immediately follows deliberately detaches the new morality Hesiod advocates from the old one, and contrasts the two. "For there was not
only one kind of Strife, but there are two on earth" (11–12), one
good, one bad. The bad one "fosters vile war and battle, being
merciless; no mortal loves her" (14–15). "But the other . . . is much
better for man. She rouses even the lazy to work" (19–20) in eager
competition with his fellow men, making "potter jealous of potter,
builder of builder, beggar envious of beggar, and singer of singer"
(25–26). "This Strife is good for man" (24).

It seems that the warlike valor of the Homeric hero, his proud,
power-bent, agonistic spirit is suddenly no longer something to be
admired, while the peaceful competition of even such lowly men
as potter and builder is extolled. In the *Erga* the mighty lords that
the *Iliad* made famous suddenly become "gift-devouring kings"
(38–39) whose ill-gotten gains and glory are easily undone by Zeus,
while the industrious common man, whom the *Iliad* hardly even
deigns to mention, is promised better rewards: easily Zeus brings
the strong man low and raises the obscure.

This impression is further reinforced by the story of the five
ages, where the low-point of degeneration is reached with the brazen
race "terrible and strong, which loved the lamentable works of Ares
and wanton violence" (145–146) so much that "they were destroyed by their own hands" (152), and where the fifth race too is
promised destruction (180) as soon as its members fall out with
one another (182–5), forsake justice and reverence (185), sack each
others' city (189), favor the evildoer and the violent (191), and

adopt the principle that might is right (189, 192). Then "bitter sorrows will be left for mortal men and there will be no defense against evil" (201). Homer's implicit criticism of Mycenean morality is made unmistakably explicit here.

The fable immediately following, told so that the kings may understand (202), sums up the aristocratic power-morality Hesiod deplores: "Thus spoke the hawk to the nightingale . . . as he carried her grasped with his claws and she cried pitifully, pierced by the curved talons. Why do you cry, you wretched thing, you are now in the power of one far stronger than you and must go where I take you. . . . I will eat you if I will, or let you go. He who wants to withstand the stronger is a fool. For he will be robbed of victory and only suffer pain beside his shame" (203–212).

What then is Hesiod's alternative? It is already implicit in the preceding and becomes clearer as the poem proceeds. The new morality Hesiod advocates rests on the twin pillars of justice and work.

"Listen to Dike, Perses, and do not foster hybris" (213), Hesiod admonishes his brother. Although in this particular passage justice and its opposite, hybris, are defined primarily in legalistic terms closely connected with dealings in law courts, it is clear that justice and injustice are for Hesiod by no means exclusively, or even primarily, legal terms. They were not such in the description of the violent bronze and iron ages, for whom might was right, and they are not such in Hesiod's mighty answer to the hawk's derision: "Listen to justice and forget violence altogether"—he repeats—"for the son of Cronos allotted this law to men that fish and beasts and winged birds should devour each other, for there is no justice among them; but to men he gave justice which is best of all" (275–279). *Bia,* violence, is the opposite of *Dike,* and man, having been given justice as his share, debases himself if he resorts to violence, the law of the beasts. What might be right for animals is brutish in man, for god gave men justice.

This shift from Homeric power-morality to the humane ethic

of peaceful competition makes even Hesiod's preoccupation with legal justice more meaningful than it would be if it were merely the result of his accidental engagement in a lawsuit with his brother. If justice is the opposite of brute force, then decision by due process of law—as the only possible alternative to decision by main strength —is not only a symbol of justice but also the most important means of its implementation by men. Thus Hesiod's insistence on justice in the law courts, and his impassioned diatribes against the "gift-devouring judges who give crooked judgments" (221, 262) and the briber, slanderer, and perjurer who twist the law to their own ends, are of a significance that far transcends the merely legalistic.

Legal justice is a means to maintaining moral justice. But what is moral justice a means to? Is it an end in itself, or at least an end for man simply because it is his inborn norm, the "human" rather than animal code of behavior? Hesiod's poem makes it clear that he has no illusions concerning man's innate goodness and no intention to leave justice with only ideal sanctions. Instead, he offers a prudential argument for being just and supports his ideal with the strongest possible sanction, that of utility. Injustice invariably leads to ruin. Retribution for transgression is inevitable. Justice brings tangible and certain rewards. If a man wants to fare well, he had better be righteous.

Hesiod never tires of repeating this. "Justice triumphs over transgression in the end" (217). "Oath keeps pace with crooked judgments" (219). Peace, prosperity, and general well-being are the rewards of the just (225–237). Famine, plague, war, death, and destruction are the punishment of the wicked (238–247). Zeus has thirty-thousand spirits to watch over the acts of men (250). The virgin Dike, honored and reverenced by the gods, reports to Zeus whenever offended (256–260), and "Zeus himself, seeing and understanding all, beholds these things" (267). "There is no way to escape the will of Zeus" (105); he gives prosperity to the just while the generation of the transgressor is left "obscure ever after" (279–285). The "gods soon blot out" the criminal and "bring his house low" (325) and "truly Zeus himself is angry and at last lays on him heavy retribution for his evil deeds" (333). As the proverb tells, "harming others you harm yourself, and evil planned harms the plotter most" (263).

The introduction of all sorts of deities to guarantee retribution (Zeus, Dike, Horkos, the Olympians, the immortal spirits) does not make Hesiod's conception of justice a naive mythical one, for these divinities are no longer the anthropomorphic, honor- and power-hungry, willful, personal, tribal gods of myth. They have become semiabstract beings: the mere guarantors of justice. As justice is transformed in Hesiod from a concrete descriptive term into an abstract universal concept (from *dikaios* through *ta dikaia* and *to dikaion* into *dike*), so the gods, too, shed their personality and individual aspirations, and instead of being opposed to or even distinguishable from *moira* (as they were in the *Iliad*), they become the embodiment of the rule of law. It is not in the least surprising that the Fates have no role to play in the *Erga,* for *dike* is nothing but a specialized *moira* concept here. As man's allotment (279), it has simply taken over the function of *moira* in the human realm.

While it is true that reward and punishment are not yet explicitly the immanent causal outcome of man's action in Hesiod, there is nevertheless quite a difference between the divine administration of justice in Hesiod and the ad hoc interventions of the gods in Homer. Though Hesiod, lacking the concept of "immanent, natural causality," still uses the traditional machinery of divine intervention, and although, strictly speaking, it is still the gods that enforce *dike,* the unbroken regularity of punishment is such that it can be regarded as automatic, the gods being, as it were, merely its mechanism, so that reward and punishment are virtually the direct outcome of man's acts and not the whim of the gods. The unjust have a short and painful life "because of their thoughtlessness" (133-4), and they destroy themselves "by their own hands" (152). Nominally it is still the gods that punish transgression, but for the most part the retribution itself is such as the acts themselves would naturally bring about. For what is more likely than that the cities of the just, who avoid violence, tend their fields, and go about their business, should prosper in peace, while those of the unjust, who practice aggression and cruelty inspired by evil Strife, should be embroiled in war, internal discord, and continual unrest with all the concomitant evils of plague, famine, death and general destruction?

In spite of this semiimmanence and quasi-natural operation of reward and punishment, however, justice does not become a purely secular concept in the poem, simply because there are no purely secular ideals in Hesiod. Moral reform is at the same time religious reform here. While divine guarantee insures justice, the function of the gods as bearers and implementors of law rationalizes religion. This process of a deliberate purification of religion already began in the *Theogony,* where the defeat of the Titans signalized the defeat of the older monstrous, cruel, and bloodthirsty gods and brought about the rule of wise, peaceful, orderly, and just deities under the unified leadership of Zeus. It is now continued in the *Erga* where Hesiod emphasizes—even in the mythical Pandora story and the tale of the five ages—that our miserable state of life is itself the direct result of Zeus's punishment of man's injustice rather than an undeserved and arbitrary doom imposed on man by some whimsical god. Since the gods have become rational, there is no need here for a "secular reason" to make man moral and give him human dignity. Divine, god-given, and god-enforced *dike* will do that.

Being just is the first essential requirement man has to fulfill if he wants to escape utter degradation and misery and lift himself above the level of beasts. The other requirement for well-being, equally important in Hesiod, is work.

"Work, high-born Perses, so that hunger may hate you and Demeter . . . fill your barn with provisions. Gods and men alike are wroth with the man who lives in idleness. . . . Through work men gain herds and wealth, and working they become much dearer to the immortals. Work is no disgrace, idleness is. . . . Whatever be your lot, work is best for you" (298–314). "Between us and well-being the immortal gods have placed the sweat of our brows" (289–90), so "work the work the gods ordained for men" (397). "Do not put it off till tomorrow and the day after, for an idle worker does not fill his barn, nor does he who puts off work; care makes work go well, while the sluggish worker is always at the brink of ruin" (409–413). Reinforcing gnomic wisdom with divine guarantee, Hesiod hammers home his truth with the subtlety of a steamroller: "If your heart desires wealth, do thus and work with work upon work" (381–382).

Although Hesiod deals with justice and work successively as if they were to some extent separate topics merely paratactically conjoined, there is an indissoluble bond between the two which makes them inseparable in this poet's thought.

Hesoid advocates justice in place of the old principle of *cheirodike,* the principle that might is right. But if warlike excellence and power are replaced by this new virtue that rules out acquisition by conquest, how will man, now gentle and peaceful, acquire a livelihood and gain honor and fame? Clearly, there is only one way: the peaceful competition that the good Eris stands for, the unceasing industry that brings material rewards. And this new road to *arete*—the farmer's success rather than the warrior's excellence—is not only required by the rule of justice, but in its own turn requires that this rule be upheld. For how is the powerless but industrious worker to safeguard the fruits of his labor, unless justice insures his possession of them? That is why *dike* is not just the opposite of violence but also the principle of right distribution and of the legal arbitration that effects and safeguards such. Only "fools do not know how much more the half (that is one's due) is than the whole (seized by force or deceit)" (40); the wise man will "take right measure from his neighbor and repay him rightly with the same measure" (349–50).

Nor is "right measure" in the *Erga* a merely legal-juridical requirement necessary for the safeguarding of one's possessions acquired by hard work. To "observe due measure" (694) is the sine qua non of work itself if it is to lead to the possessions so necessary for the maintenance of life. That is why *metra, metria, metreisthai, kata metron, hore, horaion, kosmein, eukosmos, kairos* (306, 349, 394, 409, 422, 617, 628, 630, 642, 648, 664, 694, 695, 697, 720), all words connoting the right measure, proportion, order, season, occasion, time, etc., recur with such frequency in the section dealing with work. They have to be emphasized, for they express one of Hesiod's central ideas: the due measure and order are the "best of all things" (694) in every aspect of the conduct of one's life. Some commentators deplored the inclusion of the "farmer's calendar" (383–617) in Hesiod's poem as a kind of unnecessary addition that detracts from rather than reinforces Hesiod's message. Yet, for all its being a hodgepodge assemblage of random directions for cultivating the land, the farmer's calendar has one important underlying idea: that there is a natural order of things, and that we can succeed only if we know this order and conform to it in our lives.[4] Even the "Days," whether Hesiod did in fact add them or not, have at least this much connection with the rest of the poem, that in their own way they link up with the notion that everything has its due day, time, and season.

This idea of due order in nature, and therefore in work, is in its turn connected with the idea of justice as a kind of natural order and balance whose violators prosper no more than those who fail to observe the right rules of dealing with nature. In fact, the two orders, natural and civil, have the same source in Hesiod.[5] It is Zeus who gave man justice as his portion (*Erga* 276–279) and safeguards his observance of it. It is also Zeus who distributed, fairly and equally, the portions (*moirai*) (*Theogony* 520) and functions (*timai*) (*Theogony* 885) of the gods that are the representatives of natural order in the *Theogony,* and he is thus originator and guarantee of law and order in nature. In the language of myth, Zeus' marriage with Themis (that which is laid down, established, fixed, law) brought forth the Horai (seasons, regular periods of time)

as well as Eunomia (good order); Dike and Eirene as well as the
Moirai (fates, portions) (*Theogony* 901–906). That is why the
whole of the *Erga,* the parts on justice as well as the parts on work
and on the days, the whole song about the right way of life in
the world, is, just as Hesiod announced in the proem, Zeus' praise:
a hymn to the supreme deity as the embodiment of law in the
whole—divine, human, natural—world.

The overall unity of Hesiod's poem [6] is in many ways quite unlike the unity of the Homeric epic. The *Iliad's* unity, apart from the
very loose structural and developmental coherence that the Achilles
story gave it, was above all the result of the essential sameness of
all its paratactically arranged episodes. But the sameness of the
Erga's "episodes" is no longer surface similarity. "Justice" is not the
same as "work" and neither of these is the same as the "days." What
ties all the parts of the *Erga* together is not visible identity but syn-
tactic order and an organic coherence of thought.

On the surface, the poem's composition seems even more paratactic than that of the *Iliad.* Its parts are more easily discernible since
the subject each section concentrates on is superficially quite unlike
the one before or after, and the transition between sections often
seems flimsy and illogical.[7] But the point is that beside such surface
conjunctions there is a deeper, underlying connection here. (That is
precisely why the surface transitions may be left flimsy; they are
not the only, let alone the most important, links.) Only this connection in depth is a connection of thought rather than immediate
appearance and as such must be brought to light by a reflection on
the poem as a whole.

Once the unifying principle—the idea of an orderly life in an
orderly world, of observing due measure in our dealings with men as
well as with nature—is comprehended, everything in the poem falls
into place as naturally belonging to the central theme. The invocation of Zeus as originator and preserver of order and justice; the two
Erides story contrasting peaceful competition in work with violent,
hybristic behavior; the Pandora myth accounting for the necessity to

work as a punishment for injustice; the five ages story explaining the same as the end result of a degeneration to injustice and violence; the admonitions to Perses, lazy and unjust, and to the judges and kings, crooked devourers of the product of others' work; the sections on justice and work; the farmer's calendar, the *gnomai,* and even the Days—for all surface diversity and clumsy transition between parts there is no real change of subject in the whole poem. The seemingly incoherent parts are merely so many ways of expressing, reinforcing, and expanding the same theme.

Of course the same theme—the heroic way of life in Homer's case—was also endlessly rehearsed in the *Iliad* too. But in the *Erga* the theme could not even be guessed by someone concentrating on just one or two individual parts, while in the *Iliad* it could. (A heroic exploit is a heroic exploit, be it Diomedes', Hector's or Achilles' individual *aristeia*.) Even the individual aspects of the theme—justice and work as aspects of the orderly life—are abstractions rather concrete, graphic embodiments, and the theme itself can be inferred only by further abstraction at times rejecting at times affirming what is immediately presented.

Hesiod's telling the tale of the hawk and the nightingale typifies his method of composition in the *Erga*. He introduces the fable at the end of the story of the five ages as if he were changing the subject and turning to something else: "And now I will tell a fable for princes" (202), and having concluded the story without immediately refuting the hawk's claim he turns again, this time to his brother: "But you, Perses . . ." (213). Yet, in spite of such seeming discontinuity, the relevance of the fable to what precedes and follows it, and indeed to the general theme of the poem, could not be clearer to the thoughtful reader. For all its seeming digression, indeed its apparent opposition to what immediately follows, the fable is a powerful reinforcement by antithesis of the theme. But it is a reinforcement in depth rather than immediate appearance, and this is what is so characteristic in Hesiod.

The fable explicitly says the direct opposite of what it means;

there is an inherent tension in it between surface content and hidden meaning; it is an allegory in the strict sense of the word: it proclaims (*agoreuei*) something other (*allo*) than it says. Such tension and such allegorical rather than literal truth in Hesiod's poem are completely new and unepic elements. The epic brooked no tension and required immediate, surface revelation and full disclosure with nothing concealed and merely implied. Hesiod's *ainos* is an *ainigma* [8] hiding and revealing the truth at the same time; it is a riddle that requires reflection, since its message is precisely what is not directly expressed [9] but must be added by thought. And it is, of course, inevitably added. Hesiod's abrupt silence at the end of the fable is at least as effective a reply to the hawk's contention as is his actual refutation sixty lines later. But it marks the appearance of a new technique: a technique appropriate only to a poetry directed at the mind rather than at the ear, eye, and aesthetic sensibility.

This new direction of Hesiod's poetry affects greatly the *Erga's* language and style. The oral poet lovingly embroidered his fabric, elaborating his images in all their detail until they dazzled the senses and the imagination by their ornamental splendor. In contrast to this, there is very little decorative detail in Hesiod. He is not very good at vivid, concrete, sensuously appealing presentation —the oral poet's forte—and for the most part does not even attempt it. As he himself puts it (*Erga* 106), he would rather "outline" (*ekkoryphoso*) the story, touch on the main points, and highlight the moral,[10] for that is what is important to him, not the surface appearance. That is why the simile, the Homeric device of concrete, perceptually clear characterization, can practically disappear in the *Erga*. Hesiod is intent on revealing structural rather than perceptual similarities and metaphysical rather than visual and visualizable connections. His thoughtful rather than intuitive language and style testify to this turn from visibility to intelligibility. "The visible world no longer has for him an immediate and self-evident appeal; the splendor and preciousness, which precisely the outer side of things had for Homer" [11] no longer interest Hesiod. It is the inside, the hidden meaning and thought content, the depth rather than surface of things that concern him.

It is difficult to read the *Erga* without being aware of how poor and graceless, dry and labored, its language is—measured by the Homeric standard. But this is the point: Hesiod labors at the creation of a new standard, that of thought rather than imagination. Since he wants to say something other, something more than can be said within the confines of epic poetry, the epic form itself becomes to some extent an obstacle to what Hesiod wants to say; an obstacle he begins to overcome. Although he is still using the only available poetic form—the epic hexameter—his new standard points in the direction and makes possible the future development of prose rather than verse writing and of philosophy rather than poetry. No wonder then that there is not only more beauty but also more immediate humanity in a single episode of the sixth book of the *Iliad* than can be found in the entire poetic production of Hesiod. For better or worse Homer's intuitive humanity has given way to the arid philosophic humanism of Hesiod.

All stylistic peculiarities of the *Erga* are consonant with and expressive of this new direction Hesiod takes. While poor in decorative expressions, his language is much richer in abstractions than Homer's. Words that had a concrete significance in the *Iliad* receive an abstract meaning in Hesiod and are even further abstracted by a development from the particular plural (e.g., *ethea,* particular customs) to the singular universal (*ethos,* custom as such).[12] Such abstractive conceptualization is but one aspect of Hesiod's movement away from the shining particular of the epic toward the underlying general idea of philosophic prose.

Another aspect is Hesiod's method of defining words and clarifying meaning by antitheses. This technique of achieving intellectual precision as well as greater generality has often been commented on. But Sellschopp points out [13] something less commonly emphasized: that Hesiod's definitions through antitheses gradually enrich the meaning of his abstracta and this gradual enrichment and growth in meaning is something new. In the epic, the meaning of a word or phrase had to be as transparent as possible all at once, and the same formula was used in much the same sense in much the same situation again and again. But Hesiod not only loosens formulaic use by punctuating his poem with pregnant key words (*dike, ergon, metron,* etc.) rather than formulas, with words chosen for their meaning rather than their metrical fitness, he also breaks the static rigidity of formulaic use by developing and augmenting the meaning of his words through repetition in *different* contexts with *different* antitheses. Surface sameness is no longer important now that key words have a meaning in depth that is revealed slowly in the course of the poem. With the emphasis on underlying, conceptual sameness, revelation in Hesiod becomes a process rather than a lightning flash, and growth in meaning takes the place of instant disclosure and subsequent repetition without enrichment.

Hesiod's tendency to abstract and conceptualize also explains his proneness to etymologizing. While in Homer plays on words are much more frequent than etymologies, and even the latter are almost playfully offered as ornamental flourishes adopted perhaps for the sake of their pleasing sound, Hesiod takes his explanations of names seriously and goes about them with a heavyhanded and labored deliberateness. That he should do so is not surprising. One assumption for all etymologizing is that there is more to the word than is immediately apparent, that there is a hidden meaning that only dissection will reveal, that the word is not just what it is in its conventional use but is something more. But this assumption of a tension between surface use and meaning in depth, between concrete significance and underlying, more general disclosure, is precisely the one that motivates abstraction and conceptualization in general. As for etymologizing names, the assumption here is that names are not merely denotative but also descriptive, that they do not just name the thing but also reveal its hidden nature, and that therefore if we rightly understand the name we shall also know the thing.[14] And who could be more likely to make this assumption than

Hesiod, who in his *Theogony* has already introduced a whole series of deities that are not living personalities but mere abstracta whose names indeed express their nature, the universal idea for which the name, and indeed the person, merely stand. Since he increasingly demythologized even the traditional gods of myth and made them almost impersonal embodiments of abstract spiritual principles, it is not surprising that he seeks to establish their nature even through the dissection of their names.

In the preceding I have dealt with some stylistic aspects of Hesiod's movement away from the particular instance toward the general, universal idea. What has to be emphasized is that this movement is not just a matter of style, or that it is a matter of style because it is but a stylistic aspect of Hesiod's manner of thinking. To deal with the particular, not for its own sake but as an instance of the universal, and to give this universal meaning and content through a series of more or less particular instances is the basic logical, not just stylistic, innovation of Hesiod that is characteristic of the *Erga* in all respects. Of course, all thought, no matter how imaginative and poetic, generalizes in its own way. The individual heroes of the *Iliad* are, after all, particular representations of a heroic ideal, and all individual *aristeiai* were examples of the one true *aristeia* of man that was the subject of the Homeric poem. Still the stage of abstraction is higher and generalization is more conscious and explicit in Hesiod. The "heroes" of the *Erga* are no longer individual archetypes—Achilles, Hector, Diomedes—but universals like justice and work. And even when Hesiod brings in concrete individuals or events, they are clearly unessential occasions and examples of something that is not itself concrete and cannot be represented as such. The *Erga* is written—ostensibly—on the occasion of a particular court case, but its subject is the general principle that underlies all legal arbitration. It is addressed—ostensibly—to one particular man, but its explicit aim is to teach all generations of mankind, present and future. It descends occasionally to minute directions about washing one's hands and making mortars, but its main purpose is to teach a complex yet very coherent way of life. It is written by a man emphatically insistent on his own individual insight; but this particular individual also claims to be the voice of wisdom speaking with the inspiration of something eternal. All this Hesiod can do only by virtue of his more or less conscious utilization of the logical relation between the particular and the universal.

Unlike the *Iliad,* the *Erga* does not even have an overall story to hold the poem together, yet it has more internal development than the Homeric poem, and while in the *Iliad* we find few necessary connecting links between the individual episodes, the *Erga* is full of implications and implicit references backward and forward, the understanding of which are essential to the understanding of each individual part of the poem. The parts of the *Erga* are truly parts of an organic whole. Such part-whole relationship, underlying connections, and the growth of the whole through its parts presuppose an insight by Hesiod into the relationship of the particular and the universal, the actual and the potential, the phenomenal and the ideal.

This insight inevitably affects Hesiod's sense of time too. What is structurally true of his poem is equally true of the structure of time in the poem.

The biggest time unit of any importance in the *Iliad* was the day, a concrete time-span that functioned as a kind of atomic individual without much connection to what went before and what followed after.[15] When night fell, the warriors separated, ate, and went to sleep; when rose-fingered dawn appeared, they got up, ate, and fought again. And again and again. The day itself was but a formula enabling men to go on doing the same thing day after day; it was a skeleton to be fleshed out with ever the same substance.

All this is different in Hesiod. He knows of time periods much greater than the day, and these periods are interconnected in an irreversible sequence. The seasons' yielding to one another in their settled order makes up the year; the years' passing constitutes a lifetime; generations succeed each other within cultural ages, and even these pass away never to return. For the first time, time—and its substantial content—really passes.

And because time passes, there is a season appointed for each thing which, once missed, cannot be recaptured. In the year there is a time for sowing and a time for reaping, in a man's life there is a time for marriage and a time for siring children. The seasons recur with ever the same regularity, but they punctuate *growth* in men and things: an irreversible process they measure with a discrete grid but cannot arrest. This is what makes them important: since change, organic, teleological development, is real, it is essential to seize the right moment and do the right thing at the right time. The cycle of seasons—cyclical time—is important only in a teleological context.

This sense of time pervades the poem structurally as well as materially. If a member of Homer's audience began to nod by the fire and came awake suddenly a few episodes, or, if this were possible, even a few books later, he would not be aware of how much he missed; he might feel he slept but for a moment or caught himself just on the verge of falling asleep. And the same is true of the men in the story: had one of the heroes left Troy after a few months of fighting and returned eight or nine years later, he would have found things essentially unchanged on the Scamandrean plain. The same camp by the sea, the same walls still untaken, the same interminable slaughter going on as before; victory still not in sight. Not so in Hesiod. Listening to only a part of the poem, the audience would not know what even that part, let alone the whole of the poem, was about. And returning to the scene of his labors after a long absence, the farmer would find desolation and irremediable ruin testifying to the length of time he spent away from home. A Hesiodic time-traveler would return to another cultural age, out of place, out of tune with the times, and this is something the poet of the traditional epic could not even envisage. And yet, for all particular changes that may take place in Hesiodic history, there is something universal that remains as constant as the regularity of the seasons: the rule of the law that lasts forever. So here, too, we have the historical particular over against the universal unhistorical truth.

Unity in diversity, sameness in difference, wholeness in articulate organic division, is the central principle of Hesiodic thought that governs all innovations. From the unification of Homer's anarchic collection of deities under the overall rule of Zeus in the *Theogony* it is but a short step to the further consolidation of this process in the *Erga* with its quasi-monotheistic, indeed almost monistic, view of the world in which the ruling deity is but an abstract principle regulating diverse events and phenomena. The development of unitary concepts for the whole of the human body and the totality of the sentient soul, overarching and embracing the Homeric limbs, chest, head, knees, skin—*psyche, noos, thymos, phren,* etc.; [16] the introduction of the nameless generations of the five ages, large units of mankind embracing all individuals; the elaboration of abstracta expressive of the sameness in all diverse concrete things; Hesiod's central message of the law—order, measure—inherent in all diverse and changing aspects of life and world; all are manifestations of this principle. Hesiod's language, method, and thought are themselves aspects of an organic unity.

Of course, Homer's language and thought are equally harmonious; the form and content of his poetry are as adapted to each other as are Hesiod's. But these two types of language and thought—Homer's and Hesiod's—are quite different from each other. Considering the relatively small temporal distance between the presumed dates of Homer and Hesiod, the only assumption that accounts for such radical differences is that the *Iliad* was essentially, even if not completely, oral poetry while Hesiod's poems were not.

It is generally agreed that the north Semitic alphabet was introduced into mainland Greece some time around the middle of the eighth century at the latest, so that the art of writing was certainly available at the time Hesiod composed his poems. If the *Erga* was created at about 700 B.C. some literacy undoubtedly existed on mainland Greece several generations prior to its creation. This was not a general, or even widespread literacy, of course, but some people certainly knew how to write, and that is quite sufficient for the purposes of our argument. It makes the composition of poetry with the aid of writing chronologically possible. Certainly writing had been used for these purposes in the Near East from where the Greek alphabet was derived, and the unmistakable Near Eastern influence on Hesiod's poetry makes it more than likely that Hesiod was acquainted with such use.

Of course there is no concrete way of showing that Hesiod himself knew how to write and did in fact employ writing as a method of composing his poems; the argument for Hesiod's literacy must be based on the internal evidence of his poems. But this evidence points very strongly toward Hesiod having been a literate poet.

To be sure, the *Theogony* and the *Erga* still contain formulas, a point frequently made by the proponents of the theory that Hesiod's poems are oral compositions. But by itself this argument avails nothing. For if we keep in mind that formulas are less frequent in the *Theogony* than in the *Iliad,* and even less so in the *Erga,* there is nothing in this diminished use of formulas by Hesiod that conflicts with the supposition of his literacy. If oral poems of the *Iliad's* type were the traditional, indeed the only existing, type of poetry prior to Hesiod, he would necessarily be influenced by them, and instead of creating a new language he would naturally use the available one. Thus Homer's language and the language of mainland oral poetry would survive in the *Erga* no matter how literate Hesiod himself was. We have to remember, furthermore, that the traditional poetic medium was verse, not prose, and that this verse was cast in the rather rigid framework of the epic hexameter. Now anyone writing a poem of some length in a highly prosodic language such as ancient Greek would naturally succumb to some formulaic use. The metric structure of the line together with the prosodic nature of the language makes certain expressions naturally appropriate at certain places and thus facilitates the use of formulas even if all other reasons that were of weight in oral composition have fallen by the wayside. Consequently, regardless of the presumed literacy of Hesiod, Homeric language and traditional formulas would still be present in his poems to some extent. But that this extent is smaller than in the *Iliad,* that it is diminishing in the course of Hesiod's development, and that other quasi-formulaic elements such as the stock character, the typical scene, and the repetition of long passages are completely absent in the *Erga,* make it more likely that Hesiod was a literate rather than oral poet.

Hesiod "did not use verse because he was writing poetry, but because verse was the only known medium"; [17] the use of verse was an external, rather than internal necessity for him. This is most apparent if we consider that even while using the inherited epic language Hesiod was transforming it into one much better suited to his purpose and the technique (of writing) available to him. The striking thing is that in this transformation not only epic verse but even poetry as such began to be left behind. Hesiod's ungainly and unattractive language, his unwieldy phrases, forced constructions, and technical rather than graceful expressions would have been the first to be eliminated in the course of an oral transmission, which depends on the mellifluous, well-formed and, above all, memorable phrase for its existence. But given the use of writing, Hesiod did not have to worry unduly about memorability, and aesthetic requirements were much less important to him than to the oral poet. Since writing preserved even the unpoetic, thoughtful rather than attractive and easily recited line, the poetic form, indeed the use of poetry as such, began to be a liability rather than a necessity. Writing made prose possible, and although Hesiod did not write outright prose, his prosaic rather than poetic style represents the first step in that direction.

This direction is inevitably one from image to concept, from *mythos* to *logos.* For once the beauty of one's language is no longer supremely important, one can lay more and more emphasis on the thought-content itself. This does not mean that form and content of thought become separable here. Hesiod obviously labored on his

style and language just as much as on the message he tried to convey. It means, however, that with the invention of writing a new
form of thought as well as of its—unpoetic—expression could be
cultivated.

Now that the poet—and inevitably the reader—could range back
and forth over his poem, he could insert, revise, correct, arrange,
and rearrange its parts, not as paratactic episodes but as organic
parts of a whole. He could pick up a word here and reinforce it
elsewhere, he could leave things unelaborated at one point only to
return to them with renewed emphasis and articulation at another,
he could imply what he did not directly say, he could refer backward
and forward, and he could construct and follow a line of argument
that cohered—and made the poem coherent—in spite of the diversity and seeming isolation of its parts. He could now write on
several levels, about the immediate subject and the underlying
theme at the same time, and give his poem a new dimension: depth
rather than just dazzling surface. The accent on this new dimension
almost required that he leave poetry behind. For too much splendor
in expression, too much brilliance in the well-turned phrase, too
much beauty, in fact might focus the attention at the wrong place:
on the surface expression rather than on the underlying message, on
the individual part rather than on the whole. Writing, enabling
the writer to detach himself from the particular part that the oral
poet had to concentrate on almost exclusively, fosters detachment in
both style and thought. It allows the author to think in abstract
rather than concrete terms, in universals rather than particulars, in
concepts rather than images; above all it enables him to think synoptically rather than paratactically. Thus it effects both form and
content of the writer's thought.

Writing also gives the individual poet an importance he never
had before. The oral poet had to be anonymous, since his poem, the
poem he inherited from others, would be carried on, recited, and
recreated by others. But, assured of his permanent authorship,
Hesiod can now confront us in the first person. He can announce

his name, fill his poem with personal references which would be the first thing eliminated in oral transmission; above all he can have a new pride, the author's pride in his own individual intellect and creation. With writing a new category enters into poetry: that of originality. Originality is the last thing an oral poet would have claimed for his work. But now, thinly disguising it under the mask of individual poetic inspiration, Hesiod can make the claim.

The work preserved unaltered by writing immortalizes its author, but it also lays upon him a new responsibility. He is now responsible to future, as well as present, generations. Lifted above his particular, more or less accidental, milieu, he can address, as Hesiod does, the whole world. But this makes him more than just a particular existing individual: it demands of him that he speak as an individual spokesman for all mankind. He has to become the voice of reflective intellect proclaiming not just the particular but even more the universal and the eternal. Thus the fact that his work is no longer a momentary creation radically alters the status of the writer as well as the content of his work.

Last but not least, the existence of written documents alone enables the poet to become aware of essential historical change in the way of life and view of life of succeeding generations. Hesiod's historical consciousness and his stance as a self-conscious moral reformer would be extremely hard to explain without the assumption that the Homeric epics existed, in some form or other, as a whole or in substantial parts, in writing at Hesiod's time.[18] With this assumption, however, the problem is easily solved. Since writing sealed the form, fixed the content, and arrested the development of the Homeric epics, Hesiod could neither ignore the difference between their mentality and his own, nor could he transform the Homeric stories into something more expressive of his own spirit. He had to break with tradition, detach himself from the past, and in deliberate opposition to the old morality declare his own moral reform.

In a way, this moral reform has for its content nothing but what the invention and use of writing enabled man to discover. It was writing that enabled the poet to break with tradition and made him a self-conscious, self-certain individual rather than just the bearer of the tradition which in its turn bore and supported him. But this break with tradition and insistence on one's own thought and work is also central to the new morality. Now *arete* is no longer the inherited excellence of the aristocrat embedded in and supported by a long line of noble ancestors whose achievements sustain his honor and whose honor he reinforces by his achievements. Far from being a matter of tradition—literally something handed over to the hero to be carried on and handed over by him in his turn—it is now something that can be acquired by any individual, be he ever so low-born, provided he is willing to put in the hard work that "the gods have placed between us and *arete*" (*Erga* 287) and to tread "the long and steep path to her" (290). Furthermore, *arete* is no longer the ephemeral splendor of the hero victorious in warlike agon; the new path to *arete* lays emphasis precisely on that—eternal rational rule, underlying law, order, regularity, proportion, measure —which writing, with its new dimension of depth, enabled man to think. The abstract universal is a category of literate thought, and therefore a category of literate morality. Writing gave the poem a never before attained fixity and permanence; and it is fixity and permanence—of law and order in subjective and objective events— that the new morality also proclaims. Even the new perspective of the writer—backward and forward along long lines and slowly developing wholes—is built into his morality. Instead of instant honor and episodic excellence in the moment, Hesiodic man is promised only eventual success, ultimate reward in the long run of seemingly fruitless endeavor. Virtue no longer accompanies atomic deeds; it is the gradual accomplishment of a whole life. It is only "in the end" that *arete*—prosperity and security rather than dazzling *aristeia* —comes without fail. Hesiod's new time-perspective and perspective of composition bring on a new moral perspective too. As writing enabled the poet to detach himself from the tradition formally and materially, and think in depth rather than by way of shining images, morality too became deeper, more rational, and more a matter of individual thought. The purely traditional, other-directed, and surface-oriented power-morality of the Homeric gods and men could now be left behind—together with the poetic form in which it was embodied.

3. Archilochus and Sappho

Man is not only a reflective individual, conscious of historical change and intent on discovering law. He is also subject to passion. Deeply moved by love and hate, experiencing intense joy and suffering, the individual is at once isolated from and drawn toward other human beings. As such he becomes aware of his private, personal identity as well as of his need for emotional communion, even of something in the self that it is almost impossible to share. The pathos of this discovery gives rise to and is expressed in lyric poetry.

Since lyric poetry, by virtue of its intensely subjective nature, invites a subjective and personal interpretation, it might be well to consider it at the outset as objectively and externally as possible. Even such external approach through form, vocabulary, and style reveals many of the novel aspects of the poems of Archilochus and Sappho, the two great representatives of lyric poetry that we shall discuss here.

Although Hesiod loosens the formulaic structure of the epic poem, he does not abandon its external form even though to some extent it has become a liability rather than an asset to his work. But lyric poetry breaks the bonds of the epic hexameter altogether. Instead of the one conventional metre it employs literally dozens of new verse forms and exhibits an unprecedented richness of metrical and musical invention. This variety of form is, of course, not wholly the result of the lyric poet's own creativity; choral and folk songs undoubtedly provided some models for his invention. Nevertheless the lyric poet is the first to feel sufficiently sure of his own artistic power to adopt and develop these models rather than use the traditionally accepted one, and thereby he shows a greater freedom from convention as well as a greater aesthetic sensitivity than did Hesiod. And once this form-creative process is begun, it becomes self-sustaining: the very existence of a variety of poetic forms confronts the poet with an explicit artistic decision; it forces him to choose metre and music carefully from among the many alternatives now available, and to fit verse form to content much more self-consciously than it was ever before possible. With tradition no longer sacrosanct, formal novelty becomes a poetic category, and the lyric poet not only can but must cultivate the poetic form if he wants to be heard.

But formal novelty implies experiential novelty; new forms of expression are created to suit new forms of feeling and thought. The lyric poet's loosening of the poetic form thus hints at a new existential as well as aesthetic awareness; the formal variety and irregularity of his poems indicate the variability and irregularity of experience that he feels and wants to convey.

One obvious external feature of the lyric poem that is novel as well as materially significant is its brevity. The essential unit of the oral epic, the episode, stretched over hundreds of lines, and so did the central, indivisible portion of Hesiod's *Erga*. Compared to such leisurely tempo and breadth of composition, lyric poems show a concentration and economy more akin to gnomic utterances and folk song than to the Homeric or Hesiodic song. It is almost as if the lyric poet, unlike his epic counterpart, was pressed for time, out of breath, impatient to be done with the song; as if he felt that what he wanted to say had to be said at once or else would be lost and remain forever unspoken. His new, quick, vibrant, pulsating metres are a great help to him in this new urgency of creation, and the brevity of his poems in its turn leads to the invention of an ever greater variety of metric and melodic forms, each designed to fit the mood of the passing moment. Even externally considered, this new style testifies to the emergence of a new sense of time and life: one characterized by urgency, mutability, restlessness, excitability, and a lack of faith in anything abiding.

Another significant departure from traditional language and style lies in the increasing use of the vernacular by the lyric poet. Already in Archilochus, the formal, to some extent artificial, idiom of the epic gradually yields to everyday language. In his blending of old and new the novel linguistic features begin to predominate, especially in the nonelegiac poems, and by Sappho's time a new literary language is born that is neither archaic nor traditional; its elements are almost completely those of the contemporary regional vernacular. Its use revitalizes the poet's language, but it also hints at a contraction of horizons; as if it were his Ionian contemporaries that Archilochus wrote for, while Sappho addressed an Aeolic audience. Furthermore the vernacular brings poetry close to home in another way: it gives the poem a nearness to life and makes it a better vehicle for dealing with the personal problems, cares, and joys of unheroic everyday life than the elevated language of the epic, increasingly remote and archaic now that it has been fixed by writing, would have been at this time. Thus the change of language hints at a change of subject matter: it signalizes the lyric poet's descent from the heights of heroic experience to the lowlands of a private and personal existence.

Urgency of the moment, a concentration on what is close in space and time, are not the only aspects of lyric poetry we can begin to notice by considering its language and style. The type of words the poet uses most frequently tell us something about his sense of life even when considered out of context.

Hesiod's preference for abstract rather than concrete terms, so prominent in the *Erga* as compared with the *Iliad*, has left its mark on lyric poetry, whose language, for all its closeness to life, does not revert to epic concreteness. Nevertheless the lyric poets' abstraction is quite different from Hesiod's heavyhanded and prosaic conceptualization. Sappho's favorite abstracta are not *dike, metron, ethos, kosmos* and *arete,* but *habrosyne* (youthful tenderness, freshness, grace, charm), *to lampron* (splendor, radiance, brilliance), and *to kalon* (beauty, fairness, grace of form). While even stylistically Hesiod turned from the visible, tangible, sensuous world to one of arid thought, this turn is if anything reversed in lyric language and Hesiod's aversion to intuitive presentation is no longer shared. Sappho's most frequent adjectives are *habros* (youthfully tender, graceful, fresh), *hapalos* (soft, tender, gentle, weak), *glykys* (sweet, delightful, dear), *kalos* (beautiful), *makairos* (blessed, happy), *poikilos* (many-colored, spangled, variegated, changeable), *porphyreos* (purple, red, bright), *chrysios* (gold, golden yellow). Her vocabulary betrays her addiction to the pleasures of sight, touch, and feeling and reveals her involvement in a sensuously experienced, rich, variegated and radiant, immediately lived, felt, and almost bodily embraced world. Her world is not only close, it is close enough to feel and touch. Yet it is not the Homeric world of vigorous movement—swift, sharp, clashing, soaring, crashing, or arrested in flight; it is a world in which everything is touched softly and delicately, as if with a loving caress.

One last word on word-count: the term Sappho uses more frequently than any noun, verb, adverb, or adjective is the first-person singular pronoun. I, me, mine, punctuate her poems even more than work and justice did Hesiod's. Even if we knew nothing more about the content of her poetry, this would give us a clue to the extent of Sappho's self-involvement. Hesiod already confronted us in the first person, but subjectivity was nowhere as excessive in the *Erga* as it is here, it did not yet threaten to engulf the world. But now the many-colored universe seems to contract itself to a point where it almost becomes one with the creative I. In infinite concentration it is encompassed by and reflected in the poet's own self. The central theme of lyric poetry is no longer natural order, human work, or divine justice, let alone public heroism, but the self-dramatizing (in Archilochus) or self-embracing (in Sappho) subject presenting and exploiting his own personality. For the first time in Greek literature the poet has become his own hero.[1]

Let us now turn to the poems themselves and see how Archilochus' and Sappho's new self-consciousness and untraditional subjectivity is manifested in the content rather than just the form of their poems.

Human nature is not all alike "but different things delight different hearts" (Arch. 41).[2] "Some say that knights, some that footfolk, some that ships are the most beautiful things on black earth; but I say the fairest is whatever one loves" (Sappho 27a 144).

Homer and Hesiod still assumed that all men really want the same thing, although this same thing is rather different in Hesiod from what it is in Homer. But now, more than a century before the Sophists, the lyric poets begin to find value a rather subjective thing. Instead of following public opinion—"no man who heeded the censure of the people would enjoy many delights" (Arch. 9)— or at least soberly reflecting, à la Hesiod, on our common nature, they let their immediate loves and hates, their uninhibited passions guide their judgment. With this new criterion value necessarily becomes varied and personal, and the subject in all its variability, each individual differentiated from all others present and past, begins to make its appearance.

Hesiod already rejected the Homeric ideal and extolled the simple man's virtue over against the lordly heroism of the *Iliad's* warriors. Now Archilochus and Sappho go even further and reject both Homer's heroic and Hesiod's rustic-civic paradigms, without, however, establishing a unitary ideal of their own. Through the vigorous voice of the mercenary soldier, a bastard son of nobleman and slave, the disinherited of the world begin to make their claim, while the languorous song of Sappho gives expression to the aspirations of a cultured, sensitive, and essentially idle soul.

"I am a companion of the Lord of War, who also knows the Muses' lovely gift" (1) Archilochus declares in a manner reminiscent of the epic hero, but his conception of the martial-poetic life is radically different from that of the lyre-playing Achilles. To the Homeric hero his weapons were not just symbols but almost an essential part and tangible proof of the warrior's honor and excellence. But Archilochus no longer measures his worth—even as a soldier—by such externals, and he much prefers an ignominious but pleasurable life to shining honor: "Some Saian now delights in the blameless shield I left behind unwillingly in the bush; but I saved myself. What do I care about that shield? To hell with it. I'll get me another one just as good" (6). To the Homeric hero splendid appearance was almost equivalent to virtue; Achilles was at once the best and the most beautiful, Thersites the worst and the ugliest of men. But in Archilochus appearance and being have very little to do with each other; the magnificent presence of the great warrior does not impress this soldier: "I can't stand a huge commander who strides along like a crane, curl-proud, smooth-shaven. Give me rather a small man, bow-legged, firm of feet and full of heart" (60). While Homer lovingly described his heroes' daring exploits, Archilochus looks upon martial feats with as much realism as self-mockery: "Seven men fell dead . . . we were a thousand killers" (61). The ever-living glory in the song that the epic hero so desired leaves Archilochus cold: "No one gets reverence and fame from his townsmen once he is dead. Rather we seek the favor of the living while we live. The dead always get the worst" (64). And even the favor of the living is not too assiduously courted here; Archilochus seems to hold public opinion in no higher esteem than posthumous glory: "No man who heeded the censure of the people would enjoy many delights" (9).

But Hesiodic *arete,* the lasting wealth and substance the insecure farmer would dearly love to have, has no more appeal to him than Homeric lordship. "I neither care nor strive for Gyges' wealth, nor envy the gods' works, nor aspire to tyranny; all this is beyond my vision" (22). As for the patient, plodding work that results in the slow accumulation of material possessions, the mercenary has little love for that. "By the spear (I gain) my kneaded bread, by the spear my Ismarian wine; leaning on my spear I drink" (2).

So aggressive is Archilochus' tone, so full of the underdog's revolt and resentment, that it is much easier to tell what he hates than what he loves; but on the whole both his hates and his loves move within a narrow subjective horizon. His most vicious invective is directed at those who harmed him personally: "may hairy Thracians cheerfully grab him naked, may he be wretched eating the bread of slaves. Frozen stiff, seaweed-covered, with chattering teeth may he lie like a dog on his face, helpless. . . . That I would love to see, because he did me wrong and tred on his promises, he who was once my friend" (79a). His few prayers are for his personal friends and his own safety, and all his wishes are confined to the immediate pleasures of personal life. A good fight—not so much for glory and gain as the simple fun of it—a good drink (69), a rousing song (77), sensual love's delight—that is mainly what he seems to care about. "Take delight in what is delightful" (67a6), enjoy the moment, and do not think overmuch about the past or the future, he counsels his contemporaries.

Why this lack of trust in the future and withdrawal to the immediate subjective sphere? Archilochus' view of the "rhythm that holds man" explains this.

In considering man's state on earth Hesiod already thought it wretched and insecure enough, yet he held out more than a ray of hope for salvation. Strongly believing in the rule of a natural-divine order and righteousness, he offered men justice and work as the road to well-being. Archilochus in his turn also sees human life full of misery and woe, but the law of the world Hesiod still found reassuring Archilochus finds only oppressive; an insight into it offers man scant relief.

Man is confounded with irremediable troubles (67al), he is a plaything of fate and chance (8), and the whim of the gods on whom all victory depends (57). " . . . for often they save from misfortune a man who lies on black earth, and often they overthrow him who stands assured and firm and lay him on his back; then he is engulfed by evil and wanders in mortal need, out of his mind" (58). Our fortune changes from moment to moment, misery strikes where it will, "once we are struck and groan with bloody wounds, then others take our place" (7.7-9). And no trustworthy law governs the world for the gods' deeds are arbitrary and incalculable. Archilochus uses the total eclipse of the sun (648 B.C.) as an occasion to bring home this point: "No thing can be unimaginable, impossible, or miraculous henceforth, since Zeus, father of the Olympians, turned noonday into night, hiding the light of radiant sun, and cold fear gripped men. From here on there is nothing trustworthy, nothing men might not expect" (74.1-6). No secure hold, no firm ground remains for men. "Fear comes from the unexpected" (56, 3), and now that all things can change their nature overnight (74.6-9) and *moira* has become indistinguishable from *tyche* (8), everything is unforeseen and man is a helpless prey of fear. When all is ceaseless flux, reasonless, rhymeless change, knowledge has no object and insight avails nothing.

When Homer compared the generations of men to generations of leaves, he stressed the renewal of all living things at each springtime and the ceaseless succession of essentially unchanging generations, one growing as another died (*Iliad* 6.146-9). When Hesiod spoke of the mutability of things and of time irreversibly passing, he laid emphasis on the natural and historical order that remains the same forever. But Archilochus is merely oppressed by the fragility, mutability, and precariousness of life without taking comfort from the thought of seasonal return or long-term historical lawfulness. What his lyric successors put explicitly into words—"One-day creatures we live knowing nothing" (Semonides 1.4), "One-day creatures; what is one? what is one not? man is a shadow's dream"

(Pindar *Pythian Ode* 8.95)—Archilochus already feels and indirectly articulates.

Since the world is arbitrary and contingent, all that matters to the individual is the particular moment as it immediately affects his own self. Even to speak of a lasting self might be a mistake here, for the human subject has become so ephemeral that it almost lacks substance and continuity. Not even our own minds can we safely call our own, for we have no more control over our thoughts than over external events: "The mind of mortal men is as the day Zeus sends, their thoughts are as the things they happen to meet" (68). Adrift on a sea of chance, tossed by wind and wave from mood to mood, man's being seems to be composed of accidents rather than enduring essence. To be a "subject" means not to have an underlying core, but to be subject to, to undergo and suffer, whatever may befall one from moment to moment.[3]

That is why one cannot wholly explain the lyric poet's turn to subjectivity by merely pointing to the political climate prevailing at Archilochus' and Sappho's time. To be sure, this was a time of general military defeat aggravated by internal political struggles. But if it was this military and political powerlessness that motivated the poets' inward turning and made them withdraw from the outer world to a contemplation of their own soul, how sorely disappointed they must have been to find in their own emotional experience the same powerlessness, the same lack of mastery, the same discord and incoherence as they had encountered in the "real" world. It is true that the lyric poets made their own pathos the subject of their song, and all else hardly more than an occasion for describing their own reactions, sensations, and feelings with minute care. But the point is that their internal experience was just as pathetic as was the external course of events. It certainly provided no escape from the vicissitudes of the outer world, no safe harbor in which to rest. Turning inward man simply became prey to his own emotions, victim of his own passions, a thrall to his own violent loves and hates.

Miserable I lie in longing
unsouled, cruel god-sent pain
piercing through my bones.   (Arch. 104)

For such was the desire of love that twisted itself beneath the heart
and enveloped the eyes in darkness,
stealing the gentle wits within the breast.   (Arch. 112)

but desire, looser of limbs, overwhelms me. . . .   (Arch. 118)

Archilochus complains, and Sappho suffers the same torment:

Once again Eros drives me, looser of limbs,
bitter-sweet irresistible monster   (Sappho 137)

. . . Eros has shaken my soul
like a mountain-wind falling upon oaks   (Sappho 50)

and I long and I yearn. . . .   (Sappho 20)

Only seldom does she sing of a gratification of her yearning:

You have come, oh you did well, for I longed for you;
you cooled my soul aflame with desire   (Sappho 48)

For the most part her experience of love leaves her closer to death
than to life:

Really I wish to die, since she left me, weeping   (Sappho 96.1–2)

a longing for death has me in its hold
to see the shores of Acheron, lotus-grown, bedewed. . . .
                                                   (Sappho 97.11–14)

The gods' equal seems to me
the man who sits opposite you
and listens, close, to your sweet voice

and your lovely laugher. That is
what stirred the heart within my breast so
that a brief look at you robs me of my voice

and breaks my tongue. Straighway
a subtle fire steals beneath my skin,
my eyes see nothing. I hear a confused noise.

Bathed in cold sweat I tremble
all over. Paler than grass,
I seem to be near death.

But all must be endured. . . .   (Sappho 2)

The Homeric hero was at times overwhelmed by superior force
and suffered defeat at the hand of his adversary. Lyric man is continually overwhelmed and defeated by his own emotions. The
Homeric hero's essence was manifest power; he became powerless,
was undone, only at death. But powerlessness seems to be the
essence of human life in lyric poetry, and mortals are undone by
love, not death. It is not physical injury or disease but emotional
sickness that wastes their lives. Love, the greatest force of life itself,
has become so deathlike in its effects—witness Sappho's (2.5–17)
and Archilochus' (112) descriptions [4]—that with it death, the fatal
moment of departure, the end of all power to be, is taken up into
life and experienced with an unprecedented intensity again and
again as Eros strikes the lover.

That this happens is hardly surprising. Whoever lives for the
moment must die at each moment's irretrievable passing. Whoever
invests so much of himself in each passion must be consumed at
each passion's consummation. Such tremendous concentration on
the soul's momentary delight can only bring about a thousand
deaths in the soul. In Homer death, the darkness that blotted out
the hero's brilliant life, was greatest misfortune that could ever
befall man. But now that the lyric individual is experiencing a
thousand deaths even while he lives, actual physical death promises
surcease and becomes a kind of salvation, something to be yearned
for (Sappho 96.1; 97.11–14) rather than abhorred. To a man enslaved and victimized by his own passion the moment of death cannot but appear as a moment of liberation at times.

There is something tragic in this. The lyric individual's aspirations, though profoundly un-Homeric, are in a way as self-defeating as were those of the epic hero: it is his most powerful instinct of life that turns him against life, and it is the intensity of his involvement in the moment that threatens to destroy him. Achilles too was undone by what he most cherished—his supreme moment of glory—and the fact that the external agon and other directedness of the *Iliad* are replaced by internal agony and self-directedness here does not make the lyric experience any less precarious or dangerous. Love-dominated life reveals itself as no less strife-torn, violent, and perishable than was the life of warlike contest. The external diremption of the *Iliad* has become an internal tension here that threatens to break apart the soul. "I don't know what to do, I am of two minds" (46) sings Sappho caught in the grip of contradictory emotions. Bitter-sweet, life- and death-giving love, the looser of limbs and weaver of wiles, heals and wounds her as it delights and just about drives her insane.

Even the poetic act becomes as it were schizophrenic in Sappho. For the poet, nearly out of her mind in the throes of violent emotion, describes her feelings with an almost clinical detachment. Helpless and possessed by love she may be, but verbally she is in thorough control and a master of her art.[5] Objective toward her subjectivity, dispassionate toward her own passion, delighting in her sublimated suffering, aesthetically removed from her own emotional frenzy, Sappho exhibits an inner split in the soul not just of the lover but also of the poet. At the same time, in the very act of exhibiting it, the poet also overcomes the diremption that the lover could not overcome. Consciously cultivating her own supposedly irresistible emotions, she lifts them to a level where even pain becomes pleasure, and what would otherwise be a feverish wallowing in one's own passion is purified to the point where it can be unashamedly shared by all. Self-indulgent self-enjoyment and self-pity, and a narcissistic-masochistic interest in the self are so far deepened and intensified here that they break the barriers of privacy and become public and universally shareable experiences.

For all this publicity and universality, however, the individual's

sense of uniqueness is never lost in lyric poetry. Homer's minor
heroes, and at times the major ones, were so typical that they tended
to become almost interchangeable personae acting out the typical
situation. But passion, the typical subject of lyric poetry, never lets
the subject become a mere mask; as its real experience brings people together inwardly and intimately, so its poetic presentation
evokes a deeply personal response and reinforces each individual's
private self-consciousness. Unlike the Homeric hero's power struggle, love allows no distance, no separation, no parataxis between
men; instead it tends to fuse the I and thou till each sees the other
as a personal part of himself and himself as reflected in the other.
But precisely because love tends to fuse lover and beloved in the
moment of passion, it makes them vulnerable and leaves them deso-
late and forsaken at that moment's inevitable passing. Because it
fosters a positive personal relationship—one between equals, a relation in which surrender means gain rather than loss of the self—
it makes those involved supremely sensitive to the lack or unfulfill-
ment of this relationship. Just as each lover's thought was concentrated on the beloved a moment ago, so it is now concentrated upon
himself and the absence of the beloved makes the lover conscious
of a never before felt isolation. It is this isolated, wounded self
to which lyric poetry appeals. Desire is most intense when it is not
shared, when its satisfaction is almost unattainable, and therefore
the very intensity of desire expressed in lyric poetry only intensifies
each individual's sense of isolation and makes him conscious of a
self almost consumed yet unhappily not wholly consumed by impotent passion.

Even when the poet turns outward toward things rather than
persons, everything he touches becomes a reflection of his own personality and an occasion for his own affective self-revelation. Nature
itself is seen through the inner eye here; its contemplation only leads
poet and reader alike deeper into themselves. There is no parataxis
here either; the subject's mood and emotional attitude almost overwhelms the object, the object is internalized, besouled, and sub-
merged in the self. The concrete—tree, flower, brook—does not be-

come abstract, but it becomes spiritual: so fragile and breathlike as to almost defy one's grasp, and so personal as to remain inevitably private even when revealed in the song.

> The stars around the fair moon
> hide their shining faces
> when being full she most lights up
> the earth . . .   (Sappho 4)

> Cool water sings
> through apple-branches
> and from quivering leaves
> slumber drifts down.   (Sappho 5)

> The moon has set and the Pleiades.
> It is midnight.
> The hours pass
> yet I lie alone.   (Sappho 94)

With a few light brush strokes, a few spare lines, Sappho delineates not the outer world but the brittleness of her own soul. Even her nature poems turn us inward. They spring from and require an authentic experience of the self.

This lyric self is nothing like the often flat, paratactically gathered, and largely unchanging surface image encountered in the *Iliad;* nor is it the sober, prosaic, pragmatic-rational self of the *Erga*. It is a thoroughly mutable, sensuous and sensual, affective self, abysmally deep yet ephemeral and ungraspable. Its revelation, playful or sorrowful, brings no useful, usable insight. Its discovery solves no problems and provides no cures. Its experience is self-contained; it can only be enjoyed or endured immediately. If its own freshness and radiance—"I love youthful splendor . . . and what is radiant and fair, the sun's desire, is my portion" (Sappho 65.25–6)—are not enough to justify its existence and its poetic expression not enough to give it an ephemeral eternity then there is no justification and no salvation for man, and the best advice the lyric poet can offer is a resigned "but all must be endured" (Sappho 2.17).

Complaints heal nothing, rejoicing makes no things worse
(Arch. 10.3–4)

For incurable woes, my friend, the gods gave us
the remedy of staunch endurance . . . So put off swiftly
womanish grief and endure . . .   (Arch. 7.5–7,9–10)

Soul, my soul, confounded with hopeless troubles,
rise, ward off your enemies setting a resolute front
against their attack, stand firm. Don't exult publicly
if you prevail, nor, failing, wail prostrated at home.
Enoy what is delightful and do not brood overmuch
over evil. But know what rhythm holds man.   (Arch. 67)

After all, suffering is no more permanent than is ecstasy. All is
a matter of the moment. That is the rhythm of the world.

The lyric poet's insight into this rhythm gives him a totally
different sense of time than either the *Iliad* or the *Erga* exhibited.
Not sharing Homer's faith in the forever living present, the same
moment recurring again and again eternally, the lyric poet is well
aware of the passage of time Hesiod emphasized and of the importance of the moment, the unique occasion that must be grasped
before it passes irretrievably. Yet the kind of sameness Hesiod put
all his trust in, the eternal sameness not of the moment but of the
enduring, underlying law of regular change and growth, is equally
absent from the lyric poet's experience of time. Instead of the eternal
return of the same (unchanging moment) or of identity (law) in
diversity, lyric time knows only kaleidoscopic, ever ongoing, almost
chaotic change: each unique moment slipping through our fingers
even while we try to grasp it. The world has become a delightful-
nightmarish stage of constantly shifting scenes, a theater of random
sensations following each other with no discernible pattern or organization.

The *amechania* and *akrasia* of lyric man is essentially a helplessness and powerlessness against time, his utter inability to arrest
its passage and thus master it and thereby his experience. Only

thought, subsuming all under an universal unchanging law, could arrest time now that it has been set into motion. But lyric poetry represents a step from (Homeric) *mythos* not to (Hesiodic) *logos* but to *pathos:* literally suffering, undergoing, succumbing to a welter of sensations rather than mastering them through thoughtful reflection.

That is why the passage of time leaves the lyric individual merely fearful, wistful, and forlorn. With an almost romantic intensity Sappho's poems dwell on the thought of parting and departure, on the moment never to be recaptured, on the glory of youth and the despair of aging.

> Maidenhood, maindenhood, where are you gone now that you left me?
> Never will I return to you, never again. (131)

> Like the mountain-hyacinth crushed by shepherds' feet
> on the ground lies the purple flower (117)

> . . . all my skin old age . . .
> . . . my black hair turned white
> . . . knees no longer bear
> like fawns
> . . . but what am I to do?
> . . . it cannot have happened
> . . . rose-armed Dawn
> . . . to the ends of the earth carried
> Tithonos . . .
> . . . beloved bride

> but I love youthful splendor . . .
> and what is radiant and fair, the sun's desire, is my portion
> (65.13–26)

Youth, the fleeting splendor without which the eternal life Dawn proctured Tithonos is worse than no life at all, is to the poet what immortal glory was to the Homeric hero; therefore time, not death is her bane.

With this sense of time and life it is not surprising that lyric poetry broke with the formal conventions within which Hesiod could still operate. Neither Homeric repetition nor Hesiodic continuity of theme could harmonize with a time composed of irretrievable moments. But the lyric poets' formal inventions are thoroughly in accord with it. Great variety of music and metre is expressive of the rich manifold of ever-different affective experience. Concentration and brevity of form fit the urgency and concentration of the moment. Vibrant, pulsating rhythm is in tune with the breathlessness and fitfulness of life. Fragility of line mirrors fragility of mood. Nothing is accidental here. Even the poet's conscious cultivation of the poetic form parallels his conscious cultivation of the emotions therein expressed. The new aesthetic awareness is wholly in harmony with the new awareness of the self.

This new awareness, and this cultivation bordering on a cult of the passionate self, are not an altogether harmless affair. There is a correspondence between the poet's experience, the poetic form, and the effect of the poem on the reader which threatens to endanger the autonomy of the self. Hesiodic poetry, fostering reflective thought, made the reader critical of tradition and even of Hesiod's own opinions; thereby it promoted rational self-cultivation and self-control. But the lyric poet, almost physically driven by his own emotions, succeeds in creating an almost physically compelling medium. Fostering feeling and enhancing passion, lyric poetry allows the reader no detachment; the song is chanted to enchant, it has the hypnotic effect of incantation, it seduces and subdues the reader almost against his will—just as the poet is seduced and subdued by passion almost against his own.[6] The song sings of powerlessness and makes powerless by means of its own nonrational power.

The oral epic had a kind of spellbinding effect; the quasi-unconscious transmission of a presumably forever living tradition did not allow for personal reflection and thus bound the individual to the tradition uncritically transmitted. Hesiodic poetry broke this spell. But now lyric poetry imposes on its audience a spell of its own; it makes the individual recently delivered from tradition once again captive: a captive of his own emotions. It does not deprive him of his private personality and singleness of feeling, but it undermines his autonomy by emancipating him from his own rational control. Mastering him, i.e., letting him be mastered by his own passions, it helps him lose whatever self-mastery he might have gained under the tutelage of Hesiod. Like all great poetry, the lyric song imposes on the reader its own view of life and shapes him in accordance with its own experience and vision. But therein lies the danger, for this experience and vision are that of an essentially powerless, ceaselessly changing and uncontrollable, almost blindly driven, passionate-spiritual human existence.

That this danger is not as great as it might seem is due to what made the emergence of lyric poetry possible in the first place: the art of writing.

The lyric song could not have flourished in wholly illiterate times. Oral poetry could not encompass, for the singer could never remember let alone improvise in, such a variety of metrical and musical form. Nor could such a variety of goals and aspirations have ever existed side by side in the living myth's largely homogeneous world. It was writing that enabled men to turn inward, cultivate their subjectivity, and emphasize one particular aspect of their experience—the private, emotional, sensuous one—to the exclusion of all others.

But precisely because writing allowed such concentration, it promoted the emergence not just of lyric form and content but of other specialized types of expression and thought as well, and it preserved them all impartially, existing side by side and providing a correction to each other's shortcomings. Now that the monolithic tradition of the oral era is a thing of the past, there is a new parataxis of thought that writing brings into being and at the same time enables men to overcome. While Homer—the written poem—continues forever singing of honor and glory and Hesiod of work and justice, lyric poetry can cultivate passion and Ionian and Eleatic philosophy can concentrate on a rational investigation of physical nature, without the total experience of the Greeks thereby becoming either hopelessly fragmented or one-sided. For reflection on the great variety of conflicting forms and methods of thought is also possible now that they are all preserved simultaneously, and thus thought can now mediate between its own diverse forms and begin to view them all as complementary parts of a whole. Writing, the sine qua non of both the emergence and preservation of all these paradigms of experience, also opens the way toward a grand synthesis and a synoptic vision of all—passionate and rational, private and communal, physical ad spiritual—experience. Although the Greeks have still a long way to go on this road, the process has begun and can not be arrested or reversed regardless of any attempt some particular individuals, cults, or schools of thought may undertake.

4. Solon

Solon lived in no less critical, insecure and troubled times than did
Archilochus and Sappho. Political tension was as rife, servitude as
heavy and social injustice as great in Athens at the end of the
seventh and the beginning of the sixth century as it had been on the
Ionian and Aeolic islands for several generations, and acute internal
discord made the threat of tyranny or revolution equally imminent.
But Solon's reaction to this crisis was quite different from that of
his immediate predecessors. Where Archilochus and Sappho turned
inward in lyric resignation, Solon turned outward to social and
political action. Where Archilochus and Sappho described and cultivated their own private passions, Solon spoke of and attended to
the public interest. Where Archilochus and Sappho were crushed
by each moment's misfortune, Solon rose above the particular occasion and took a long-term view of events. Archilochus and Sappho
merely bewailed man's helplessness; Solon attempted to do something about it, and instead of offering their pale remedy, "but all
must be endured," he sought real solutions to the problems of individual and state. Even as a lyric poet he did not merely adopt
the poetic forms developed by his predecessors; he adapted them to
his own purpose by transforming the lyric song of impotent lamentation, delightful-woeful self-revelation and personal invective into
an efficient educational tool for social and political reform.

Solon was no less conscious of his own individuality than were his lyric predecessors; yet his self-consciousness is more reminiscent of Hesiod's than of Archilochus' and Sappho's. It is not as a help-less, passionate, emotionally driven, mood-torn self but as a self-confident, rational, reflective-critical individual that he confronts us in his writing: others may deceive you, "the poets tell many lies" (21), he echoes Hesiod, but I tell you the truth. Others in my place would have done otherwise (23.5–7; 24.20–22; 25.6–7), but I, Solon, did what I had to do. Had I listened to others (24.23–4) I would have acted differently, but I did as I thought best. Had I sided with either of the opposing parties, things would have come out differ-ently, but I, Solon, stood my ground against them all (5.1–6; 24.26–7); like a wolf at bay among a pack of hounds (24.27), like a boundary stone on a disputed frontier (25.8–9), I stood alone. There-fore others may think me mad, yet time will show that I was right (9); others may despise me, but "I feel no shame at all, for this way I think I shall triumph more fully over all mankind" (23.11–12).

Archilochus' and Sappho's concentration on the passionate ex-perience of the immediate moment was consistent with their dis-belief in trustworthy knowledge of enduring, intelligible laws. Solon is no less consistent, though his attitudes are quite different: his rising above the occasion and taking a long-term view of human events goes hand in hand with his affirmation of the rule of law and his faith in the power of human intelligence.

To be sure, this power is far from unlimited. "It is most hard to know the hidden measure of judgment which alone holds the ends of all things" (16). "The mind of immortals is ever hidden from mankind" (17). Yet man can learn—"I grow older ever learn-ing many things" (22.6)—and in time the truth comes forth into the public view (9). Though most men are ignorant, ignorance is not irremediable. If men only used their minds and instead of being swayed by wily rhetoric looked to the deeds done before their eyes, they would not have empty minds (8.6–8) but would recognize the truths Solon knows and wants to teach.

These truths are as simple as they are important. They assert the rule of Dike, the inevitability of a retribution that comes as a result of men's evil-doing and not as a whim of the gods, and the fact that man's ignorance and inordinate desire for wealth are the most prevalent causes of ruin. "Our city will never be destroyed by the dispensation of Zeus or the design of the blessed immortal gods. . . . It is the citizens themselves who in their thoughtlessness seek to destroy the great city, prompted by greed; and their unjust-minded leaders who will thereafter suffer many woes for their great transgressions. For they do not know how to check surfeit nor how to enjoy in an orderly and sober manner the feast before them. . . . But many are rich following unjust courses. . . . Neither sacred nor public possessions do they spare, and they steal each other blind, rapaciously, paying no heed to the holy foundations of Dike" (3.1–14). In these opening lines of his elegy on Eunomia the central themes of Solon's teaching are outlined. We shall deal with them one by one.

There is no exception to the rule of justice. Punishment may not be immediate, but it is universal and inevitable. In the long run justice necessarily prevails. With the relentlessness of Hesiod, Solon reiterates this theme: "in time [Dike] comes unfailingly to exact payment" (3.16), "without fail Dike comes following" unjust deeds (1.7–8). "No man of unjust heart escapes notice forever, but in the end without fail he is brought to light. One man pays right away, another later . . . but unfailingly (punishment) comes" in the course of time (1.27–31).

Hesiod had already insisted on the inevitability of retribution, but he still employed thirty-thousand spirits, the virgin Dike, all the gods, and Zeus himself to enforce justice. Solon dispenses with much of this divine apparatus and explains that justice is the automatic and natural result of one's crime and not something arbitrarily imposed by the gods. The criminal, disturbing the balance of things by his transgression, starts a chain of events which in the end recoil on him and bring about his destruction.

"That which man pursue by crime does not come in the order of things . . . and swiftly it is joined by ruin. Its origin, like that of fire, is small and paltry at first but grievous in the end. Criminal works do not last long. . . . Like a sudden spring wind swiftly scattering clouds and moving the depths of the swelling, barren sea . . . such is divine retribution" (1.11–25). As "from the cloud comes the force of snow and hail, and thunder springs from lightning-flash, so from great men comes destruction to the state, and through their own ignorance do people sink into servitude . . ." (10.1–4). Solon's natural similes are more than a mere poetic device. He conceives of justice as a kind of natural and objective order immanent in human affairs, whose disturbance has as inevitable consequences as any event has in the usual course of nature.[1] As the sea is "most just" when it is not disturbed by winds (11), so the city is peaceful when untroubled by injustice.

Solon does not oppose this natural order of things to a supernatural one, since for him, as already for Hesiod, all order is one, natural and divine at the same time. Nevertheless he takes great care in eliminating all divine arbitrariness from its operation. As a man who starts a fire should not wonder, let alone blame the gods, if his house burns down, so "if you have suffered dismally through your own evil-doing, do not charge the gods with having brought about your fate (*moiran*); you yourselves" have caused your own ruin (8.1–3; see also 3.1–8). Moira no longer needs for its enforcement a special spontaneous, divine intervention; it is the natural order within which men operate, foolishly or wisely, with appropriate results. It is not the gods, but man's *"dysnomia* (lawlessness, transgression) that brings innumerable ills to the state, while *eunomia* (good order, lawfulness) displays all things well-ordered and sound" (3.31–2). It is "the citizens themselves who in their thoughtlessness seek to destroy the great city" (3.5–6). Homeric *ate,* heaven-sent blindness and ruin, is replaced here by simple human ignorance followed by ruin.

Although Solon does not yet use the powerful metaphor of a

"body politic" explicitly, its conception underlies his view of the state as a social organism and of injustice as a kind of pollution and disease of the whole community. Homer and Hesiod knew only of physical pollution; Solon extends the idea into the moral-political realm. In Homer and Hesiod one had to avoid uncleanliness only if one wanted to deal with the gods; now Solon extends the avoidance of pollution to one's dealings with men. In Homer and Hesiod "pollution" could be cleansed simply by washing oneself with cold water; now social pollution is almost indelible and its effects are dangerous not only for the individual but for the whole community.

It is this idea of injustice as a disease of the body politic, a "pathological condition"[2] of the social organism, and of justice as health, integrity, and harmonious functioning of the state, that enables Solon to account for certain apparent anomalies in the operation of Dike: that punishment does not necessarily come immediately upon the commission of crime; that one man pays straightaway, another later; that even the innocent suffer, and one's escape from retribution may be paid for by one's children and children's children—all this makes sense now. For in Solon's conception the transgressor inflicts grievous, often fatal wounds on himself, his family, and the state. Though these wounds may be hidden for a while, they fester and corrupt, and sooner or later their disastrous effect appears plain to sight. Injustice is like a contagious, even hereditary disease; that is why a whole town may suffer for one man's crime (3.17) and descendants pay for their ancestors' transgression (1.31). The unjust man's deed pollutes the whole community. Lawlessness is a miasma which, unchecked, naturally ends in an epidemic of disaster.

The idea of innocents suffering for others' wrongdoing may strike us as going a bit too far in the cause of justice, yet what could be a more realistic appraisal of the results of social evil? As a few germs may destroy whole cities, or a small fire consume an entire town, so from negligible beginnings social discord spreads till cities fall. In Hesiod, evil strife already led to war, famine, and pestilence affecting all, while honest work brought peace and general well-being to all men. Now in Solon injustice naturally leads to widespread discord, civil war, tyranny, and slavery, and what could be more evident than the fact that from this everyone suffers, not only the criminal, just as everyone benefits from general order and harmony? The truth is that no matter who caused it "the public evil comes home to every man" (3.26). Like the plague "it is not kept out by courtyard gates but leaps over towering walls, and without fail finds (every man) even though he be fled to the inmost corners of his chamber" (3.27–29). This is precisely what makes injustice so dangerous to the whole community, and why every man must be constantly on the alert to avert general disaster. The idea is as realistic as it is rational. What Homer presented mythically—Apollo's plague killing the Greeks, but not Agamemnon, for Agamemnon's misdeeds—and Hesiod without explanation, Solon now discusses in the manner of a physician dispassionately describing the causes, symptoms, and case history of a disease.

The main cause of social injustice is *pleonexia*[3]—insatiable greed, man's forever wanting more than he already has—and Solon never ceases to inveigh against it (e.g., 1.11; 11.71–76; 3.6–14; 5.9). *Koros—hybris—ate:* satiety and excess in abundance breed transgression which brings on ruin. That this is the natural course of events became a commonplace in later Greek literature, but it was Solon who first explained why this sequence is unalterable. "In wealth there is no limit apparent to men. Even those of us who have the most means of livelihood are exerting ourselves with redoubled energy; what would satisfy all?" (1.71–3). It is its character of having no limit, end, boundary, or set measure that makes *pleonexia,* literally 'wanting to have more,' so ruinous. That which has no measure, no measure of striving can satisfy, and a desire that can never be sated is by its very nature a poison to the soul, a cancerous tissue in the body—individual or politic—that corrupts the organism without fail.

Fortunately, the remedy for this evil was as evident to the

Greeks as was its presence. "Observe due measure; proportion is best in all" (*Erga* 694) Hesiod urged; and this is what Solon, too, advocates with all the eloquence in his power. Hard as it may be "to know the hidden measure of judgment that alone holds the limits of all things" (16), this knowledge is the strongest of the holy foundations of Dike, it is the very essence of *eunomia* which makes all things "well-ordered and right as it fetters the unjust, smoothes what is rough, checks surfeit, reduces transgression, withers the unfolding flowers of blind delusion, straightens crooked judgment, softens arrogant deeds, stops the works of discord, and ends the wrath of grievous strife. Under her rule all is sound and prudent among men" (3.32–39). Therefore "tame your strong hearts, you who have made your way to an abundance of many goods; keep your grand designs within bounds" (4.5–7). Moderate, limit, check, restrain, still your excessive greed—the repetitiousness of Solon's advice may not make great poetry, but it certainly gets the point across.

Solon does not despise wealth altogether; he merely emphasizes the uncertainties and risks of its pursuit even by honest, let alone dishonest means (1.32–36, 43–48, 63–70). Since wealth has no measure or limit, its direct pursuit is not subject to rational principles, and thus one had best accept possessions as a—sometime fateful but always dangerous— gift from the gods rather than as the necessary result of one's own effort. Certainly wealth is no evidence of virtue, and material gifts, human or divine—the Homeric *time* and *geras* —are not equivalent to honor. "Many bad men are rich while good men are poor; but we will not exchange our virtue for their wealth, for the one is forever firm while riches go unstably from men to men" (4.9–13). Treasures "in silver and gold, wheat-bearing ground and horses and mules" (14.1–3) are not even "true wealth for mortals, for no man can take vast possessions with him to Hades, nor can he by ransom escape death or baneful disease or the misery of approaching old age" (14.7–10). True treasures for men are rather "the pleasant sensations of stomach, lungs, and feet, the youthful prime of boys and women, when these things come; every season brings what is appropriate to it" (14.4–6; see also 13; 20; and Herodotus 1.30–31). It is, after all, for the sake of these that we pursue wealth itself and not the other way around; they are the end to which wealth is but an uncertain means. And they can be had even without wealth; that is why Solon thinks men of modest competence, like Tellus, Cleobis, and Biton, to be better off and richer than Croesus himself. For they had this true treasure as well as what was sufficient for the needs of daily life (Herodotus 1.31). Sufficiency is the key word here: while wealth has no limit and therefore greed cannot be satisfied, the natural desires of men have a built-in, natural measure or limit and that makes them capable of fulfilment. Since they can be given their due, it is their satisfaction that we ought to pursue—in moderation.

Solon's view of political power is very similar to his view of wealth. Since the desire for power is characterized by the same limitlessness and lack of measure that made material greed so disruptive to social harmony, the pursuit of power naturally leads to excess, and Solon regards such excess of domination, tending toward the joint evils of tyranny and slavery, no less dangerous to society than are excessive wealth and poverty. Too great an unbalance in the distribution of power is as responsible for the class conflict that ruins the state as is too unequal a distribution of wealth. That is why in the political domain, too, Solon advocates moderation. He hates tyranny and refuses to assume tyrannical powers even though he could easily make himself absolute master of Athens (23). In opposition to public opinion he regards the "relentless violence of tyranny" (23.9) a dishonor to himself (23.10) as well as a danger to the community. Yet unlike Hesiod he is not a naive champion of the underdog either and refuses to take up arms for the people's overly one-sided claims. Aware that the uninhibited, quasi-tyrannical rule of the people is a not unmixed blessing, he assumes the role of mediator setting limits to rich and poor, noble and base alike. Due measure, moderation, sufficiency, and the avoidance of excess are the keys to his political program too: "To the people I have given as much privilege as is sufficient, neither diminishing their due nor offering more; but I also thought of those who held power and were honored for their wealth, that they too should not be abused. I stood with a strong shield held over both sides, not letting either win an unjust victory. . . . The people will follow its leaders best if it is neither excessively free nor too oppressed; for surfeit breeds transgression when prosperity comes upon men of unsound minds" (5.1–10). Therefore, while he freed the slaves at home and brought back those sold into bondage abroad or driven by destitution into exile (24.7–15), he also "held the people back" (24.22; 25.6) and "wrote laws for base and noble alike fitting straight justice to each and every man" (24.18–20). Thus "I stood at bay like a wolf amidst a pack of hounds, defending myself against all comers" (24.26–7), "I took a stand like a boundary stone on a disputed frontier" (25.8–9).

Solon's appointment as *diallaktes,* mediator, suited his frame of mind exactly. For although he was against excessive imbalance in distribution, he thought absolute equality—in wealth and power—equally wrong. *Isomoiria,* the idea that "worthy and unworthy should have equal share" (23.21) and that wise and ignorant should be treated alike, was as repugnant to him as were the extremes of tyranny and slavery, and for much the same reason. The tyrant far exceeds, the slave falls far short of his natural due. But *isomoiria,* the absolute equality of all regardless of all inherent, natural inequality among men, also violates the notion of giving each man his due. Excessive equality, the forced equality of the naturally unequal, disregards due measure, limit, harmony, and balance, and consequently disturbs the ideal order of the state just as much as excessive inequality. Solon, a worthy precursor of Plato and Aristotle, is resolved to avoid both types of excess in his legislation.

Some commentators [4] separate sharply the economic and political aspects of Solon's reform and find the latter to be far more liberal than the former. But what strikes me most in Solon's treat--

ment of distributive and political justice is precisely the similarity of his argument and of his measures in both cases and the overall unity of his thought. He legislates against excess—in both wealth and power—and against utter deprivation—of both wealth and power. He is against political as well as economic *isomoiria*. Some of his political reforms—e.g., limiting the power of the aristocracy —he achieves through economic legislation, others are bound up with it. He extends franchise and most important judicial powers to all citizens, but restricts eligibility for office to those of higher economic status. He realizes that the community cannot flourish while some of its members labor in total economic and political servitude; at the same time he is bent on preserving the economic and political incentives that enable men to rise above their present status. Economic and political measures are inseparable here, because they are governed by the same principles and directed at the same end: social-legal-political-economic justice.

This is why the controversy [5] concerning *eunomia* and *dysnomia* in Solon, which terms some scholars translate as lawfulness and lawlessness while others as right and wrong material allotment, the state of things being well or badly distributed, seems largely verbal. To be sure, *eunomia* means lawfulness, political order, and harmony, the foremost characteristic of the just state. But to legislate and act justly means to observe due measure, to harmonize claims, not to diminish or inflate anyone's due, not to let anyone encroach on others' portions, not to transgress limits by wanting or giving more than is fit, right, appropriate. Thus *eunomia,* whether it is translated as lawfulness or due allotment, legal-political or distributive justice, comes to the same thing: proportion and right balance between man and man in possession, freedom, and power. This is, at any rate, what Solon's legislation was intended to bring about in the service of justice—legal, political, and economic.

Not only is there a thoroughgoing correspondence between the diverse aspects of Solon's conception of *eunomia,* but there is an equal harmony between his thought and his practical action. While

Hesiod had laid the foundations for much of Solon's theory of the well-ordered state, he could not do anything to put his theories into effect on the practical level. But Solon, elected as archon with almost unrestricted legislative powers, was in a unique position to bring about legislative reform and promptly proceeded to do so. Through the cancellation of debts, the outlawing of mortgages on one's person, the liberation of those thus enslaved, and the prohibition on exporting scarce agricultural products, he relieved the worst economic pressure on the poorest classes. Through the assertion of individual property rights over those of the clan, the outlawing of conspicuous waste, and the limits imposed on the amount of land anyone could acquire, he tried to weaken the position of the landed aristocracy. Through the encouragement of trade he strengthened the middle class and even opened the way into it to all by requiring parents to teach their children some craft. By introducing general franchise and judicial powers, extending eligibility to office, and making public officials publicly accountable, he matched his economic legislation by his judicial-political measures. Above all, by neither seeking material aggrandizement nor assuming the tyranny, he demonstrated that he was an advocate of moderation and due measure in deed as well as word. Though he lived in what we call the archaic age of Greece, the harmony and balance of Solon's thought and action make him a prime example of what later became the classical ideal of man.

He was neither a hidebound traditionalist nor a reckless innovator. Building on tradition, he modified it, unified diverse trends —the individualism of Archilochus and Sappho, and Hesiod's concern for communal existence; Archilochus' and Sappho's insight into the contingency of life and Hesiod's trust in an abiding world-order —and above all he clarified much that was available before in a crude form only. He expanded the traditional religious idea of pollution and made it a rationally and empirically verifiable one. He retained Hesiod's notion of the lawfulness and justice of divinity, but he relied more on rational and empirical argument than on supernatural religious sanctions to support his concept of the rule of law. Hesiod already contrasted violence and justice and advocated legality as the only viable alternative to settling disputes by brute force. But while this gave at best a negative definition of justice, Solon's insistence on due allotment, natural limit, and rational measure gave the rule of law a more positive content.

That Solon deepened Hesiod's notion of justice had far-reaching consequences. Hesiod, failing to distinguish clearly between legality and justice, naively assumed that positive law was necessarily harmonious with that which it was designed to promote: social order and harmony. But Solon saw that this was far from being the case; that even as measured by Hesiod's own criteria—using violence and discord as touchstones of injustice—positive laws could themselves be unjust. The mortgage law allowing for the enslavement of the mortgagee, for instance, was itself a source of social discord and violence: promoting excessive servitude on the one hand and the accumulation of too much wealth and power on the other, this law tended to increase faction and conflict within the city and foster the conditions which led to civil war, anarchy, and tyranny. This law then defeated the very purpose which all laws and legal institutions were designed to serve; because it did not fulfill the law's general function it was a bad and unjust law.

The importance of this Solonic distinction between mere legality and true justice cannot be overestimated. By introducing a conflict between seeming and being (just) into the realm of law itself, Solon's jurisprudential and legislative thought laid a rational foundation for both the criticism and the correction of positive law. Since not all laws were necessarily just, no particular law was above criticism and conventional law could be attacked even by the champions of justice. At the same time since the law itself served a clearly defined purpose—promoting the city's well-being—the legislator had rational guidelines not just for criticizing but for reforming the law with a view to making it more adequate to fulfilling its function. Solon's thought opened the way for both the

Sophistic nature-convention controversy and its philosophical resolution.

With his more sophisticated insight into the nature and function of law, Solon could also take a more sophisticated and realistic attitude toward the use and abuse of force. Force (*bia*) for Hesiod was an evil in itself; as used by men it amounted to violence, the antithesis of god-given, god-enforced justice. But for Solon, force is evil only when excessive and unlimited: when it is used by the self-seeking individual with blind passion rather than rational restraint to subvert rather than promote the ends of justice. Therefore Solon not only seeks to impose measure on force; but in order to impose measure, check violence, and set limits to antisocial conduct, he will gladly use force himself. Only this force is something new: it is the force of law that Solon harnessed "by main strength forging force and justice [Hesiod's antithetical *bia* and *dike*] into an harmonious whole" (24.15–17).

In language and style Solon seems at first more of a traditionalist than an innovator. Unlike Archilochus and Sappho he creates no new verse forms; from the vast array of lyric examples he selects as his favorite the most traditional form, the elegy, itself an offshoot of the epic hexameter. Nor does he use the vernacular, whose closeness to life Archilochus and Sappho exploited with such success; instead of writing in his own Attic tongue, he borrows the by now traditional Ionian language of the elegy and uses it with little Attic admixture. And even though he writes elegies, his style is more reminiscent of Hesiod's than of his immediate lyric predecessors'. His poems are longer than those of Archilochus and Sappho, and, instead of running swiftly like the breathless lyric song, they move along massively in long sentences and with long lines of argument. Instead of showing variety and diversity, they present one single theme that grows organically—Hesiodically—all through the poem, indeed all through his poems as a whole. On the whole, his poems are prosaic and show as little sensitivity to form and as little poetic imagination as did Hesiod's.

Paradoxically, it is this return to Hesiod that makes Solon, if not altogether an innovator, at least a modifier and developer of tradition. For, like Hesiod, he subordinates poetic form to thought-content, and poetry itself to social-political education; as a result his poems represent a further step toward the ultimate development of prose writing and of legal-political rhetoric. The stylistic peculiarities of his poems can be best understood if we approach them while keeping Solon's educational-political priorities in mind. Since he wants to speak of the universal, impersonal order of things, he generally employs the least personal verse form, the elegy. Since he wants to awaken people to social-political consciousness, he transforms the elegy from a song of helpless lamentation and the iambus from a song of personal invective into tools of active social-political reform. Since he wants to teach all men at all times, he spurns the immediacy of the vernacular and chooses a more distant, loftier, and widerspread idiom as his vehicle. Since he is more concerned with content than with form, he pays less attention to music and sound than to meaning. He is not even averse to a monotonous repetition of the same word—*pauei* appears three times in five lines in 3.34-38 —as long as it gets his message across. It is not so much that Solon's ability to think was far in advance of his ability to express himself, as Wilamowitz thought; rather his thought required a different expression than did that of Archilochus and Sappho, and this accounts for his noticeable divergence from their styles. Linforth surmises [6] that even Solon's choice of poetry rather than prose as a vehicle for his teaching may have been governed more by didactic-political considerations than by a blind adherence to literary tradition. Finding the "ordered song of words" (2.2) more memorable and persuasive, of greater emotional appeal and mind-molding power than prose, Solon may have chosen it deliberately as a better instrument for broad political education than prose could ever be. If Solon did indeed think this, time proved him wrong, for in the fifth century the Sophists developed a kind of prose that was an even more powerful instrument of legal-political persuasion than

Solon's artless poetry. However, even Solon's rhetorical and poetic shortcomings furthered rather than hindered his cause; they saved him from a danger to which late Sophistry succumbed precisely because of its accomplishments. The Sophists spoke so beautifully on any subject that the artfulness of their words overshadowed the thought-content of their speeches and took attention away from the truth or falsity of what they said. In Solon at least there is little danger of that; certainly even his grateful compatriots who were exceedingly proud of him as their sage and legislator never regarded him a great and accomplished poet.

On the whole, there is probably no need to bring in political considerations to account for the fact that Solon, the mediator, the transmitter and modifier of tradition, did not initiate an entirely new form of literature. As for his artlessness in the form of writing he did adopt, little more explanation is necessary. The later Sophists, like their lyric predecessors Archilochus and Sappho, with whom they have many a trait in common, concentrated on the cultivation of language and form because they had little faith in man's capacity to arrive at trustworthy knowledge of abiding universal truths. Solon, on the contrary, believed in and aimed at the acquisition and imparting of such knowledge, and therefore he cultivated the measure of judgment, *metron gnomosynes,* rather than the poetic and musical metre. It is certainly not accidental that the only new abstraction original with Solon—*gnomosyne*—refers to thought rather than feeling and emotion, and that the traditional term *sophia* in Solon no longer connotes skill in carpentry (*Iliad* 15.412), or navigation (*Erga* 649; Archilochus 44), or even poetry (Sappho 60, Alcman 13), but like *gnomosyne* it is connected with *metron* (1.52) and becomes an intellectual skill, a knowledge of measure, order, and limit.[7]

Solon's faith in and insistence on knowledge is very much in harmony with his sense of time too. Knowledge is possible only if there is something abiding in the passage of time; certainty of insight presupposes order and necessity in the temporal world. Accordingly, once again in Solon the flow of time expands far beyond the moment Archilochus and Sappho concentrated on, and, since the world is approached not emotionally but rationally, time becomes once again the lawful dimension of orderly change and growth. In Archilochus and Sappho, utter temporal mutability made each moment's revelation forever useless. In Solon, however, time itself becomes the agent for revealing timeless truths (9) as well as the "court of law" before which the testimony of black earth, the most enduring thing known to man, witnesses the justice of Solon's case (24.3–5). Archilochus' and Sappho's helplessness in life was, as we saw, a helplessness against time, whose irretrievable passing they could neither master nor arrest. Now Solon's self-assurance as knower and teacher stems from his overcoming time through reason's quest for timeless law.

With the reinstatement of abiding law, and the making of time itself both court and judge of world history, the ephemeral moment is radically deemphasized. Zeus looks not to the moment but to the end (1.17); he does not swiftly punish each instant's transgression (1.25–6) yet "in the end, without fail" (1.28) the transgressor is brought to light. Justice too, "silently notes what happens and what has gone before" (3.14–5), and though one may escape it for a time retribution comes sooner or later, but unfailingly in the end. Solon personally endures momentary set-backs and passing injustice with composure. Unlike the fool who would "want to rule, seizing boundless wealth and tyrannizing Athens, for one single day, even though he be flayed for it and his race be destroyed thereafter" (23.5–7), Solon wants "good reputation among men forever" (1.4) rather than instant success and glory; he wants not victory now but "a fuller triumph over all mankind" (23.11–12) in the end.

With abiding law paramount, the lyric emphasis on youth is also gone; the never-to-be-recaptured moment of freshness and delicate grace is no longer the only worthwhile time of life. Now each season has its own suitable joy and work (19; 14.6), its own inherent worth. Even death comes "not out of season" (19.18) when "a man, having completed his tenth seven-year period, according to measure, reaches the end" (19.17). Solon's poem on the hebdomads of life emphasizes precisely what Hesiod insisted on and what Archilochus and Sappho disregarded: lawful change and organic growth in the life of man. Although the right moment and the right season remain important—for once missed their advantages are not easily regained at a later time (10.5–6)—even here it is Solon's insight into lawful organic change in the life of men and states that leads to his stressing the suitable occasion. The same insight, however, also enables him to rise above the occasion and take a long-term view of human and divine affairs, which is more than Archilochus and Sappho could do.

Solon's language and style are suited to his view of time. His rising above the particular occasion by way of an intelligent grasp of universal law enduring in time is parallelled by his avoiding the regional and contemporary vernacular and writing in a more elevated idiom, distant from his own in space and time. His conception of organic growth and gradual development in the course of time is matched by the stately flow of his longer poems in which the central theme is gradually expanded and reinforced. Even his position as transmitter and modifier of tradition makes sense only in view of his belief in organic growth and abiding patterns in history. Now that time is a dimension of orderly change and growth, one can build on what is of lasting value in tradition, yet remain responsive to the needs of the changing situation and still hope to establish something that will last foreveer. Solon's thought and deeds, style, and sense of time and life are but so many different aspects of the same unitary view of the world as a whole. Although a poet and statesman, rather than a systematic thinker, Solon still managed to make his thought, life, and work a more harmonious whole than many a philosopher in later times.

5. Dionysus

"No man prays to a concept," [1] but that is almost what the gods have become in the Hesiodic-Solonic reform of Homeric myth. In answer to the rational demand for unity and consistency the gods have been reduced to being little more than the embodiment and sanction of law, and this new conception, though more appropriate to the intellect than Homer's anthropomorphic deities, was even less gratifying to the need for emotional involvement. It is no wonder then that a type of religious worship which provided just such gratification spread all over Greece with an almost irresistible force during this period.

Little is known for certain about the origin of the cult of Dionysus. Until recently most scholars believed the god to have been a Thracian-Phrygian import, a relative latecomer to Greece, and there seemed to be a great deal of evidence in support of their view. For Homer, who knew Dionysus, excluded him from the Olympus; Herodotus, who knew of his Thracian worship, derived his cult from Egypt; vase-painters often depicted the god in Oriental garb; and the majority of the stories concerning his arrival in Greece tell

Material in this chapter also appeared in "Dionysus and Tragedy" *Review of Metaphysics* (September 1962) and is republished by permission.

us how much resistance Dionysus encountered on his entry—or reentry—to the mainland.

With the decipherment of Linear B, however, new evidence came to light which shows that Dionysus was worshiped in Crete as well as on the mainland in Minoan-Mycenean times. Therefore his appearance in Greece in the eighth century constitutes a religious revival rather than a first import or a new creation, and the Greeks' reluctance to own him as native and to accept him as god must be explained as resulting from the fact that the worship of Dionysus, in its most essential aspects, ran counter to the moral, religious, and intellectual tendencies that were dominant at the time. This explains at the same time why the cult of Dionysus, appealing to what was otherwise left out of account, found such a fertile soil in Greece and, spreading like an epidemic through the land, could firmly establish itself there by the beginning of the seventh century.

Who is this strange god who exerted, in defiance of all opposition, such a great influence on the life of Greece? What was the power of Dionysus that poets, artists, philosophers, and kings, and above all the masses of common people felt and responded to in so many different ways?

According to myth, Dionysus is the son of Zeus, an immortal god, and of Semele, a mortal woman of Thebes. His mother is burnt to death by the god's thunderbolt before Dionysus' birth, but Zeus saves Dionysus from the ashes, sews him up in his thigh and gives birth to him. Changed into a kid or a ram to escape Hera's anger, Dionysus is given to the nymphs to be brought up in Nysa— or else to Ino and Athamas, who bring him up disguised as a girl. In his youth Dionysus and the nymphs, accompanied by wild animals, wander freely through the woods filling them with the sound of their joyful revels. Later Dionysus goes down to Hades to rescue his mother, who is then made immortal. He marries Ariadne, another mortal woman, whom Zeus makes ageless and deathless for him.

Harmless enough. But a disturbing note soon enters the stories

of the god's epiphanies. The myth of Lycourgos tells of the Edonian
king's resistance to Dionysus *mainomenos,* the mad god. Lycourgos
drives Dionysus into the sea and makes his Nysean nurses captive.
In retribution the god drives Lycourgos mad, whereupon the king
kills his own son with an axe and chops off the corpse's extremities
before he comes to his senses. At Dionysus' command the Edonians
then bind Lycourgos on Mt. Pangaeus where he is torn apart by
horses. Boutes, Lycourgos' brother who catches one of Dionysus'
followers and makes her his wife, is also driven mad; he commits
suicide by throwing himself into a well.

The story of Pentheus, king of Thebes, is equally rich in horror.
When Dionysus comes to Thebes with a band of maenads and
drives the initially resisting women of the city from their looms into
the mountains where they engage in wild, orgiastic, nocturnal
revelry, Pentheus has the bacchants bound and imprisons the god
himself. Dionysus dissolves the bonds and, leaving prison with his
followers, takes possession of the king and turns him into a bac-
chant. Disguised as a woman, Pentheus is led to spy on the revellers
until at Dionysus' command he is torn apart, limb from limb, by
his own mother and aunts. In their madness the women believe they
are dismembering a lion's whelp, play ball with chunks of his
flesh, and proceed to invite their relatives to a raw feast. When they
come to their senses, they, too, are punished for their initial resistance.

On and on Dionysus wanders, and each epiphany brings new
disaster. At Argos where Perseus first opposes him, the Argive
women are driven mad and devour their infants raw. At Orchome-
nos vines sprout from the looms of king Minyas' resisting daughters
and strange music fills the air as Dionysus, changing his shape from
girl to lion, bull, and panther, takes away their senses and inspires
them to kill one of their offspring, tear him to pieces, and eat his
flesh raw. At Tiryns Proetus' daughters are driven mad because
they would not receive the god of their own volition; in Attica the
same thing happens to the daughters of Eleuther; and the Icarian

women, turned insane, hang themselves from trees. In Thrace Orpheus is torn apart by the bacchants for offending the god and his limbs are scattered; in India King Damascus is flayed alive for opposing Dionysus; the Amazons too are killed for the same reason.

But the dangers of Dionysus' coming are not confined to those who resist the god; even those who receive him with kindness seem to do so at their own peril. Hera strikes Athamas and Ino with madness for bringing up Dionysus, and Athamas, distracted, kills one of his sons, mistaking him for a lion, and throws another into a kettle of boiling water. Nor is madness primarily a *punishment* that comes upon those who are exposed to Dionysus; the god's most devoted worshipers and willing followers are the maenads, madwomen possessed by Dionysus. Finally, madness is not even confined to mortals: the god himself is Dionysus *mainomenos,* the mad god, and the madness of the human beings possessed by him merely reflects the madness of the god.

We might begin an appraisal of Dionysian myth by noting this all-important difference between Dionysus and the Olympians. Homer's anthropomorphic deities mirrored in their exalted forms the characters and ideal traits of Homeric man. But Dionysus, instead of mirroring man, transforms his worshipers in his own image. Homer's gods, despite their all-too-human characteristics, or perhaps because of them, insisted on the distance separating gods and men. Though occasionally they entered the human arena, they knew their rightful place to be the Olympus and by and large that is where they stayed. Certainly they would have regarded any man's attempt to enter their domain and equate himself with the gods as sacrilegious and unholy. In contrast to this, un-Olympian Dionysus dwells exclusively on earth, surrounded by men and beasts, and instead of emphasizing the unbridgeable gulf between mortals and immortals, he is intent on abolishing it. His worshipers become ecstatic: they are taken out of themselves, released from human bondage. They are possessed: the god claims and takes over their whole being and fills them with his own substance. In Dionysian enthusiasm men become *entheoi,* literally full of god. The communion between man and god is complete, with nothing reserved and kept apart on either side.[2]

The immediate result of such divine possession is a complete self-abandonment and loss of individuality on the part of man. The lyric poet almost deified his own passion and cultivated, just about exclusively, his individual personality; all this is given up in Dionysian enthusiasm. "To the *thiasos* of Dionysus everything is surrendered"[3] and in transcending his own limitations man achieves a radical freedom, a freedom from the self. Released from the bonds of separate individual existence, elevated beyond all that is human, the ecstatic is one with god. Dionysus *lusios* is a looser, dissolver, deliverer: his worshipers are delivered from themselves, distracted from what they were as individuals, taken out of their own minds and personality. In divine transport they are carried into a region where the bonds of the self no longer hold, where there is only god. Humanity itself has become an unessential trait, from which the follower of Dionysus is delivered in ecstasy.

The horrifying rites of *sparagmos* (tearing apart) and *omophagia* (raw-eating) are, as it were, literal representations of this aspect of the Dionysian cult. Since the living human person is no more than an unessential envelope that conceals the divine substance, it has to be torn apart in the pursuit of the essence of divinity. At the same time, since man is *entheos,* since the god dwells in man as his ultimate substance, the ritual devouring of raw flesh is a devouring, and thereby literally an embodying, of the god himself. *Sparagmos* and *omophagia* are enactments of ecstasy (delivery from the self) and enthusiasm (being filled with god).

Even apart from its horribly literal aspects, the ecstatic union with god is also a union with one's fellow beings. Since all separate, individual existence is abolished, all men are perforce united. In the ecstatic band of Dionysus all souls merge and each worshiper is "one with those who belong to the holy body of god."[4] The *thiasos* is not a social group; it is an undifferentiated mass of emotionally united revellers who are essentially indistinguishable from each other.

Nor is that all. Dionysian apotheosis is a dehumanization of man in the worst as well as in the best sense. It is not only the distance between man and god, and concomitantly between men and men, that is annulled here: the distinction between man and beast is equally dissolved. Dionysus changes not only his opponents (e.g., Cadmus and Harmonia; Leucippe, Alcithoe, and Arsippe; the Tyrsenian pirates) into beasts; his followers seem even more intent on becoming like animals in every way. The maenads clothe themselves in animal hides, twine serpents around their heads and necks, cradle and suckle wild animals, and romp wildly through the woods. But more important than these superficial aspects is the fact that their behavior is beastly in the worst sense of the word. In Hesiod, violence—"that fishes and beasts and winged birds should devour one another"—was the law of the beasts, and the Hesiodic-Solonic reform of human conduct was designed to lift men above such brutish behavior. Now Dionysus, lifting men above humanity, also lowers man to the level of brute animals and if possible even below. Certainly nothing could surpass the maenads' violence in tearing animals and men apart with bare hands, rending the squirming flesh with tooth and claw, tossing back and forth the steaming, reeking bits, and devouring them raw. While animals normally kill out of hunger or self-defense, the maenads kill like rabid beasts for sport; while animals normally spare their own young, it is precisely their own offspring that the followers of Dionysus hunt, kill, and devour in ecstasy. "Oh beautiful agon, to plunge reeking hands into the blood of one's own child . . ." (Euripides, *Bacchae* 1163).

It is an almost unnecessary symbolism that Dionysus' cortege is composed of animals and half-human, half-animal creatures as well as of men. For his human followers are even more bestial than the satyrs, sileni, and the beasts themselves. The worship of Dionysus is unanthropomorphic with a vengeance; the bacchants' human exterior only underscores the degree to which they are divested of all humanity and, in exaltation above man's state, are debased below the beasts. The point is, of course, that none of these divisions hold here, and human value judgments concerning higher and lower states of being have become irrelevant.

Although in the Dionysian fusion of god, man, and beast, nature herself seems to join the maenads' *baccheia*—"the mountain and the beasts all shared their ecstasy and nothing remained unmoved" (Euripides, *Bacchae* 726-7)—the cult of Dionysus is not a movement designed to reintegrate man into an idyllic natural existence. To be sure, there are elements of nature, fertility, and vegetation worship in this cult, but they are probably later accretions,[5] and the essentially ecstatic-enthusiastic character of Dionysian religion is antithetical to Dionysus being a vegetation and fertility god. For it is not only the bonds of the self and those of civilized social life that Dionysus dissolves; the very bonds of nature seem to give way at the god's coming. More than any other god, Dionysus is a miracle-worker, wizard, and enchanter (Euripides, *Bacchae* 449-50, 234), who plays havoc with the rhythm of nature and confounds the orderly seasonal growth and flow of things. Earthquake, miraculous fire, and lightning out of clear sky accompany the god's epiphanies, strange music fills the air, and shipmasts bloom. Wine, milk, and honey flow from the soil, water wells forth from barren rock, and vines sprout on looms. The maenads acquire superhuman strength and are unscathed by fire, spear, or sword, while their wands deal grievous wounds. Mothers leave their offspring to fondle wolf cubs, virgins suckle fawns, and parents turn in frenzy against their children. What has all this to do with the settled order of nature? Juenger aptly compared Minyas' daughters weaving at their loom to Clotho, Athropos, and Lachesis working at the loom of fate,[6] for, just as Dionysus puts an end to the Minydes' work, so he tears apart the woof and warp of *moira* too. It is *moira*—the natural allotment, portion, constitution, and way of things—that makes everything what it is, that defines limits and bounds and separates each thing from the next. But Dionysus cancels all portions, dissolves all limits, and brings all settled order to naught. Dissolver, perverter, destroyer, his coming throws nature out of joint as if things shared the ecstasy of the maenads. Time itself gives way, for what is time without rhythmic endurance and orderly change and growth? What is time for the possessed who, oblivious of past, present, and future, experience eternity in the moment? The ecstatic is beyond nature and time, or would be if he still existed in his own right. But, strictly speaking, the individual no longer does. In the region into which he is transported there is only god.

This god may be called a god of life, but only in a special sense. He represents life exploding beyond all boundaries,[7] life undifferentiated and formless,[8] life disjointed, disoriented, disorganized—a life that is hardly distinguishable from death. Supremely indifferent to any form of life here and now, or even hostile to its confining particular manifestations from which Dionysian ecstasy saves man, Dionysus is, as Heracleitus saw, as much a god of death as of life.[9]

What makes any clear-cut and unequivocal characterization of the god impossible is that Dionysus is an essentially self-contradictory divinity. A god of life, generation, and creative power *and* a god of death, degeneration, and destruction; a god of exaltation, exultation, otherworldly peace and bliss *and* of debasement, terror, frenzied violence, and bestial excess. He is healer, benefactor, good counselor, leader, savior, joy of mortals, god of many delights—some of his many epithets—*and* man-dismemberer, raw-devourer, mad maddener of man, beast, and even of mountains. Man-woman— *gynnis*—is one of his apter names, for Dionysus is, as it were, a form of being that defies the separation of opposites. "Gay yet menacing, eternally the same yet eternally the other,"[10] joyous yet grim, raging-orgiastic yet of an "uncanny stillness and calm"[11] he is, and accordingly his worship is full of things "which bring man bliss or tear his life to shreds without a break in their own serenity,"[12] it is equally "compounded of beauty and terror"[13]—as some of the most acute interpreters have clearly seen. It is not only his worshipers who undergo such fearful, contradictory experiences as are reported by myth; Dionysus himself suffers the same fate. As a hunter he is hunted, as dismemberer dismembered, possessor possessed, killer killed, dead reborn. As nothing abides and endures in the world into which Dionysus erupts, so the god himself changes his form with lightning swiftness, and even such contradictory characteristics as we are forced to ascribe to him in the attempt to grasp his essence tend to merge and to dissolve in the mad whirl of the god's metamorphoses.

Metamorphosis is an essential trait of the god.[14] He is pure becoming rather than being; he transforms himself—as well as man and world—"in any manner he pleases" (Euripides, *Bacchae* 477). As man, woman, boy, girl; bull, lion, snake, panther, mule, ram, kid;[15] Dionysus *polumorphos, polueides,*[16] *poluonumos*[17] glitters in a kaleidoscopic variability of form. The god's physical *sparagmos* is paralleled by a metaphysical-conceptual one; Plutarch's Delphic theologians already "spoke darkly of his (Dionysus') transformation as a kind of tearing apart (*diaspasmos*) and dismemberment (*diamelismos*)."[18] This conceptual diremption of Dionysus leaves the god essentially formless; he is a multiplicity of forms none of which are essential to him. Dionysus *lusios,* the dissolver of persons, dissolves before our eyes.

One of the most compelling symbols of Dionysus is the mask, and in its way the mask symbolizes everything the god stands for. The mask is deceptive surface and unessential appearance. It can be put on and discarded at will. It can be filled with any manner of content. The same person can wear different masks and the same mask can be worn by different people. Depending on its use, the mask can make both form and content irrelevant. Its face hides and reveals at the same time: it hides the substance but also reveals it— once the mask is seen as mere mask—as that which is hidden. The mask is a true symbol; in presenting itself it points beyond what it presents toward that which is unpresented and yet alone essential in the presentation.

In Dionysus' hands all men become mere masks, *personae,* possessed, inspired and filled by nothing but the god. The ecstatic experience reveals the individual to himself as an unessential vessel and vehicle of divinity, and accordingly we see the possessed frantically tearing at the bonds that tie them to this unsubstantial, mask-like existence. Yet their attempt to stand out beyond the mask, shed the mask and become more than mask is doomed to fail. For the god with whom the ecstatic is united, the god for whom man is a mere mask, the god that is revealed in the unmasking of man, is nothing but a mask himself. Like a mask he is all there; immediate, tangible, concrete presence with nothing withheld. But that is just the point: no matter how deep the intellect probes beyond the masks there is nothing else to find. The god is all there, but what is there completely and without reservation is just a mask; lift it and you encounter nothing. The faceless, formless, impersonal reverse of the mask only reveals the ineffability of Dionysus, the purely mimetic god. This is precisely the function of the mask as a Dionysian instrument and symbol: to turn everything (men and the god) into a mask and to reveal it as such (i.e., as unessential). In this dissolution of the mask (revealed as mask) we are left with nothing intelligible; reason despairs.

That is why the ecstatic experience which may be sheer joy to the enthusiast is at the same time inexpressible terror to the intellect. Reason can grasp the unchanging law, the universal form that underlies all the changing, particular manifestations of things. But here nothing abides, no law is unbroken, and for all his manifold appearance the god has no essential form. Reason insists on measure, boundary, limit, and here all measure is exceeded, all bounds are broken, and all limits transcended. Reason demands unity and consistency, Dionysus is dirempt and self-contradictory. Reason separates and distinguishes according to kinds, Dionysus abolishes all distinctions and merges all into one. Reason seeks reality and here all is appearance, and while appearance, epiphany as such, seems essential to Dionysus, no particular appearance is; the very visibility of the god—qua multiform mask—makes him invisible, undefinable, and unintelligible.

In Euripides' *Bacchae* the inadequacy of a rational approach to the god is justly emphasized (e.g., 200, 395–99, 1005), and the relatively sane Pentheus is scorned as lacking true insight. "Being in your right mind you know nothing" (332), "you don't know what you speak; you were out of your mind before but now you are raving" (358), "you don't know what you live, what you do, nor what you are" (506). But while the sane Pentheus is accused of ignorance—of his own and the god's essential nature—Pentheus turned mad, the self-alienated Pentheus, Pentheus out of his mind and possessed by the god, is conceded to be at least on the road to wisdom: "now you see as you ought to see" (924), "your mind was not healthy before but now it is as it should be" (947–8). All is inverted here; sanity has become madness and madness sanity, knowledge ignorance and irrationality true wisdom.

We can understand now why the worship of Dionysus so strongly attracted and repelled the Greeks at the same time. To the emotionally starved, whose need for passionate involvement the increasingly rationalized Hesiodic-Solonic notion of divinity failed to satisfy, Dionysus brought release and a promise of salvation. Women, whose lives were most curtailed and regimented, felt Dionysus' liberative power most strongly, but the common people responded with an almost equal abandon to the coming of this unintellectual god. Appealing to the emotions—that wherein everyone could claim to be all others' equal—and abolishing all distinctions between men, Dionysus seemed to be a positively democratic deity. His rites helped to release men from the responsibilities of thought as well as the often insufferable bonds that custom and convention imposed on their behavior. Even mortality that has ever been another name for man's fate seemed to be overcome in the union with Dionysus, and the greatest distinction between gods and men seemed to disappear. If this was madness, clearly it was a "divinely inspired one which was a noble thing . . . a madness superior to health of mind, for the one is only of human, the other of divine origin" (Plato, *Phaedrus* 244C–D). To be out of one's mind in this manner was therefore "neither shameful nor disgraceful" (244B), it was not an evil or a disease; on the contrary it appeared that "the greatest of goods come to us through (this) madness" (244A) and "he who has it is made whole and safe for the present and the after-time . . . and finds release from the evils of the day" (244E). There had never been a salvation religion such as this in Greece before.

On the other hand, there had never been such a wild, dark, antisocial, and antirational religion either, as far as anyone could remember. The Homeric world was one of clarity and visibility, but here all that was clear and visible was but a mask hiding the void. And what most of the post-Homeric Greeks searched for in the world was some sort of immutable, universal identity; rational measure, proportion, harmony, balance, law. But Dionysian religion, dissolving all intelligible distinctions, transported men into a realm where such things had no meaning, where meaning, based on the separation and combination of kinds, on boundaries, limits, definition, was itself dissolved. This meaningless realm, this unnameable divine ground, could it be anything but an abyss before which reason recoiled? Certainly not all the Greeks were ready to step out of their minds and relinquish what they regarded as man's most essential and most divine trait: human-divine reason.

For centuries poets and thinkers had been trying to find a human alternative to bestial violence and had praised peace, harmony, and the rule of law in human affairs. Now Dionysus threatened to return man to a prehistoric, presocial, even prehuman state of unparalleled violence. For centuries the poets and thinkers counselled men to avoid hybris and to reverence holiness and justice. Now Dionysus' followers combined hybris and holiness into one concept (Euripides, *Bacchae* 113–4). The killing of one's own flesh and blood—not to speak of its particularly horrifying manner (*spa-*

ragmos) and aftermath (*omophagia*)—had always been the worst crime, the most polluted-polluting act the Greeks could ever conceive of. Now this quintessence of horror began to be celebrated as a holy act, and the frenzy that led to it became a "sacred purification" (Euripides, *Bacchae* 77). The most deep-seated moral-religious convictions of the Greeks were suddenly inverted and perverted here. Dionysus, the liberator, threatened to liberate man from all he ever believed in and stood for.

The Greek response to this double—attractive and repulsive—aspect of Dionysian worship was a characteristically realistic one. Since it was beyond the power of post-Homeric man to resist Dionysus directly, his cult had to be accepted. But as the radical form of this cult tended to subvert all order, it had to be modified till it became harmless or even serviceable to the ends of organized communal life.

So Dionysus triumphed over all initial resistance in eighth-century Greece. The mass of people surrendered themselves to the god, the poets began to extol his divinity, the cities gradually sanctioned and institutionalized his cult, and in the end Apollo, the god of proportion, measure, harmony, and the controlled, temperate life, joined hands with him at Delphi. But this triumph was at the same time a defeat for Dionysus, inasmuch as the process of acceptance subtly changed and tempered his character and in some cases almost completely reversed it.

Dionysus' merger with Apollo influenced the latter's worship. While there are no previous instances of ecstasy or enthusiasm recorded in Apolline cult, from the sixth century on we hear of frenzied prophetesses at Delphi and ecstatic priests of Apollo wandering, rapt in Bacchic fury, all over Greece. Melampus, a favorite of Apollo, is so Dionysiac in some respects that Herodotus credits him with introducing the cult of Dionysus into Greece; Aeschylus calls Apollo "the ivy-crowned Bacchic prophet"; [19] and by Plato's time Apollo is regarded the god of prophetic madness.

On the other hand, Apollo, the god of measure, had an equally strong influence on Dionysus. The hitherto spontaneous and un-regulated outbursts of Dionysian ecstasy were gradually brought under control and made safe by being given a periodic outlet. The cathartic practices of Apolline priests—and the similar rites of cory-bantism—began to be associated with the cult of Dionysus. Melam-pus combined Apolline purification and Dionysian ecstasy so far that he ended up purifying people of Dionysian ecstasy by an in-tensification of this frenzied state. By the fifth century bacchants and corybants, the cathartic priests and priestesses of Cybele who "cure Bacchic women of their madness" (Plato, *Laws* 790D) and produce in them "a sound mind to take the place of their frenzy" (*Laws* 791 A), can hardly be kept apart.[20] By the fourth century the taming of Dionysus and his amalgamation with Apollo are so complete that Plato who makes Apollo the god of one kind of madness identifies Dionysus as the lord of those "purifications and mysteries" (Plato, *Phaedrus* 244) which release men from affliction and presumably restore them to a state of everyday normalcy.

But where was there purification of pollution and exorcism of madness in the original worship of Dionysus? If one can speak at all of a catharsis in connection with Dionysian enthusiasm, this is a purification from the cares and customs of everyday existence, the bonds and laws of communal life, the mask of individuality and even the confining order of nature. Purified of all this, the ecstatic ascends to a realm of radically, inexpressibly heightened life. In union with the divine and lost to his unsubstantial humanity, he returns to the original, fundamental ground of all; purified of a merely human nature, he regains his ultimate essence, the god. Far from being something shameful, deplorable, or privative, Dionysian madness is the richest, fullest, highest experience for a human being.

There could not be a greater contrast between this kind of experience and Apolline catharsis. What Dionysian catharsis delivers man from, Apolline and corybantic catharses deliver men to: the everyday life of custom and convention, the life of *meden agan,* of knowing one's place and not transcending the bounds of *moira, dike, nomos.* What would be called miasma from the point of view of Dionysus—the quotidian welter—is the end in view of the purificatory rites of Apollo. While ecstasy, divine abandon, and exaltation are the height of experience in Dionysus' cult, Melampus and the corybants only heighten madness homeopathically in order to get rid of it. Madness, the real health of mind in Dionysus, becomes a disease in corybantism, and although both types of catharsis, Dionysian and Apolline, are aimed at restoring man to his nature, the two conceptions of the ultimate nature of man are diametrically opposed. For Dionysus, the essence of man is ultimately freedom in god, reached in divine ecstasy. For the Apolline variant, man is fulfilled only within the bonds of a rational, social-political existence. Dionysus *soter* saves us from being merely human. Salvation through Apollo consists in a return to humanity. The original Dionysus *lusios* dissolves all bondage in ecstatic transport. The Apolline Dionysus delivers from madness.

That such a radical inversion of the cult of Dionysus could take place without seeming to be an out-and-out denial and suppression of the cult is, however, not so strange. After all, one of the *observable* effects of Dionysian frenzy was that the ecstatic, utterly spent through the orgiastic outburst, sank to the ground as if burnt out and fell into a deep exhausted sleep. Intense madness apparently consumed itself and gave way to a relative state of peace. Now those who did not know that ecstasy itself was the sole purpose of the original experience and rest merely its irrelevant by-product, could be easily persuaded that this externally observable effect was in fact the essential goal of such practices. And those who were intent on taming the cult and converting it into a means for the preservation of society, certainly had a great interest in fostering such inversion of ends (i.e., of unessential by-product into ostensible purpose).

A similar process may have led to the association of wine and viticulture with the name of Dionysus. Although probably a later accretion, such association was not implausible. To begin with, wine is a means to removing inhibitions and increasing emotional fervor

(though there is little early evidence that wine was ever used to in-
duce Dionysian ecstasy). Then, the state of intoxication and its aftermath bear a certain resemblance to Bacchic enthusiasm. Wine, too,
lifts a man above the cares of the world and releases him temporarily
from the problems and responsibilities of everyday life. It "puts an
end to long-suffering mortals' grief; brings sleep and with it oblivion
of our daily ills" (Euripides, *Bacchae* 280-2), "stills the troubles of
the mind" (*Bacchae* 381) and gives "grief-free delight" (*Bacchae*
423). Furthermore the association of wine with the cult of Dionysus
was not only plausible, it was also serviceable for the taming of the
cult. Drunkenness was a far less harmful state of intoxication than
true Dionysian ecstasy, and making Dionysus the god of the cultivation of the vine turns him into a deity supporting honest work and a
socially useful activity.

In general, this is what explains the gradual amalgamation of
Dionysus' worship with such a great variety of religious beliefs and
practices: since Dionysus was polymorph to begin with, a few more
traits could easily be attached, or different aspects of his "personality"
could easily be emphasized, in response to different individual and
social needs and in line with the interests and aspirations of the
different sections of the community. Accordingly we can observe
increasing accretion and fusion (Dionysus is associated with Apollo,
Rhea, Cybele, Demeter, the Cretan Mother-Goddess, Sabazios,
Zagreus, Pan; Curetes and corybants, Muses, nymphs, maenads,
satyrs, sileni, and animals are joined in his *thiasos;* he becomes god
of purification, vegetation, fertility, viticulture; of private, secret
cults as well as communal, public performances; wine-cup, phallus,
and *liknon* are added to his customary emblems of mask, ivy,
thyrsus, and *nebris*) as well as increasing diremption and dispersion
in his cult. In the end the most antithetical practices (e.g., the most
stylized, dignified, and stately forms of art and the wildest orgiastic
rites) exist side by side, all connected in one way or another with his
worship.

The development of the Greek theater out of Dionysus' cult is an especially instructive illustration of how the Dionysiac experience was gradually modified, purified, and ultimately inverted between the eighth and fifth centuries.

The original worship of Dionysus, in its purest and most radical state, was not only antiintellectual, it was also eminently antiartistic. For art, even in its least intellectual forms, involves form-giving, discipline, and control, and the Dionysian experience is characterized by formlessness and unrestraint. The maenads do not speak, they whirl in silence [21] or emitting ecstatic cries. The invocation of Iacchus is not a song, it is a formless shriek or howl. The approach to Dionysus *bromios, eribromos,* is not tuneful and harmonious, but is a wild, inarticulate, clashing, gnashing, roaring-uproarious, far-sounding thundering noise. The Dionysian utterance is an unuttering utterance, it has no specifiable content; it establishes communion but it communicates nothing. Similarly, the convulsive, delirious, violent, jerking movement of the maenads is not yet a dance; it is a mad, ecstatic, abandoned, orgiastic, uncontrolled whirl. And the individual (artist) who might impose rhythm and measure on this chaos of howling convulsion and give it form does not exist here: the goal of the Dionysian experience is precisely to get rid of all autonomous personality and dissolve the separate individual in the undifferentiated mass.

But once the community, which has to tame and channel the cult in the interest of its own survival, begins to regulate it, all this changes. The limiting of orgiastic worship to certain times and places at which it has to be performed robs it of much of its spontaneity. To make up for this loss of self-propelling inspiration, a formal ritual begins to be elaborated. The howl becomes song, the wild turbulence measured rhythm, the convulsive movement dance, the spontaneous outburst planned ritual, and the original orgiastic transport mere enactment of enthusiasm. Since enthusiasm is now merely *performed* and the god is no longer immediately present in his rites, he has to be symbolically represented by effigies, emblems, masks, and by having his epiphany *acted out*. The regulation and channelling of the worship of Dionysus makes it mimetic: an imitation of the experience, a performance of the epiphany, an enactment of the birth and death of Dionysus.

Of course, this is a slow, gradual process, and occasionally even the mere enactment of ecstasy might degenerate into the real thing. The transition is easy, and of hard and fast dividing lines there are none. The emotional energy liberated in true Dionysian ecstasy lies close to the surface, and the less efficient its sublimation the more likely it is to break through the bonds of ritual and carry all before it. The orgiastic experience is never completely channelled let alone suppressed, and we witness its occasional reemergence all through the history of antiquity.

Still the transformation of Dionysian frenzy into artistic inspiration and creative experience is also accomplished in the seventh century, and in the following two centuries the worship of this god leads to and culminates in some of the greatest artistic creations in the history of man.

The first art-form to develop from the cult was the dithyramb, a combination of music, dance, and song in a choral performance. Although its early form can be described only conjecturally, it seems to have been frenzied and full of movement; [22] the song was "shout-mingled" [23] and the dance characterized by *turbasia*—confusion, tumult, disorder.[24] It was accompanied by the flute, an enthusiastic orgiastic instrument [25] playing music in the Phrygian mode that was wild, orgiastic, and thus specially suited to the dithyramb.[26]

At this stage the dithyramb was probably largely improvisational, but it soon lost its impromptu character and became a planned public performance, a spectacle directed at the audience rather than performed primarily for the enjoyment of the participants themselves.

By the end of the seventh century the dithyramb became an art-form in its own right: the song is now composed rather than improvised; the dance a stately, orderly, stylized movement around a central altar rather than a free, riotous, turbulent discharge; and even the music may have become more temperate to accommodate itself to the other changes.[27] As for its content, the original invocation of Dionysus, the celebration of his birth,[28] and the telling of stories associated with his epiphanies are gradually eliminated, and the dithyramb becomes a short choral narrative of heroic myths. By the time the dithyramb attains its position as a permanent feature of the Great Dionysia at Athens, its Dionysian content and its quasi-Dionysian form have just about disappeared, and the reproach that it has "nothing to do with Dionysus" is almost completely justified.[29] The first Dionysian art-form has become eminently un-Dionysian.

Tragedy, the next form of art associated with the name of Dionysus, most probably developed from the early dithyramb. According to Aristotle, tragedy had an improvisational beginning, originating "with the leaders-off of the dithyramb" (*Poetics* 1449a9–11). Although Aristotle may be theorizing here, rather than giving a historical account based on first-hand evidence, this is no reason for rejecting his theory. Even if he had no first-hand knowledge of the early form of either dithyramb or tragedy, "he was much nearer the origin of tragedy than we are" and had access to "sources which we no longer possess." [30] And, above all, his theory is still the most plausible one we can construct on the basis of the available evidence.

Whether the original "leaders-off" of the dithyramb led off the song which was then taken up, echoed, or elaborated on by the chorus in response,[31] or were, instead of merely invoking the god, enacting his presence and leading the chorus in the manner Dionysus led his *thiasos,*[32] in either case the dithyramb had a leader who was at least minimally detached from the chorus and to some extent stood outside it. It already had a kind of orchestra, the place of the circular dance; it was already mimetic (whether in the sense of the *exarchon* representing Dionysus, the chorus at times wearing a minimal disguise, or in the more general sense mentioned above pp. 122–23); it already had non-Dionysian myth-content and was a communal performance that had left behind its spontaneous and anonymous ritual origin and was the autonomous artistic creation of an individual performed by trained executors. No matter how many other forms of art would yet contribute formally and materially to the creation of full-fledged tragedy, and no matter how much the total moral, religious, political, and intellectual climate—all the forces alive in the sixth and fifth centuries—would affect its development, the minimal means for this development were already there in the dithyramb, and genuine drama—in our sense of the word—was but a step away.

How important this next step was I shall discuss later in connection with Aeschylean tragedy. At this point it is more germane to take a look forward to see if there are any traces of the original ecstatic-enthusiastic worship of Dionysus observable in the fully developed form of classical tragedy. Given the dithyramb as the immediate source and occasion of its birth, were the Greeks right in complaining that in the end tragedy, too, lost all its connection, other than the institutional one, with the cult of the god and had "nothing to do with Dionysus"?

To begin with the aspect of the theater that lies closest to the surface, tragic drama is related to Dionysus not just through the fact that the Greeks actually used masks, a ritual symbol of Dionysus, on the stage, but because the mask symbolized, as it does even today, the mimetic art. The actor acts not on his own behalf, but stepping out of (*ekstasis*) his own character he assumes another personality. Though he seldom embodies and speaks directly on behalf of a god (as literally *entheos*), he is nevertheless possessed by his role, is out of *his* mind and individual nature. "Are you not carried out of yourself and does not your soul in ecstasy seem to be among the persons (acted)?" Socrates asks the rhapsode Ion (Plato, *Ion* 535), and the answer is that the actor, even more than the rhapsode, is qua actor and mask always ecstatic and possessed. Although he is not literally raving in the manner of Dionysus' followers but may be coolly calculating and emotionally detached from his role, formally he is beside himself: acting different parts, assuming and shedding masks, impersonating ever different persons, he partakes of the metamorphic, polymorph, and at the same time formless character of Dionysus.

The theater is the realm of the mask, furthermore, not only because the actor acts a role other than his everyday one, but because the role itself is a mask standing for something else, and the whole play is mask-like symbolic inasmuch as it always points toward something other than what is actually performed on the stage. As in the epiphanies of Dionysus the actual appearance of the god only served to manifest the essential divine nature which could not be directly revealed, so the play makes manifest something more essential and universal than what it actually presents. (The subject of *Oedipus* is not just the fate of a particular Theban tyrant who happened to kill his father and marry his mother, etc.)

The second Dionysian aspect of fifth-century theater is the intense involvement and participation of the audience in the play. The actor surrounded by the chorus and the stage by the viewers remind us of Dionysus accompanied by his *thiasos,* and the distance between the stage and the audience dissolves during the performance of great plays just as inevitably as does the distance between Dionysus and his revellers in the ecstatic-enthusiastic experience. Quite apart from its institutional character, the Athenian theater is a communal event because, as great theater, it is a communion of playwright, actors, chorus, audience, and ultimately of all these with the power that inspires this communion. Plato compared the dramatic performance to a magnetic field in which everything responds to the same central force, transmitted by a kind of chain reaction from god to playwright to actor to audience, until in the end all are possessed by the same (god) and move in harmony with the same (divine substance).[33] For the duration of the performance at least, Dionysus *lusios* breaks down all barriers, abolishes all reservation, and unites all participants in the theater too.

To achieve this communion only one thing is necessary; that the man in the audience identify himself with what is enacted on the stage. Can he, if the theater dissolves the personal and individual character of all participants and, taking them out of themselves, fills them with something other than their own private nature? He can and does by virtue of the Dionysian dissolution of the mask, in which the mask itself is revealed as mere mask, as unessential surface, so that in the unmasking man confronts, is implemented in and united with, his essential nature. Like the sudden advent of Dionysus, great tragedy seizes man, claims him in his innermost being, and transforms him into something more than just this or that isolated individual person living out his uninspired everyday life as he had done before.

This matter of a metamorphosis into something other than what one has been, brings us to the third Dionysian characteristic of tragedy. In the earliest Greek treatise exclusively devoted to the poetic arts that is still available to us, Aristotle defined tragedy as the kind of imitation which, through pity and fear, accomplishes a catharsis of some sort. What exactly Aristotle meant by catharsis has been endlessly debated, but we need not enter the controversy here. For whether we interpret Aristotelian catharsis on the basis of *Politics* 134a21–b40 as a therapeutic purification of the emotional part of the soul,[34] or, concentrating on the *Poetics* itself, regard it a moral-intellectual purification tied up with recognition and learning,[35] in either case the Aristotelian conception involves a substantial modification of the Dionysian one.

Catharsis as a quasi-medical cure that removes certain harmful elements which would interfere with the orderly functioning of the soul and thereby effects a return to normalcy on the part of the patient, is clearly an Apolline-corybantic process. As I have tried to show above (pp. 119–20), this is an inversion rather than a direct carrying on of the original Dionysian experience. But catharsis as a clarification of events or experience is more authentically Dionysian as to its form—though not in its content or the direction the cathartic movement takes.

In Aristotle, catharsis is accomplished through the structure of the plot, and this structure is characterized by *hamartia, peripeteia,* and *anagnorisis.* In a way nothing could be more Dionysian than this structure. For what is *anagnorisis* but an unmasking, the recognition of the mask as mask, and what causes all *peripeteia* but our —and the world's—mask-existence, the hiddenness of the essential under the everyday surface, the "tragic flaw" in the world and in our own nature? *Hamartia,* the great error, is not an incidental act of man but a state of being: our being hidden to ourselves by the mask. It is at once intellectual and moral self-alienation; the erring individual does not know his true essence and is not truly what he is. Being dirempt by nature, a visible mask on the invisible face of the god, he mistakes the obvious, the mask, for his essence and, trying to hold on to it, he works at his own destruction (qua essentially divine). Aiming at one thing—to become truly what he is—he brings about its opposite—becomes more and more masklike—without recognizing it. Yet man is not merely mask but also that which the mask conceals, and thus all his efforts to remain mere mask are doomed to fail, and *anagnorisis,* the unmasking, is inevitable. Recognition is a reversal of the individual's state of knowledge and being. Where at first man worked away from his ultimate nature and brought about the opposite of what he intended (true self-fulfillment), it is this opposite state that is now reversed in turn. All former efforts at self-assertion are revealed as failure, the hero—in terms of his previous conception of himself—falls. But he falls as mask—he lets the mask fall—and thus in his defeat achieves victory. The final unmasking makes him truly what he is.

This structure is Dionysian, but its tragic content is not. For what the individual learns in tragic *anagnorisis* is that he is not only, not even primarily, divine, but also human, not only hidden essence, but also mask, not only undifferentiated common substance, but also separate personal existence. Therefore the absolute dissolution and destruction of all "persons" in Dionysian ecstasy is rejected in tragedy as ultimately inhuman. Being a mask as well, man must live as mask. This, and not Dionysian ecstasy, makes his dirempt existence tragic. If the mask is also essential, man can become neither mere mask nor pure divine substance. To be human means to exist as both, as ultimately dirempt, living with, rather than abolishing, this diremption. Hence tragedy.[36]

As *anagnorisis* presupposes *hamartia,* catharsis presupposes pollution as a prior state. Dionysian religion and tragedy share the idea of an essential pollution of man. But Dionysian catharsis purifies of this pollution by getting rid of humanity itself: Dionysus *anthroporraistes* tears apart the human shell. Tragedy offers no easy solutions of this sort; rather, it comes to terms with man's failure to extinguish his essential taint and offers man a way to endure his impure existence with dignity. Like most Dionysian myths, tragedies are stories of resistance against a power immeasurably more powerful than man. But while in the Dionysus myths all resistance is crushed and only the power of the god is affirmed, in tragedy the resister is affirmed and acclaimed—even while he is crushed. Dionysian worship celebrates only the god. Tragedy, in the end, celebrates man. So once again the artistic offshoot of the Dionysus cult has inverted its original source. It had to, for Dionysian ecstasy was not an experience man could *live* with.

It is not too much to say that for all its Dionysian origin fully developed tragedy is essentially un-Dionysian. Its Dionysian aspects—mask, ecstasy, enthusiasm, *hamartia-catharsis-anagnorisis*—are technical at best; pale remainders of what was once vital in the worship of the god. Though historically and formally its connection with the cult of Dionysus is noticeable, its content and main thrust of thought, its conception of man and world, owe more to Homer's notion of the paradoxical hero and to Hesiodic-Solonic moral reform than to Dionysian enthusiasm.

This is not to say that the essentials of Dionysian worship ever disappear from the Greek scene. Orgiastic-enthusiastic religion and its ecstatic soul-expanding experience are never completely suppressed for all their artistic and philosophic channelling and inversion. But they remain vital only as a lurking undercurrent, as an ever present seduction to and possibility of an at times dangerous at times saving but always spasmodic emotional release. The main trend of Greek thought, the crystallized imaginative or reflective expression of the Greeks' experience, the day rather than night life of the Greek spirit remain, as we shall see, rational-humanistic as opposed to the inhumanity and irrationality of Dionysian religion.

6. Xenophanes-Heracleitus-Parmenides

Dionysian religion, in its attempt to bridge the gulf between the human and divine, merely succeeded in widening this gulf; its god was in fact a counterconcept to just about everything humanity stood for, and the approach to Dionysus, the ineffable god, turned out to be a thoroughly dehumanizing experience. Paradoxically, the first explicit attempt at dehumanizing the gods, undertaken by Xenophanes, had the opposite effect: its deanthropomorphized god turned out to be very like the human intellect that approached the problem of divinity so critically.

Xenophanes' critical reappraisal, which divested the gods of the last vestiges of their mythical character, was no more an attack on religion than was the emotional-enthusiastic worship of Dionysus. As the Dionysian cult attempted to deepen religious experience, so the Xenophantic reform aimed at purifying and intellectualizing it. The two movements, the Dionysian and the Hesiodic-Solonic-Xenophantic, were in fact complementary. Diametrically opposed to each other they labored at revitalizing and de-Homericizing religion and making it conformable to that aspect of human experience—emotional or rational—which each regarded as paramount.

"It is good always to show respect for the gods" (1.24) [1] Xenophanes writes, and showing respect for the gods means to him
above all to speak of them in a manner appropriate to the true nature of divinity. This is something Homer and Hesiod failed to do
in Xenophanes' opinion. "Men of good sense ought to praise god
first with well-spoken accounts and pure words" (1.13), yet what
had Homer and Hesiod done? They "ascribed to the gods all that
is shame and blame among men: stealing, adultery, and deceiving
each other" (11). Such an approach to the gods demeans rather
than exalts them. True piety requires true discrimination and judgment. ". . . of men one must praise him who . . . [unlike Homer
and Hesiod] brings to light what is noble . . . and does not dwell
on the battles of the Titans and Giants and Centaurs—the figments
of our predecessors' imagination—nor on violent discord, for there
is nothing useful in this" (1.19–23).

To make god-talk useful and educational and to eliminate all
poetic abuse, Xenophanes first strikes at what seems to him the
root of the problem: the ascription of an anthropomorphic nature to
the gods. If gods are like men, they will always be subject to men's
faults. Indeed, human imperfection will be only magnified on the
divine scale. Where men's misdeeds are small because of the limits
of human power, divine crimes are truly awful on account of the
incomparably greater strength of the gods. Xenophanes' *silloi* sati-
rize anthropomorphism brilliantly: ". . . men believe that gods are
born and that they have clothes and voices and bodies like their own"
(14) because it is in their image that they create gods. "The Ethi-
opians assert their gods to be snub-nosed and black, the Thracians
blue-eyed and red-haired" (16), and so does each nation and race
inject its own characteristics into divine nature. Dissatisfied with
such obvious relativism, Xenophanes exposes its absurdity: "but if
oxen and horses and lions had hands and with their hands could
draw and accomplish works like men, then horses would draw images of horses and oxen of oxen, and each species would frame [di-
vine] shapes just like its own" (15).

How are we to think of the gods then? Xenophanes' answer to this question completes the development of the Greek conception of divinity that we have been following from Homer to Solon. The epic emphasis on visibility led to the creation of embodied gods manifesting in their person all that was excellent in man—his bodily beauty and visible strength and power. With the gradual shift in Greek thought from image to concept, from visibility to intelligibility, however, the gods too began to undergo a metamorphosis from splendid bodily forms to beings of pure intellect. As the shift from *mythos* to *logos* gradually led to a replacement of epic parataxis by Hesiodic-Solonic unity of thought, so, too, the fragmentation of divinity in epic yielded to a new, unitary conception of god. Xenophanes' theologizing brings this movement to completion.

"God is one, greatest among gods and men, neither in shape like men nor in thought" (23). God is an undivided unity, not an aggregate of paratactically ordered parts: "as a whole he sees, as a whole he thinks, as a whole he hears" (24). Unlike the whimsical and volatile Homeric deities, he is unmoved and immovable: "forever he abides in the same, without movement; nor is it fitting for him to go around from place to place" (26). Nor is it necessary that he should do so, for "without toil he makes all things tremble by the thought of his mind" (25).

Xenophanes' insistence on the motionlessness of the deity is more than just a reaction against the undignified manner in which the Homeric gods kept running about. Motion, if not synonymous with change, is nevertheless a kind of change. What is capable of movement is therefore unstable and mutable. What is born—also a kind of movement from nonbeing to being—is liable to pass away. Whatever is or has a sensible, observable body is subject to change in time. Only thought, grasping the unchanging universal, transcends all temporal change. Hence Xenophanes' god had to be motionless, eternal, ungenerated-undying (A 12, 13, 31.4), and unembodied in the ordinary sense of the word [2] to serve the purposes he had in mind.

This notion of one god, an undivided, motionless, emotionless whole that governs all by the thought of his mind, was thoroughly in line with the intellectual demands of the time. Since divinity in Hesiod and Solon became gradually identified with the one—divine and natural—law, way, and order of things, it was logical for Xenophanes to reduce the diversity of gods to a unity. Since the law (*dike*) that the Hesiodic and, to a lesser extent, Solonic gods were to enforce became more and more a universal, unchanging principle inherent in the world, an unchanging, unmoving god was more appropriate to its symbolic representation than the vast array of Homeric-Hesiodic deities. The intellect demands identity in change, unity in diversity, and endurance in time. Xenophanes yields to this demand by fashioning his one, abiding, immutable, whole god that is or at least functions as a pure intellect—ironically very like the intellect with which Xenophanes, the opponent of anthropomorphic relativism, approached the problem of divinity.

Whether Xenophanes was aware of the hidden anthropomorphism of his own conception and failed to eliminate it merely because that would have required dispensing with the notion of divinity altogether, we do not know. Certainly he was aware of the limits of human knowledge, insisted on god not being like men either in shape or thought, and tried to guard against anyone taking even his own words too literally: "As to the exact truth about the gods and all the things I speak of, no man knows or will ever know it; for even if one chanced to express best the perfect truth, he would still not know it himself, for seeming permeates all" (34). Therefore "let these things be held as opinions only, similar to the truth" (35) rather than the absolute truth itself.

But this warning against complacent dogmatism did not lead to a despair of all knowledge and a thoroughgoing skepticism in Xenophanes any more than it did in Solon. "The gods have not revealed all things to men from the beginning, yet, seeking, men find out better in time" (18). Since god is pure intellect presiding over or identical with the intelligible order of the world, man can hope at least to approximate knowledge—of god and reality—by the use of his own intellect. Although human knowing is fallible—since the divine intellect is to some extent beyond our limited powers of conception—it is still the most rewarding and noblest pursuit for man (cf. 2.11–12).

More explicitly than anyone before him Xenophanes combines the two attitudes toward knowledge which once joined helped to make the Greeks' intellectual achievements unsurpassed: self-assurance and self-criticism; a faith in the power of the human intellect to grasp what is real and a critical attitude toward the power of man's mind to encompass absolute reality. In this combination even the shortcomings of human knowledge spur us on to more rather than less inquiry: an inquiry into our own seemingly certain opinions, a critical reflection on our own—and others'—thought.

* * * * * *

Heracleitus, sometimes said to have been a student of Xenophanes, heeded the latter's warning against the easy acceptance of others' views all to well. With a grandiose sweep of the hand he brushed aside his predecessors—including Xenophanes himself—as well as his contemporaries: "The learning of many things does not teach understanding, or it would have taught Hesiod and Pythagoras and Xenophanes and Hecataeus" (40). "Homer deserves to be thrown out of the contests and to be whipped, and so does Archilochus" (42). And so do most men, "for what is their reason or sense? They believe the folksingers and have the crowd for their teacher, not knowing that the many are bad and only the few good" (104). "The many are like sated cattle" (29), "they know neither how to listen nor how to speak" (19). "Like Homer, they are deceived [even] in the knowledge of visible things" (56), and much more so in matters not immediately open to sight. They use their senses without understanding; to such "barbarous souls" eyes and ears are bad witnesses (107). No matter how often they see, hear or experience something, they fail to understand it. Though they hear they are like deaf, though awake they are as unaware as when asleep, though present they are as if absent. Even when they learn they acquire no knowledge; instead of gaining insight they merely imagine things and hold on to opinions that are like the playthings of a child (1, 17, 34, 70, 72).

For all this emphasis on the untrustworthiness of traditional and popular beliefs, however, Heracleitus is no less convinced that some men at least may acquire knowledge than were Hesiod, Solon, and Xenophanes. The world—physical, human, divine—is rational and men have a share, at least potentially, in cosmic reason. If they only used their faculties right and concentrated on what is essential, they could gain essential wisdom. How to do this is precisely what Hercleitus is intent on teaching his fellow men.

Listen "not to me but to the *logos*" (50), Heracleitus writes. But what is the *logos* if it is more than or other than Heracleitus' word? It cannot be unequivocally defined, for it is so all-embracing a notion that no particular collection of words is fully adequate for expressing it. The *logos* is that which is common (2), yet common *logos* is not merely human or divine reason; it is not a mere faculty but also that which this faculty is directed toward. It is reason in man as well as in the world, it is that which understands as well as that which is understood. It is the eternal law according to which all things happen (1), the invisible but intelligible principle and ground of all that is. The *logos* is the common: it is that in the light of which all differences are reconciled, all discord is reduced to harmony, and all changes are but aspects of eternal sameness. The *logos* is the One; it unites everything—things as well as men— because it is the unity, order, constitution, and fundamental nature of all, the way of things, their measure, balance, and law. Directed by and toward the *logos,* men are brought together in a common understanding of all.

One of Heracleitus' most pregnant sentences expresses this succinctly: "Listening not to me but to the *logos,* it is wise to agree (*homologein*): all is one (*hen panta*)" (50). Right listening, being guided not by any particular man but by the *logos,* involves *homologein:* the saying of the same. *Homologein,* however, is not only saying the same as all essentially thinking men would say; it is also seeing all things in the same light, seeing that wherein they are all the same and thus saying the same of all things. *Homologein* means nothing other than saying "*hen panta,*" all is one. "*Hen panta*" is not just what the *logos* says, but above all what the *logos* is and does: the function of the *logos* is precisely to bring together, collect (*legein*) all into one, to make one out of many, to reveal and lay open to sight all things in their essential unity.[3] At first sight, *logos, homologein,* and *hen panta* seem different and distinct parts of the same sentence here; yet they mean essentially the same if we read them in a Heracleitean sense. This peculiarity of the sentence itself brings to light the basic message of Heracleitus: that what seems to be distinct on the surface and is seen as distinct by those who are not rightly listening is the same fundamentally and is seen as the same by those whose intellect is rightly directed at the *logos,* i.e., at the ground rather than the surface of things.

This is what Heracleitus keeps repeating: "*Harmonie aphanes phaneres kreitton,*" the invisible, intellegible harmony of all things is stronger than all apparent harmony, and men fail to see this only because they are looking at the surface. Totally involved with the visible, they use only their eyes and not their intelligence, and thus what is most intelligible remains hidden to them. Lacking a more profound vision "they are like people of no experience even when they experience" (1), "they are furthest from the *logos* even though in constant contact with it, and what they light upon every day remains strange to them" (72). Though "present they are absent" (34), though awake they live as in a dream. They are unaware of the fact that all that can be seen, even the greatest visible harmony and "fairest order is like a randomly poured out garbage heap" (124) in comparison with the invisible order. They ignore that what matters most is the underlying intelligible *logos,* i.e., precisely that which never appears itself but can be seen only through the phenomena. They fail to realize that in the *logos* all that is "brought apart is brought together with itself" (51), all that is at variance agrees with itself, and all that is separate is collected in the same: "Bringing together the whole and the unwhole, the convergent and the divergent, the attuned and the discordant: out of all one and out of one all" (10), "out of the divergent: the fairest harmony" (8). "One thing alone is wise: to understand the insight how all things are governed through all" (41). The intellectual demand for universality, for finding the common principle and ground of all diversity, and seeing all things as partial and fragmentary manifestations of a unitary whole, leads to an all-embracing vision in Heracleitus.

As everything is but a manifestation of the same *logos,* the *logos* may and may not be called by any name. "The One that is alone wise wants and does not want to be assigned the name of God" (32). It may be called divine if divinity means the ultimate power and substance of all; at the same time, if by God we mean something less than and only part of the whole, the name is inadequate. To overcome this inadequacy of names Heracleitus uses a plethora of them almost interchangeably: *logos, xynon, kosmos, physis, hen, sophon, metron, harmonie, dike, chreon* are but so many words for the same thing in his thought. The inevitable necessity that Homeric *moira* stood for, the power and insight vested in the Olympians, Hesiod's *dike* and proportion, Archilochean rhythm as well as Sapphic variegatedness, Anaximandrean *chreon* as well as Solonic *eunomia*—all this Heracleitus compresses into One.

Even Fire is an appropriate name for the reality he speaks of: "This world-order (*kosmos*), that is the same for all, no god or man created but it always was and is and shall be forever living Fire, kindling in measures and extinguishing in measures" (30). Fire, here, is obviously not just one of the physical elements; it is more the underlying, invisible but intelligible substance which is "fair exchange for all, just as all is fair exchange for it" (90). All change and diversity in the world is, as it were, "Fire's turnings" in which the overall balance is preserved, and that which changes is "measured according to the same *logos* as existed before" (31). Fire is measure, that which is measured, as well as that which measures "judges and sentences all" (66). Forever living, light-giving, life-preserving, warming, nourishing, destroying, and consuming cosmic-intellectual Fire is but another name for what is common in all—*logos, kosmos, theos, hen*. "Like Fire, which when mixed with incense is named according to the scent of each" (67), the One embraces and is embodied by all that is and thus may be called by any name.

At the same time it is important to remember that particular names are but symbols in Heracleitus—just as particular things are merely fragments in his world; they are fragments (*symbola*) that point toward the Whole but are not the Whole. The *logos* is more than, other than, any of its names or manifestations; as the *sophon*, the quintessence of all wisdom, it is "set apart from all" (108). It brings together all only when distinguished from each thing as its transcendental principle and substance.

Transcendental does not mean thoroughly transcendent here; the *logos* is not postulated to exist by itself and on its own apart from the phenomena which make it manifest. The Heraclitean emphasis on the unchanging, eternal One does not lead to an exclusion of the Many and a disregard for all the changing, particular, and varied components of the world. On the contrary, the One manifests itself only in the Many, the *logos* is only in and through the beings whose *logos* it is, the Common is common to all the particulars without which it could not be (common), and forever living Fire is kept alive in and by all that it nourishes and consumes. Identity in Heracleitus is meaningless without diversity and harmony impossible without tension and strife: tension not only on the surface between diverse, conflicting phenomena but also between surface (phenomena) and depth (underlying *logos*). Heracleitus' world is as dynamic, rich, and manifold as that of any Greek. It is only in such a world that the *logos* has a function: gathering and collecting together (*legein*) that into which it unfolds and uniting all into one common ground.

If this is the *logos* of which Heracleitus speaks, what is our proper relationship to it? It can be expressed in one word, *homologein*: agreement with and correspondence to the *logos*. Since the *logos* is the one substantial ground of all, we can acquire wisdom and become substantial ourselves only by listening to and corresponding with the *logos* as Heracleitus counsels in 50.

Although most men do not listen, i.e., do not think rightly, such thinking is both possible and necessary for man. It is possible, because the *logos* is not altogether transcendent to us but is at the same time our *logos*. Human reason being the subjective correlate and partial manifestation of cosmic-divine rationality,[4] we are not cut off from the underlying ground of all as if from an alien reality, but are essentially attuned to it. Consequently we are not inevitably caught in a solipsistic world of private sense-perception and opinion, but, for all the particularity and relativity of perception and opinion, we can enter into and participate in the common world of reason by making universal, rational judgments. Such judgments lift us above the level of unconnected, fragmented, and isolated phenomena—the world as viewed by "barbarous souls"—to a higher and more essential vision which views all things synoptically as interconnected parts and members of a unitary whole. Right thinking requires only that we do not act as "children of our parents" (74), i. e., rely on tradition and thus "make rash judgments about the greatest things" (47), nor pursue worthless *polymathie,* the frantic, undirected search into many things, but use our *logos* in such a way that it is directed toward the *Logos* common to all. If we only live up to this requirement we are, as much as it is humanly possible, in the truth: our insight corresponds with because it responds to ultimate reality.

Such *homologia*—correspondence with the *logos*—is essential to us not just epistemologically but also ethically; thinking essentially and becoming essential are one and the same thing in Heracleitus.

In the first place such thinking—the proper use of our *logos*—is our essence, so that in engaging in it we perform our essential function; by using our *logos* we correspond not only to the *Logos* but also to our own nature. In the second place, by corresponding to the *Logos* we enter into harmony with all and can thus lead a harmonious existence. These two aspects of becoming essential can in the end never be separated. Since the *Logos,* the ultimate ground of all, is our own foundation as well as that of all other things, in corresponding with it we are not abandoning ourselves to an alien reality but find our authentic self within a true reality for the first time.

"Ethos anthropo daimon" (119). In the spirit of Heracleitus these words are best rendered: "the essential nature of man is the Divine, the *logos,* the Common." Man is essential only when he dwells near God, i.e., grounds himself in that *logos* which is his ultimate ground.

Such is the correspondence between Heracleitus' theoretical and practical teaching, that even his political theory is harmonious with and derivable from the foregoing. Listening to the *logos* not only lifts man above the privacy and relativity of opinions and makes him harmonious with nature. It also lifts him above the isolation of a merely private existence, which divides him from his fellow men, and brings him, politically as well as intellectually, into harmony with others. By using what is common—his *logos*—man enters into the community.

"It is necessary to follow what is common. But although the *logos* is common, the many behave as if they each had a purely private insight" (2). "To speak with sense one must rely on what is common to all, just as the city must rely on the laws, only more so. For all human laws are nourished by the one, divine (law)" (114). The comparison between the individual's reliance on what is common and the city's on the laws is more than a poetic analogy in Heracleitus. The two are philosophically analogous too, because the laws of the city are reliable only to the extent that they are based on the common *logos;* actual human legislative attempts to express what is common to men succeed in their aim only to the extent that they correspond to and are approximations of their one, all-nourishing ground. Human justice can harmonize human activity only if it is in harmony with cosmic law.

This being so, true legislation is no more dependent on consensus and convention than true knowledge is the outcome of traditional and popular opinion. Both are proportionate to and the result of men's insight into the *logos.* Since this insight is exceedingly rare, the ideal form of government is aristocratic rather than democratic, the rule of the best, rather than that of the majority. "One man is worth a thousand, if he be the best" (49), and the Ephesians who "expelled their most worthwhile man, saying: among us no one must be most worthwhile, or, if one should be, let him be elsewhere, among others" (121) had better "hang themselves" and let their children govern the town. For obviously they do not know that it may be "law to follow the will of one man" (33) provided he is guided not by what is private but by what is common. If he is, the resulting human legislation is guaranteed to make the city healthy even though it is the work of one man. And in a healthy city it is right that "the people should fight for the laws as they fight for the city walls" (44) and should "extinguish transgression even more urgently than conflagration" (43).

Civil and natural order and disorder are as analogous conceptions in Heracleitus as they were in Solon. As Vlastos points out: "Cosmic justice is a conception of nature at large as a harmonious association, whose members observe, or are compelled to observe, the law. . . ."[5] Just such a conception is that of human justice in Heracleitus; the justice that guarantees the harmonious operation of the smaller cosmos of the political organism. Solon's conception of natural law is not only reaffirmed here, but it is given a deeper foundation in universal *logos.* There is no break in the transition from one to the other, since to act in accordance with the *logos* is to act in accordance with the nature of whatever—or whoever—is involved, and this means to respect its particular nature,[6] to treat it fittingly, appropriately, harmoniously with its constitution, and thereby to strengthen its—and the entire organism's—health and harmonious operation. This is precisely what we call justice even on the human level.

But this is justice and *phronesis,* right action and thought, on the individual level too. Seeking support in what is common—reason, law, *logos*—one is in harmony not only with all men but with oneself, one's essential nature as well. That is why *sophronein,* essential thought, the thinking of the *logos,* is equivalent to health of mind, the greatest excellence of the individual: "Thinking wisely is the greatest virtue, and wisdom consists in speaking what is true and acting in accordance with nature, hearkening to it" (112). Whether one interprets "nature" here as that of the individual or of the universe makes little difference, since the two, though not the same, are essentially in harmony. To know and follow nature is to know and follow the *logos,* to think and live truly, to be a true individual as well as a harmonious member of the social-physical world.

The greatness of Heracleitus consists in this: that he does not separate man and nature but insists on the indissoluble unity of all; nature and man, macrocosm and microcosm, the divine and the human are but so many aspects of the One in his thought. "Immortals mortals, mortals immortals; living each others' death, dying each others' life" (62), "it is all the same [substance] in us, living and dead, waking and sleeping, young and old; for these having turned are those and those having turned again are these" (88). "We live their death and they live our death" (77). Since the essential constitution of all is the same, all transition—even of seeming opposites metamorphosing into each other—is easy and natural; it is but superficial change in which the underlying substance and law is preserved unchanged.

Hesiod already spoke of divine justice turning kings into beggars and beggars into kings, of changes taking place in accordance with immutable laws in human affairs as well as in natural events, and Solon already conceived of civic, historical processes in natural terms, as events governed by quasi-natural law. Now Heracleitus explicitly extends their conception of lawful change and makes it all inclusive: "It is necessary to know that war is common and strife is right, and all things take place in accordance with strife and necessity" (80). "War is the father of all and ruler of all; some it shows forth as gods, some as men, some it makes slaves and others free" (53). As in physical nature (76, 90) so in human-divine events such warring is but "fire's turnings" (31): ceaseless change in which for all superficial conflict harmony prevails and for all superficial alteration everything remains essentially the same. Constantly "changing (all) is at rest" (84a).

"I searched for myself" (101) Heracleitus says, but he might just as well have said "I searched for the logos, for nature, for god," for the inquiry into the self is not merely self-directed; it is, at the same time, an inquiry into that which animates all inquiry as its subject and object, motivating force, and ultimate end: daimonic, human-divine, forever living, cosmic *logos*. That is why "you cannot find the limits of the soul even by travelling all roads —so deep is its *logos*" (45). The true self as the correlate of divine *logos* is not limited to the self but embraces all. The search for it is simultaneously an ethical, physical, logical, cosmological, and ontological inquiry. By reflecting on himself, and thus on that in which he is grounded, man attains to the sum of theoretical and practical wisdom, to true self-consciousness and self-fulfillment as well as to a consciousness of and harmony with all. "It is given to all men to know themselves and to think wisely" (116), to grow in self-consciousness as well as in being. If men use their *logos* properly, "the *logos* proper to the soul is self-increasing" (115): it increases as the self increases for the two are essentially the same.

The preceding account of Heracleitus' thought could not help being repetitious; there is a grand *homologia* in this man's thinking; incessantly circling around the same, Heracleitus manages to say the same. *Homologein* is not only a favorite word of this thinker; it is thoroughly characteristic of his thought. To show this, even at the risk of making this account more homologous than it already is, I shall deal briefly with the correspondence between the form and content of Heracleitus' writings.

Although most pre-Socratic thought has come down to us in the form of fragments laboriously collected from a great variety of ancient sources, we know that the fragmentary character of Heracleitus' sayings is not due to the mere historical accident of their preservation. The earliest commentators already complained about Heracleitus' aphoristic, epigrammatic mode of speaking and ridiculed his terse utterances and his seemingly incoherent style. Although the epithets "Heracleitus the Riddler," the "Obscure," are of later origin, there is ample evidence that Heracleitus was neither understood nor even regarded as comprehensible by most of his contemporaries and immediate successors. Plato already made fun of the "enigmatic little sayings" Heracleiteans let fly in the manner of their master and declared it as little possible to discuss matters with them as with madmen (Plato, *Theaetetus* 180A, 179E). Aristotle found Heracleitus' writings difficult to read, his punctuation unclear, and his wording obscure (Aristotle, *Rhetoric* 1407b 11). Plotinus remarked on Heracleitus' speaking in "images, heedless of making his meaning clear" (Plotinus, *Enneads* 4.8), and Diogenes Laertius noted the "incomparable brevity and weight of his expression" (Diogenes Laertius 9.7). "What I understood [of Heracleitus' thought] was fine, and no doubt what I did not understand also; but it takes a diver to get to the bottom of it"—the comment Diogenes Laertius attributes to Socrates is apocryphal; still it expresses the ancient reader's bewilderment when confronted with Heracleitus' *gnomai*.

Gnomic utterances were, of course, not the invention of Heracleitus; they were a traditional mode of transmitting popular wisdom. Nevertheless the fact that out of the many by now available forms of communication Heracleitus deliberately chose such brief, pithy sayings as the vehicle of his teaching makes it incumbent on us to ask why he should have found this form of transmission particularly appropriate to the content of his thought. What makes this question especially important is that quite unlike popular *gnomai* Heracleitus' aphorisms were prima facie not only singularly unsuccessful in communication, as witnessed by his contemporaries' and immediate successors' comments, but they almost deliberately defied popular understanding, courted incomprehension, and invited the generally negative response which they duly received.

To understand why Heracleitus wrote in a cryptic, enigmatic, oracular style, it might be best to consider at the outset what he himself said about the oracle as a medium of cryptic revelation: "The Lord to whom the oracle at Delphi belongs, neither speaks outright (*legei*) nor hides (*kryptei*) but gives a sign (*semainei*)" (93). A sign is something incomplete that does not stand for itself but points beyond. It is a symbol, a fragment (*symbolon*): something unwhole that points toward the whole, something that is clearly visible yet in appearing only serves to make something else visible, something that is open to sight only to bring to mind something else that never itself appears on the surface. By "giving a sign" the oracle neither hides (ultimately) nor reveals (immediately), yet it both hides and reveals surface and depth in its turn depending on the receiver's attitude—superficial or profound—in listening to it.

Now if this is the function of the oracle, then Heracleitus was indeed a consummate artist in whose work "form and content coincide completely,"[7] for oracular utterance is *the* way of communicating what Heracleitus wants to say, i. e., that the world as we see it is itself an oracle constituted in an oracular fashion: all that we see is merely a sign, a symbol for the invisible underlying *logos*. Heracleitus speaks in incomplete sentences, fragments, because in his view the things as they immediately appear in the world are themselves incomplete manifestations and fragments of a whole and must thus be viewed only in reference to what they represent, must be understood in reference to and in terms of the whole. Everything in the visible world is but a symbol for the *logos,* the One, the Common; therefore the world is best approached symbolically; in a manner designed to carry us beyond immediate appearances to the underlying reality. Since the "unapparent harmony is stronger than the apparent" (54), since "nature loves to hide itself" (123), i.e., the true constitution of things is hidden from sight, there is such a thing as the necessary metaphor,[8] and Heracleitus' mode of speaking is not an external ornament but the only mode of expression adequate to what he wants to say.[9]

Heracleitus does speak like a madman, if to be mad is to speak paradoxically, out of step, out of tune with popular opinion. But Solon already was held mad by his contemporaries because he insisted on his own superior insight, and Heracleitus defends his "madness" in a similar way: "The Sybil who with mad-raving mouth utters mirthless, unadorned and unanointed things reaches over a thousand years with her voice—*dia ton theon"* (92): because she speaks on behalf of, driven by and hearkening to the god, the divine *logos* on whose behalf and with whose inspiration Heracleitus himself claims to speak.

Heracleitus speaks paradoxically; but in his thought the world itself is a paradox: what appears conflicts with what does not appear; what is essential wars with what lies nearest at hand; what is most true is incoherent with and contrary to popular vision. Heracleitus' words are obscure; but in his view the world itself is obscure and needs to be illuminated in a manner appropriate to its constitution. Heracleitus' *gnomai* are enigmatic; but so is the world an enigma to be solved rather than something to be viewed in its immediacy and taken to be no more than it appears to be. Heracleitus speaks in contradictions; he no longer uses antitheses in a Hesiodic manner merely to reinforce the meaning of each term by opposing it to its contrary. He combines antitheses into a unity, because what he wants to affirm is precisely the underlying unity of all seeming contraries, the unity which can be grasped only by the intellect able to go beyond all surface contradiction. How much Heracleitus' style helps him get his message across is shown by the fact that even as we attempt to unravel his sentences—e.g., "the name of the bow (*bios*) is life (*bios*), its work death" (48)—and in the process step from level to level of meaning—*bios/bios:* the same (as to sound) and not the same (qua life and instrument of death) and yet the same (for life and death are but forms of the same substance)—we undergo the dynamic experience and dialectical movement that all things undergo in Heracleitus' world as they harmonize with and at the same time oppose each other, ceaselessly transmuting into one another as parts of the same divided yet undivided whole. His very manner of speaking makes us correspond to and be like the *logos* he speaks about and thus helps to bring home the truth of his teaching.

Heracleitus writes in prose, yet his use of language is as creative, vivid, sensitive, and imaginative as that of any poet. Frequently "reinforcing sense by sound"[10] while at the same time contrasting the two, combining the intuitive, felt significance of his words with their underlying meaning in such a way that the two conflict even while they harmonize with each other, utilizing the immediate, emotional power of speech to counterpoint as well as to minimize the coldness of the most abstract thought, Heracleitus exploits the full power of language. By punning—*xun no-xuno* (114), *bios-bios* (48), *miainomenoi-mainesthai* (5), *moroi-moiras* (25)—by giving the same word—e.g., *homologein*—several distinct yet homologous meanings at once, by almost exploding the word at times through investing it with a variety of irreconcilable meanings, he forces us to listen and to think always on more than one level. Though he writes prose, prosaic univocity is not one of his vices; Heracleitus scorns the everyday use of language which fastens on every word a meaning of just this and no more. His words always mean more than what they first seem to mean, and while at times they almost break from the tension between surface and depth, in the end they are marvelously equal to carrying the immense burden he lays upon them.

Heracleitus' words are ambiguous and intentionally equivocal, not because he is irrational but because his conception of the *logos* is richer and more advanced than that of any of his predecessors. In dealing with the Homeric simile we noted the appropriateness of this clear, concrete, limited, and precise paratactic device of symbolic fixation to the possibilities and necessities of oral presentation (pp. 9-10). In Hesiod's *Erga* we witnessed the beginnings of abstraction, of allegorical rather than tautegorical presentation, and the concomitant shift from immediate surface-revelation to that of an underlying and not immediately perceptible truth (pp. 45-46). It is this shift that Heracleitus consciously exploits and further develops here. He knows that the making of simple distinctions, the careful separation of this from that in Homeric or everyday language, is a necessary step of thought. But he also knows that it is but an initial step; a step that is in itself inadequate because it is inappropriate to the *logos* qua *hen panta,* the *logos* in whose light all is set apart and brought together (10, 51), one and manifold at the same time. Since the function of the *logos* is not only to reveal the particular in its concreteness but also to gather all particulars together and carry us beyond immediate distinction and paratactic fragmentation to an all-embracing vision, one cannot stop with immediate presentation but has to go beyond: one has to speak and think metaphysically—going beyond the particular to its universal ground—and metaphorically—fusing the disparate particulars into a deeper unity without, however, robbing them of their particularity.[11] Only this type of language and thought is for Heracleitus truly logical—adequate to the *logos;* and it is logical not in spite of but because of its poetic-symbolic character.

Nonetheless this language, though poetic, also guards against a purely esthetic response and immediate enjoyment in passive acceptance. It is not only appropriate to its subject (the *logos*); it also fosters in the listener the appropriate attitude to what is said. It communicates indirectly, resists being taken at face value; without interpretation it makes no sense, and thus it repels rather than attracts those who would profit from it without undergoing hard intellectual labor. That is why Heracleitus' language has so little appeal to the many: it requires too much from the ordinary receiver. It requires that he himself think rather than merely believe, that he travel the arduous path Heracleitus traversed rather than merely assent to what he says, that he overcome all seeming parataxis and incoherence and conceive, i. e., view synoptically, these fragments rather than merely receive them as an aggregate of vibrant staccato statements without continuity or connection. As Plotinus acutely remarked: "He seems to speak in images, heedless of making his meaning clear to us, in order that we too should have to search ourselves for what he found out in his own search" (*Enneads* 4.8). The very nature of Heracleitus' language asks for and almost enforces *homologia*: a likemindedness in thought, a correspondence in our own spiritual attitude. And it does this without reducing the reader to a slavish obedience to the teacher's thought. Instead, it turns the listener toward himself, toward his own *logos,* which he must exercise in autonomous thought if he is to follow not Heracleitus—for that is unessential—but the *logos* of which Heracleitus speaks.

Whether Heracleitus believed this *logos* to be completely accessible to men and held man's autonomous thought to be capable of totally unveiling the mysteries of nature is doubtful. Although he thought nothing else even approximately adequate to the task, he seemed to hold that autonomous, essential thinking itself had its limits beyond which it could not go.

"You cannot find the limits of the soul even though you traverse all roads, so deep is its *logos*" (45) we hear him say. Does this mean that human *logos* is in the end inadequate to fully knowing the divine, universal *logos* that dwells in the soul and of which man's *logos* is but a fragment and pale reflection? There are passages in Heracleitus that seem to support this interpretation.

"Human nature has no insight; divine nature has it" (78). "Man is childish compared to God, just like a child is compared to man" (79). "Compared to God the wisest man seems like an ape in wisdom, beauty, and everything else" (83). In fragment 18 the possibility of knowing the ultimate seems at once affirmed and denied: "if one does not hope for the unhoped for, one will not find it; for it is not to be searched out and there is no access to it".

In the case of someone other than Heracleitus one might be inclined to regard such sayings as no more than a pious repetition of traditional-religious wisdom. But Heracleitus is not only too critical of tradition to allow that; his very manner of speaking as well as the content of his thought as a whole indicate that there is more to these fragments than traditional piety. After all, oracular, symbolic, analogical thinking and speaking are necessary only if what is spoken and thought about is not directly sayable and think-able. And that seems to be true of Heracleitean *logos*. Words, even in their most abstract usage, define and delimit; as such they are not wholly adequate to that (*logos*) which pervading all transcends all limit and definition. As there are no names fully appropriate to the divine substance (32), so the absolute underlying *logos* must always remain to some extent ineffable; words can only point to it and human knowledge can only adumbrate it negatively as its own undiscoverable ground (18). Precisely because that to which all in-telligence is directed (*to sophon*) is inherent in all things, it is at least to some extent set apart from all its embodiments (108) and as such not totally accessible to a merely human wisdom. The very nature of *logos* makes it at once knowable—since manifest in all—and unknowable—absolutely. Like nature it hides itself—in itself—even as it reveals itself—in terms of finite human knowing.

The fact that even while Heracleitus strains thought and language to its limits he still recognizes that there are limits to language and thought is perhaps his greatest intellectual achieve-ment. While his most distinguished contemporary, Parmenides, came perilously close to disregarding these limits and going too far beyond the conditioned in his search for the unconditional, Hera-cleitus seems to realize that the rational demand for an ultimate synthesis becomes irrational and excessive itself if unbridled and unchecked. Though a spokesman for divine *logos*, Heracleitus never became its quasi-Dionysian enthusiast: he never became so possessed with it that he succumbed to the temptation of following it ecstatically beyond what is humanly reasonable and into a realm of thought that thought itself could not encompass.

Heracleitus is as aware of the difference between absolute and finite knowledge in his practical thought as he is in his theoretical reflections. He emphasizes the relativity of human sensation and value judgment—"sickness makes health pleasant and good, hunger satiety and toil rest" (111); men "would not even know the name of justice if this [injustice] did not exist" (23)—as well as the natural relativity of what is good for each particular finite species or creature: "the sea is at once the purest and most defiled water; for fishes drinkable and life-giving, for men undrinkable and deadly" (61). "Asses prefer sweepings to gold" (9), pigs prefer mire to clear water (13). Long before the Sophists he warns against thoughtlessly extending particular judgments, no matter how true in their limited context, into general, universal ones: "The way up and down is one and the same" (60) depending on the viewer's position; "the path of the carding-screw is straight and crooked" (59) depending on what aspect of it is considered; the same point on the circle can be called beginning and end (103) and the same thing good and evil (58) depending on our point of view.

Heracleitus knows that taken out of their context and viewed under the aspect of eternity, value judgments lose their meaning— "to God all is fair and good and just, but men have held some things to be unjust and others just" (102)—just as all opposites coincide and all contradiction is reconciled in God—"God is day night, winter summer, war peace, satiety hunger" (67). But nowhere does he imply that men should therefore abandon making distinctions and rise altogether above their finite human judgment in practical life. It is clear to him that being finite, men must also fulfill themselves as finite beings for whom good and evil, justice and injustice, war and peace are not at all the same. Not because good and evil have suddenly become absolute terms independent of their context, but bcause man is not an absolute being independent of his context: the particulars of his natural and social condition. Though value is relative, it is relative not only to private opinion and false convention—this relativity can and must be overcome—but also to the natural constitution and environment of each organism which inevitably determine what is good and evil, beneficial and harmful for each. And this relativity must never be lost sight of either in judgment or in action. True judgment requires that we should know within what limits, in relation to what, on what level of particularity or generality we assert what we assert. And right action likewise depends on this: that we should never confuse what is good for one individual with what is good for another or what is good for them all as a collection of individuals working together in the state or as a species. In Heracleitus one can and must move up and down the line between the polar opposites of the most general and the most particular without ever losing sight of either pole. The generality of the *logos*—as the ground and interrelation of all particulars—does not cancel the particularity of each being, rather it embraces them all and makes each essential to the whole.

From a divine point of view, of course, even life and death are the same (62, 77, 88), and the ceaseless interchange of contraries, the back and forth turnings of forever living Fire (*logos,* god, the One) are themselves without reason or end: *"Aion* [lifetime, time, eternity?] is a child playing, playing at draughts; a child's dominion" (52). Heracleitus is well aware of the fact that *ultimately* all is without purpose inasmuch as the Ultimate cannot itself be justified (if all value, purpose, and justification is relative). But he can appreciate this without therefore negating all human purpose by simply identifying men and god. To do the latter and thereby to transfer what is true in one context (the divine) to another (the human) would be to deny the relativity of judgment and the manifoldness of the one *logos* that he is so intent on affirming. Heracleitus' insight into the relativity of all value judgment does not make finite practical human reasoning any more unfunctional than his affirmation of the ultimate ineffability of the *logos* made finite human knowledge worthless. In both theory and practice Heracleitus accepts human limitation and is willing to remain within the limits of what is human. It is in this way, corresponding to the *logos* yet living up to his own measure without becoming one with the divine, that in his view man can best harmonize with the divine *logos* of which he is a vital but limited part.

This is what distinguishes Heraclitean thought from Dionysian enthusiasm. Not just that it is rational rather than emotional, for there are, as we shall shortly see, excesses of reason that are hardly distinguishable from excesses of unreason; at their extreme both pure rationality and irrationality tend to become life-negating and lead to the absolute dissolution—intellectual or emotional—of all in One. But Heraclitean thought, though more abstract than anyone else's before, never abstracts us from human life. With a magnificent conceptual effort Heracleitus has brought about a grand synthesis of all, but he never lets it engulf and annihilate man by volatilizing the finite self and making it lose its precarious foothold in what is, after all, a finite rather than infinite existence.

This is not to say that the world of Heracleitus bears no resemblance to that of Dionysian religion. In both, men are embodiments of something divine (*logos*/Dionysus), animated and sustained by something more powerful and more essential than their individual, private persons. And so are all things but fragments participating in and manifesting their common ground (*logos*/Dionysus). Like Dionysus in his epiphanies, the very constitution of things in Heracleitus neither reveals nor fully conceals itself; the world leads a masked existence as it were, nature hiding itself behind appearances and disclosing itself only to those who are capable of seeing beyond the mask. All is full of god—*entheos*—in both worlds, and Heracleitus himself is in a sense but the spokesman of the god speaking not on his own behalf but on behalf of the One which, like Dionysus *polyonymos,* may or may not be called by any name.

Still this does not make Heracleitus a Dionysian, for he also insists on what the Dionysian experience seeks to abolish: finitude, measure, and limit, individual particularity, separateness and diversity, as well as the type of unity that only imagination and intellect can provide. Nor does he ignore all previous thought in the Dionysian manner, but for all his ostensible contempt for his predecessors he learns from them and builds on their achievements.

Like Archilochus and Sappho he recognizes the relativity and subjectivity of finite experience, yet like Hesiod and Solon he searches for the law governing human life and attempts to give all individual existence a foundation in something universal. Like Anaximander he seeks for what is common and necessary in a world of ceaseless change, and gives all diverse phenomena a common principle and a nonsensuous underlying ground. Like Xenophanes he is aware of the limits of knowledge as well as of the importance of its determined pursuit. Like all his great predecessors he rises above popular opinion and poetic-religious tradition critically and claims as well as tries to impart an uncommon insight into the common.

For all its seeming discontinuity, his writing does not represent a return to Homeric parataxis; his fragments cohere and fuse into an indivisible whole and his random arrows find the same mark, again and again, with an awesome precision. Although unsystematically presented, his philosophy has an organic unity and in its turn unites all the separate trends of thought current at the time and reveals them as interconnected aspects and manifestations of the same *logos*. It is this unity and complexity, simplicity and manifoldness of Heracleitus' thought that makes him the equal of any other Greek thinker and poet considered in this study.[12]

* * * * * *

To appreciate fully the richness and manifoldness of Heracleitus' rational yet impassioned, philosophical yet poetic, reflective yet imaginative thought, it is useful to consider briefly the work of his greatest contemporary, Parmenides. Parmenides was also driven by the Greek demand for a grand intellectual synthesis reducing all change to identity and all diversity to unity; nevertheless the bareness and barrenness of his logic contrast extraordinarily with the wealth and fertility of the Heraclitean *logos*.

"It is all the same to me where I begin," says Parmenides, "for I shall come back there again" (5), and the reader of his poem may easily get the impression that in the major portion of his work Parmenides not only comes back to where he began but never even left the supposed point of departure for a moment. To illustrate, I shall give a brief paraphrase of this philosopher's Way of Truth.

The only ways of inquiry to be thought of are: that (what is) is and (what) is not is not—this is the way of persuasion for it follows truth; that (what is) is not and it is necessary (for it) not to be—this path is altogether unknowable, for you could neither know nor say what is not. . . . For it is the same (what can be) thought and (what can) be. . . . It is necessary to say and to think that what is is; for (what) is is and nothing is not. . . . And never shall it be proved that what is not is. . . . The only path of inquiry that remains is that (what is) is and on this path there are many signs: that being ungenerated (it) is also indestructible, whole, immovable, and without end. (It) never was nor will be, for (it) is now altogether, one, continuous. For what origin would you seek for it? How, whence could it grow? I will not allow you to say or to think (that it grows) from what is not. For it is not possible to say or to think that (something) is not. And what need would have made it emerge later rather than sooner if it began in nothing? Thus it must either be altogether or not at all. For out of nothing . . . nothing can come. . . . How then could what is perish? How could it come to be? If it came into being it is not, nor (is it) if it is only going to be. Thus coming into being is extinguished and perishing is unknown. Nor is it divisible, for it is all alike. . . . It is altogether continuous, for what is draws nigh what is. . . . Motionless (it) is in the limits of mighty bonds without beginning or ceasing to be. . . . It rests selfsame in the same by itself abiding, remaining steadfast where it is . . . for it needs nothing; if it did it would need all. The same is thinking and that wherefor thought is. For not without what is . . . will you find thought. . . . Therefore all that mortals laid down, convinced of its truth, are but mere names: genesis and destruction, being and nonbeing, change of place and alteration of brilliant color. . . .

There are several points of interest for us in the preceding. The first is that instead of dogmatically stating his conclusions Parmenides argues for them. Such an explicitly nondogmatic presentation of one's thought is something novel in Greek literature. While Xenophanes' *silloi* already contained a kind of argument—the *reductio ad absurdum* of the anthropomorphic approach—his positive description of divinity was still dogmatic and unargued. And while Heracleitus' fragments were in a sense undogmatic—in that they required critical reflection on the part of the receiver and discouraged uncritical acceptance—they were still stated without an express attempt at justification and remained superficially incoherent and unconnected. Parmenides is the first Greek thinker to offer concise and explicit arguments in support of his thesis and to establish what he asserts by way of a logical deduction.

Though Parmenides uses the Homeric haxameter as a vehicle for conveying his thought, the composition of his "epic" is anything but paratactic. The poem as a whole has an organic unity, it is a structure constructed in accordance with a carefully elaborated hierarchial plan,[13] and the composition of the individual sentences as well as the sequence of individual sentences is strongly hypotactic. Parmenides' intention to make the connection and the logical succession of his ideas explicit and clear is always evident.[14] His poem is undoubtedly the first example of a sustained philosophical argument in the history of Western thought.

A second point of equal interest is that the purely rational nature of Parmenides' poem is at once its greatest achievement and its most striking defect. By yielding to reason's demand for a thoroughgoing logical consistency and the elimination of all that could not be derived from rational thought itself, Parmenides not only fulfilled but also subverted this demand. His Way of Truth is at once an admirable exercise in logical deduction and a philosophical monstrosity; its creation marks both the invention of a purely philosophical argument and its most incredible abuse.

For in its radical reduction of all to One and in its complete denial of all existence other than the Parmenidean Is, of which nothing positive can be said except that it is—and Plato's *Parmenides* soon shows that even that is to say too much—the poem demonstrates that unaided reason with its demand for absolute unity and consistency necessarily ends up with an abstraction lacking all content. The poem shows the Way of Truth to be indeed the only path open to pure reason, but it makes equally evident that on this path there is nowhere to go. The Way offers no concrete knowledge, has no bearing on action, gives no guidance for life, leaves no scope for the imagination, and yields no outlet for the emotions, no pleasure for the senses, and no object for worship. From every human point of view—in the end even from that of reason—the Parmenidean One, his Is, might as well not be. "It" is certainly no different from nothing at all.

In his introduction (1) to the Way of Truth Parmenides describes his way to enlightenment as a celestial or infernal journey. Whether we interpret the journey as celestial or infernal, the image is all too appropriate, for Parmenides' flight of reason literally transports him out of this world. It is an ecstatic journey which, for all the difference between the purely rational and the purely emotional modes of transport, bears a strange resemblance to Dionysian ecstasy. Both the Parmenidean dissolution of all in One and the Dionysian dissolution of all in the god are a nightmare for the living human being. Both regard every aspect of man's existence —other than the one each insists on—as unauthentic, as a kind of falsity or pollution; both deem the world here and now as unessential and unreal; and both elevate man above and beyond all time and change and individual human existence. For all their different points of departure and way of approach the two journeys end in the same place: in a total void where all life and all thought are extinct. The logical end of both Dionysian enthusiasm and Parmenidean logic is total silence. Whereas Heracleitus' thought, for all its superficial resemblance to Dionysian worship, was in essence profoundly opposed to it (see above pp. 154–55), Parmenides' thought is in fact its exact intellectual counterpart.

Although Parmenides is not notably silent, it is clear that no language available or conceivable could be appropriate to what he wants to say—just as all formalized expression was alien to Dionysian ecstasy. For the function of language is to order and articulate experience, to identify and differentiate the whole and its parts, to gather the many into one and to separate the one into the many at the same time. But the Parmenidean unity, like the Dionysian divinity, excludes all diversity and thus defies articulation. It is a purely negative concept to which no experience can correspond or give content. Therefore it can be expressed only negatively, as other than any conceivable—particular or general but not altogether empty—idea.

While any language can be pressed into the service of this type of negative ontology—the argument that gradually empties "being" of all content—there is a kind of logic in Parmenides' adoption of the epic idiom as his vehicle. For what he wanted to convey was that which was furthest removed from everyday language and experience, and by his time the Homeric verse-form and phraseology were further removed from contemporary language and experience than any other available form of literature. The fact that compared to Homeric poetry the Parmenidean versification is utterly unpoetic—clumsy, dry, inept, unimaginative, lifeless —is a help rather than a hindrance here: by producing a kind of shock effect, it helps to detach this poem even from its own model and thereby brings home its message of being *sui generis*.

This does not mean, of course, that Parmenides deliberately wrote bad poetry. He was simply uninterested in those aspects of experience—concrete, sensuous, emotional, and imaginative—to which poetry appeals. Since his subject matter was totally unesthetic, he had no reason to care about and cultivate his own or his audience's esthetic sensibilities. We have observed a similar antipoetic frame of mind at work in Hesiod's quasi-epic *Erga* (see pp. 65–66 above). But while Hesiod used the only available language of other than everyday discourse, Parmenides' return to the epic form was a matter of choice. Although he may not have aimed consciously at producing a kind of poetic monstrosity as a means for subverting poetry itself, the end result of this creation was certainly in line with his explicit intentions.

Before leaving Parmenides it is only fair to point out that the preceding discussion does not do full justice to his Way of Truth. But those logical and ontological aspects of Parmenides' thought which proved most influential and fruitful in the development of fifth- and fourth-century Greek philosophy lie outside the scope of this study. We are concerned here only with the contribution of Parmenides to the development of the Greek view of man. And this contribution is twofold: Parmenides showed that men could think coherently, argue deductively, and follow a train of thought rigorously no matter where it led. But he also showed that men were capable of following a train of thought excessively and ecstatically even to life-denying conclusions. By committing what might be called an extraordinary hybris of the rational faculty, Parmenides demonstrated that not only passion but reason too could lead to a corrosive inhumanity and an abstraction from all life; that rationality was at once an endowment man could cultivate for his own benefit and a temptation to which he could succumb to his own lasting harm.

Although post-Parmenidean philosophy, Ionian and Eleatic, was aware of some of these dangers, its investigation of physical nature contributed little to the Greeks' understanding of human nature and need not therefore be considered here. The next chapter in the development of the Greek concept of man was written by the dramatists who made human life, in all its depth and breadth, the central problem of their creative work.

7. *The* Oresteia

"It is peculiarly fitting to begin a study of Aeschylus by a consideration of the trilogy, which clearly demonstrates that the poet is interested not in a person but in a doom and that the doom need not fall on one individual, but can affect a whole family. In his tragedies man is not the chief problem: man is merely a vehicle of destiny and that destiny is the real problem."[1] Jaeger's remark may serve as our starting point for considering the Aeschylean view of man.

Aeschylus' only extant trilogy is the *Oresteia*. Does this trilogy bear out Jaeger's observation that Aeschylus' subject is not the individual agent in his own right but the fate of mankind as a whole? To decide this question we have to deal first of all with the problem of personal responsibility on the part of the individual protagonists in these plays. Do the protagonists themselves accept responsibility for what they are about to do and what they have done? Is such responsibility ascribed to them by the chorus? Do they act entirely under compulsion, or are there real alternatives open to them to act otherwise than they do in the *Oresteia?*

To the question do the protagonists accept responsibility for their acts we must answer with an unqualified no. Every one of the actors pleads "not mine the deed" and claims to be caught up in a cycle of events almost completely beyond his own initiative and control. As Paris was "forced by wretched Peitho, the overmastering child of designing destruction" (*Agamemnon* 385-46) to do the deed that resulted in irremediable ruin for Troy, so without choice or remedy Agamemnon claims to have followed the gods' command (*Ag.* 812ff., 206) in committing the acts through which he dealt himself, as it were, his own deathblow.

To be sure, Clytemnestra blames Agamemnon—"He filled the bowl in his house with so many curse-laden ills, and now he drained it to the dregs" (*Ag.* 1397-8); "Did he not set Ate afoot in the house?" (*Ag.* 1523-4) so that now he only "paid with death for what he first began" (*Ag.* 1529)—but this is more an expression of her own refusal to shoulder any blame than a clear ascription of personal culpability to Agamemnon. To what extent Agamemnon could be said to have begun the whole bloody sequence of acts is questionable even in Clytemnestra's own terms. "Can you affirm that this deed is mine?" (*Ag.* 1497) she asks rhetorically, only to claim that she, and by implication Agamemnon himself, was merely a tool of higher powers: "Assuming the shape of this corpse's wife the ancient stark avenging spirit of Atreus . . . offered this man in payment, a last sacrifice" (*Ag.* 1500-04)—for Thyestes' children, with whose murder Agamemnon had nothing to do.

Aegisthus, the other murderer of Agamemnon, not only disclaims personal responsibilty for his own part, but he, too, unwittingly absolves Agememnon of personal guilt: it was the Erinyes that spun the bloody robe to make Agamemnon pay, not for his own acts but "for the deeds contrived by his father's hand" (*Ag.* 1582).

Without exception the protagonists claim to be agents of avenging justice, delivering well-deserved punishment "justly and more than justly" (*Ag.* 1396). "By Dike, exacted for my child, by Ate and Erinys, to whom I sacrificed this man" (*Ag.* 1423-33), Clytemnestra claims to be guiltless—and so does Orestes, her slayer. "Fate, my child, has helped to bring this [Agamemnon's death] about" (*Choephoroi* 910), Clytemnestra pleads with Orestes, only to hear him reply "then it is also Fate that has worked your death" (*Cho.* 911). And how reminiscent of Clytemnestra's disclaimer (*Ag.* 1529) is Orestes' own: "It is you who will kill yourself, not I" (*Cho.* 923). To Zeus, Dike, Peitho, Erinys, and Ate, whose support the others claimed for their deed, Orestes has one more deity to add in excusing himself: he acted, persuaded and advised "by this god's [Apollo's] command; he is my witness" (*Eumenides* 594); a blameless servant of divine justice Orestes was, no more. Indeed, Clytemnestra seems to speak not just for herself and Aegisthus but for all the protagonists in the *Oresteia:* "What we did had to be done . . . let us accept it, ill-struck as we are by the heavy claws of Fate" (*Ag.* 1659–69).

That the protagonists disclaim responsibility is, perhaps, not too surprising. What is striking is that the chorus, too, seems to agree with them to a large extent. Of Orestes' innocence the chorus is never in doubt; fully convinced of the justice of his case it urges Orestes on to matricide. Of Agamemnon the chorus is more critical, and even more so of Clytemnestra. Yet for all its negative attitude toward this ill-fated pair, the chorus is not averse to joining them in their disclaimer. On hearing Clytemnestra's arguments for example, it is Helen, not Clytemnestra, that the chorus blames, and above all it blames the "evil Spirit that fell upon the house and Tantalus' descendents . . . and standing on the corpse like a hateful crow chants her discordant chant of triumph" (*Ag.* 1468–74); the "thrice-gorged demon of this race" (*Ag.* 1476–7) who inspires men with ever fresh blood lust to spill new blood before the old wound is healed (*Ag.* 1478–81); the "mighty, haunting, wrath-bent demon" of insatiate doom (*Ag.* 1481–4) in whose toils men are caught as in a "spider's web" (*Ag.* 1492), "fast-bound to ruin" (*Ag.* 1566).

What is this curse, this "pain bred into the race" (*Cho.* 466) not just of Pleisthenes but, as we shall see, of all mankind? On the surface, it is the ancient law of blood-vengeance repeatedly affirmed in the *Agememnon* and the *Choephoroi.* "It is the law that drops of blood spilt upon the ground demand more blood. Murder cries aloud for the Erinyes to bring from those slain-before new ruin upon old" (*Cho.* 400–404). The law of blood-pollution is, as it were, a law of nature: when spilt blood seeps into the nourishing earth it congeals into black gore, a fertile ground from which further ruin grows. Indissoluble, not to be washed away, spilt blood infects the very soil with a deadly disease (*Cho.* 66–74) until the "earth herself that brings all to birth" (*Cho.* 127) brings forth a deadly bloom. Black blood spilt on earth cannot be recalled (*Ag.* 1019) nor "ransomed once it has fallen on the ground" (*Cho.* 48); "even if a man poured out his all [in sacrifice] to undo one deed of blood, it would be in vain" (*Cho.* 520–21). Since blood can be washed away only by blood, each act of purification is necessarily a new pollution so that pollution spreads in the very process of its being wiped away and crime breeds crime in an ever widening circle (*Ag.* 758, 763). Under the rule of this law "the dead are killing the living" (*Cho.* 886) almost literally, as each agent and sufferer, each executioner and victim "pays in blood for other blood shed before, and, dying for the dead, passes death-sentence on others yet to come" (*Ag.* 1338–40).

"The spoiler despoiled, the slayer paying in turn . . . to the doer the deed; that is the law" (*Ag.* 1562), and *antapoktanein,* to kill in turn (*Cho.* 121), is its supreme principle. "As justice turns, let words of hate be paid in words of hate . . . and murderous stroke in murderous stroke; let the doer suffer . . ." (*Cho.* 208–13), "the slayer be justly slain in turn" (*Cho.* 144) and "evil be requited with evil" (*Cho.* 123), till all who "killed by wile . . . will die by wile, caught in the selfsame snare" (*Cho.* 556–7).

So primitive, so pervaded with netherworldly gloom, does this vision of retributive justice seem at this point in the development of the Greek spirit, that the reader almost involuntarily seeks for signs of a more enlightened, Olympian rather than chthonic justice, a Zeus-given Dike to counter the blood-law and thereby provide relief. Yet in the *Agamemnon* and the *Choephoroi* one searches in vain for such a rival conception. There is but one justice in these plays, and Zeus and the Erinyes, the Olympian and the chthonic deities, the gods and the *moirai* are wholly united in affirming and enforcing its rule.[2]

In the *Agamemnon,* it is Apollo, Pan, or Zeus himself who sends the avenging Erinys (*Ag.* 55, 461ff., 748), and, in speaking of the bloody Spirit haunting the house of Atreus, the chorus makes it an agent, an aspect almost, of the will of "Zeus, all-mover, all-worker. For what is accomplished among mortals without Zeus? What of all these things is not god-wrought?" (1485-88). Dike and Moira, far from being opposed, are joint guardians (1535-36) of the blood-law which "holds good while Zeus abides on his throne" (1563). In the *Choephoroi,* Moira, Zeus, and Dike work hand in hand (309-11), and Dike, Aisa, and Erinys are conjoined: "The root of Justice is planted firm, Fate preforges her sword, and in time deep-brooding Erinys brings the son into the house to avenge ancient blood-pollution" (646-51). Nor is Apollo a new god opposed to the bloody rule of the old here; he himself threatens Orestes with death, destruction, and the Erinyes if he should fail to repay murder with murder (269ff.).

Since we are dealing with the problem of individual responsibility, it is important to emphasize this unitary hyperouranian-chthonic support for the blood-law. For if it is this law which is the curse under which the individuals labor, and if this law has the entire weight of divine sanction behind it, in what sense can we still speak of individual choice, responsibility and guilt in the case of agents confronted with such crushing power and such overwhelming odds as seem to be arrayed against them in the *Agamemnon* and the *Choephoroi?*

To speak of guilt and responsibility in the modern sense of these terms would require that the agents with whom we deal should have had some real alternatives between better and worse ways of acting open to them. But did any of the protagonists of the *Oresteia* have meaningful choices to make between alternatives that differed significantly in moral worth? Let us consider briefly

Agamemnon's case, which is more ambiguous than either Orestes' or Clytemnestra's and seems to lie halfway between the two in terms of being morally problematic.

Zeus had sent the sons of Atreus against Troy to avenge Paris' crime. To disobey Zeus' command would have meant for Agamemnon and Menelaos to transgress against divine justice as well as to fail to uphold their personal and family honor. That this would have been a wholesome alternative to the course of action they adopted can hardly be suggested. On the way to Troy adverse winds hold up the fleet and Agamemnon is confronted with the fateful choice between abandoning his mission and sacrificing his daughter Iphigenia; two equally bitter alternatives to Agamemnon's mind: "Grievous is my fate if I disobey, and grievous if I slay my child, the glory of my house, polluting at the altar here these father's hands with streams of maiden blood. Which of these courses is without evil? How can I desert the fleet and fail in my duty to my allies? For that they should urge such sacrifice . . . is right" (*Ag.* 206–16). The scales are evenly balanced between two intolerable courses of action. To try to unbalance them by making one of the alternatives much more appealing is to miss the point of the tragedy. Agamemnon may have been a moral monster in real life, but that is not how Aeschylus presents him; rather it is his choice, the options open to him that are monstrous here. Faced with equally impossible options, Agamemnon, half-distracted and in tears, decides; he "dons the yoke of necessity" (217) and moves on toward Troy and his doom.

But then, can we blame him for acting as he did? Is it possible that the intolerable decision imposed on him by the gods was itself not so much the cause as it was the result of his criminal behavior? This is not as far-fetched a theory as it sounds. Perhaps Artemis was angry at Agamemnon on account of his trangressions and demanded Iphigenia's sacrifice as the price Agamemnon had to pay for his crimes. Yet what crimes? To answer this we have to ignore exact chronology and linear causal sequence and begin to treat concrete events figuratively and symbolically, as Aeschylus may well have intended us to do.

If we take the omen of the two kingly eagles devouring a hare with unborn brood as symbolizing the ravages Atreus' sons would inflict on the innocent inhabitants of Troy, this might explain why Artemis, ever the defender of the young and the helpless, would want to punish Agamemnon. The fact that the crime is here avenged long before it takes place could be disregarded if the eagle-omen is viewed as a "timeless emblem of the recurring crime for which Artemis has a long-enduring wrath." [3] Such recurring crime —the slaying of Thyestes' children, of Iphigenia, of the children at Troy—is without doubt endemic in Atreus' house, and Agamemnon himself is without doubt engaged in a course of action that will necessarily result in the killing of young innocents.

Viewed in this manner, the sacrifice of his virgin daughter becomes both the penalty for and the symbolic preenactment of the brutal child-devouring justice Agamemnon is on the way to exact. Since it is foredoomed that the innocent as well as the guilty will suffer at Troy, it hardly matters that Agamemnon's punishment begins long before and ends some time after the commission of his crime (at Troy), or indeed that the punishment at Aulis (Iphigenia's sacrifice), preceding the crime at Troy, is itself a crime for which Agamemnon will pay with his life at Argos. Such is the fore- and aft-entanglement of events here that a morally relevant temporal sequence is impossible to establish, as crime and punishment, agent and victim gradually fuse, and crucial events (e.g., Iphigenia's sacrifice) are revealed as both preenactment of what is to come (the Trojan slaughter) and reenactment of what had taken place (the slaying of Thyestes' children). [4]

This entanglement of events is characteristic of the *Agamemnon* and the *Choephoroi,* where actual happenings and things so often tend to become timeless paradigms. The purple path Agamemnon treads on his homecoming prefigures the blood bath to which it leads as well as it symbolizes the path of blood he began to tread as soon as he left home. (And is his treading on purple a crime itself or merely the symbol of a crime?) The net thrown over him just before the knife descends is symbolic of the net of fate in which he and his race have been ensnared all along and will be ensnared even after his death. The "unhoped for home" he is about to enter is not just the house Agamemnon despaired of ever seeing, nor just his grave, but also a symbol for the world: a homeless home for him and all mankind who under the rule of such justice are doomed to find no rest.

Particular agents and acts gradually lose their concreteness and become archetypal masks and stylized gestures here, as we recognize how "blood shed propagates a nearly exact image of itself in each generation . . . [and] the members of the family become largely interchangeable with each other." [5] Parent slaying child, child slaying parent, the dead slaying the living, the living reenacting the deeds of the dead—who can untangle the intersecting lines of blood and point to where the blood-guilt began? All we see is a cursed race, worn away by time, turning back on itself in a circle; a timeless masque in which persons are *personae,* not autonomous agents but play-actors on the stage of life—a stage not of their own choosing—acting the parts assigned to them by fate, involved in movements they do not half comprehend, directed and sustained by something far more powerful than their own individual will and design.

If this interpretation is correct, it is pointless to try to isolate, let alone single out for blame, any agent or act. For what they are all entangled in is, of course, the web of retributive justice. Not any single act but the law of blood dooms not any single agent but the whole race. Under its rule there are no wholesome alternatives for action; every act and agent is just and unjust, cathartic and polluted at the same time. Justice may seem monolithic as sanctioned by all the powers above and below the earth—but from the point of view of man and for the purposes of action it is also dirempt and antinomical: action splits the world and pits law against law, duty against duty, divine command against divine command, "Ares against Ares, Dike against Dike" (*Cho.* 461), and "Fate against Fate" (*Ag.* 1026).

In such a world human action is forever ambiguous, and there is such a thing as the necessary crime. This Lesky regarded as one fundamental trait in Aeschylean tragedy. "Human action is danger, and again and again it leads to a situation from which there is no way out, in which the same act means necessity, duty, merit, and at the same time most grievous guilt. . . . Man stands under the horrible necessity to act and knows that this action will be a crime." [6]

In his analysis of dramatic action in Aeschylus [7] Snell emphasized the teleological, forward-looking character of *dran* in drama, and contrasted *dran,* as the critical moment of decision in which all hangs in the balance, with *prattein* as the temporal process of the execution of an already determined upon plan. However, in his effort to explain guilt and responsibility in the *Oresteia,* he laid too great an emphasis on the openness of alternatives at the moment of decision and too little on the nature of these alternatives themselves. But this, the intolerable nature of both alternatives rather than the choice itself, is what most characterizes Aeschylean *dran.* Orestes' question *"ti draso?"* ("What am I to do?") (parallelled by Electra's *"ti pho?"*—"What am I to say?") is tragic not because the guilt or innocence of the questioner depend on the answer but precisely because they do not; because no decision is without guilt. The Aeschylean *ti draso?* is not the moment of consciousness of freedom but the moment of consciousness of dreadful necessity. *Ti draso?* implies not that the choice is regarded as free but that the acts contemplated are seen at the same time as necessary and horrible—no matter what alternative is to be adopted. This is what makes *dran* tragic: the agent's consciousness of the antinomical nature of all action, his realization of man's *aporia* in the face of open alternatives and *amechania* in the midst of action. Contrary to Snell, *dran* and *paschein,* action and intolerable suffering, are more identical than opposed terms in the *Agamemnon* and the *Choephoroi,* and the actors' cries *"ti draso?, ti tonde aneu kakon?"* ("which of these [choices] is without evil?") merely reveal the protagonists' agonizing consciousness of this.

How then can one account for the famous Aeschylean dictum "through suffering, knowledge" that is twice intoned in the first choral ode of the *Agamemnon?* In line with the preceding interpretation this celebrated pronouncement can hardly be taken to be more than a piece of traditional gnomic wisdom fondly but vainly recalled by the chorus; for Aeschylus more a pious hope than a deeply felt reality in the *Agamemnon* and the *Choephoroi.* None of the protagonists learn anything worth knowing by suffering here, nor could they have avoided suffering had they had more knowledge before the deed. Since the only insight they could possibly gain through their suffering is an "insight into the rules of the nightmare world (they) inhabit," [8] and thus into the uselessness and powerlessness of knowledge itself—an insight more likely to torture than to save them—Cassandra's tortured vision conveys Aschylus' real message in the *Agamemnon* much better than the chorus's pious pronouncement.[9]

Cassandra, more than anyone in the plays, is cursed with knowledge, and knowledge is truly a curse for her. We first become aware of her on the stage as she stands there, an alien figure, silent, unresponsive even when addressed, as if what she would have to say were more than could be said: an unutterable, world-shattering wisdom that bends her mind and seals her lips. Then the mounting tension breaks as, god-crazed, she breaks out in an inhuman howl—"Woe, woe, woe Apollo; Woe, woe, woe, Apollo; Apollo, Apollo, guardian of the ways, my destroyer; Thou hast destroyed me utterly, once again" (*Ag.* 1072-82)—followed by a raving utterance of her unbearable vision of an atrocious past, present, and future. Finally, exhausted, her madness subsides, and Cassandra walks toward her doom "like a god-driven ox to the altar" (1297-98) open-eyed, without hope. "There is no escape, there is none . . . the day has come, there is no gain in flight" (1299–31). We can understand now why Agamemnon, too, wordlessly "dons the yoke of necessity" after his one brief outburst of impotent knowledge. In an irrational world where justice itself is antinomical, action and knowledge are irreconcilable rather than harmonious elements mutually reinforcing each other. In such a world man might act best, i.e., with least pain, by not thinking at all. Certainly the chorus's realization of the contradictory nature of justice leaves it not only inactive but at times even speechless (*Ag.* 1026–33), while Clytemnestra, the strongest, most active figure on the stage, never deliberates before the deed nor wavers in doubtful thought but is driven by thoughtless passion to action.

Though Aeschylus echoes Hesiod's and Solon's insight into the natural history of crime and the inevitability of punishment (*Ag.* 54–59, 367–77, 433, 461–68, 533; *Cho.* 61–65, 639–51; *Eum.* 540, etc.), it is not their rather optimistic message about the rule of Dike and the advantages of wisdom and moderation that he transmits in the *Agamemnon* and the *Choephoroi*.[10] Instead of teaching "avoid crime, for punishment comes without fail," what he seems to be saying is that all warning is futile since, no matter what man does, he cannot avoid crime—or punishment. The righteous might indeed prosper, but who can still be righteous in the face of man's evil destiny? The fate of the *Agamemnon*'s and the *Choephoroi*'s protagonists more than nullifies the chorus's gnomic "through suffering, knowledge"; it reverses it into "through knowledge, suffering" and teaches that in this world knowledge promotes not action but passion, not tranquility but fear, as the chorus itself comes to see when confronted with Cassandra: "From oracles what message of good ever comes to men? Through evils do the wordy arts of prophecy bring us to learn fear" (*Ag.* 1132–35).

It is no wonder that fear is the dominant mood of the *Agamemnon* and the *Choephoroi*,[11] and that it affects not so much the protagonists, who act for the most part without much deliberation, as it infects the chorus that stands back inactively pondering the meaning of events. Characteristically, the chorus's fear is not a fear of particular evils more or less reasonably expected. "Muttering in the dark, sore at heart," the chorus has "no hope of ever unravelling aught to timely purpose" (1020-33). But precisely because it can know nothing beyond the inevitability of disaster, the chorus is troubled by an indefinite dread of impending doom. This dread is so intense and oppressive that the actual moments of death and disaster come almost as moments of relief, while actual moments of apparent victory and safe homecoming only nurture and strengthen fear: "I have seen with my own eyes [Agamemnon's] return; I witnessed it myself. And still my soul, self-taught, intones the unmusical dirge of the Erinys, feeling no confidence of hope at all" (*Ag.* 988-94).

"Aeschylean fear is, in general, brutal, physical, mysterious, involuntary"; [12] it is an irrational uncalculative fear that is, nevertheless, the result of a certain inarticulable insight into the way of things. It is a demonic fear, dully responsive to the "demon hovering over the house" (*Ag.* 1467, 1481-2), a fear "unbidden, unhired yet chanting prophetic" (*Ag.* 979). It is "pure fear in itself," [13] a miasmatic atmosphere expressive of and responsive to the miasmatic rule of the Law; a suffocating, paralyzing fear that is the emotional counterpart of the web of justice that strangles men. Since this fear infects the inactive even more than those who act, it reveals the true nature of man's plight: inaction is no less doom-laden than action. Man cannot be saved. "Alas for mortal things . . . what mortal can claim to have been born unscathed by god?" (*Ag.* 1327-41).

If in spite of this general hopelessness of human fortune we can still speak of guilt in the *Agamemnon* and the *Choephoroi*, that is simply because in the Aeschylean scheme of things guilt does not presuppose responsible—in our sense of the word—choice between wholesome and ruinous alternatives. Though Agamemnon "dons the yoke of necessity" without ever having been offered a better option, his deed is no less "impious, impure, and unholy" (*Ag.* 219-20) for that, and it is no less subject to punishment; for guilt—

the price one has to pay, the penalty to be exacted—is attached to the act and not the intention.

We have seen how the Homeric Agamemnon offered payment for his deed even while disclaiming all responsibility for its commission. In the *Iliad* divine causation in no way excused and made guiltless the doer of the deed. Much the same situation obtains in the *Oresteia*. Blood spilt, for whatever reason, cries out for vengeance. The Erinyes simply pursue those *"upon whom have fallen"* (*toisin sympesosin, Eum.* 336–37) kinfolk-murderous deeds (*autourgiai*). That Orestes was to a large extent Apollo's tool, and that Clytemnestra deserved punishment, does not excuse Orestes' deed. The deed is in the world and objectively deserves punishment regardless of the subjective intention and attitude of the doer. Willing or unwilling, knowing or unwitting, every criminal act gives rise to an equal and opposite reaction; that is the chthonic law of nature. Innocence (of intention) is not a counterconcept to guilt (of action). The innocently guilty owe just as great a price for spilling blood as the utterly depraved. The pollution is the same.

Anaximander, in his one surviving fragment, described the operation of natural law in this manner: whatever happens—the generation of things and their destruction—happens "according to necessity; for they pay penalty and retribution to each other for their injustice according to the assessment of time." Just such a natural order is retributive justice in Aeschylus.[14] Transgression, however committed, not only disturbs the order and balance of things but it also starts a chain reaction which will reestablish this balance.[15] In this chain reaction—Thyestes-Atreus-Agamemnon-Clytemnestra-Aegisthus-Orestes—the individuals pay each other penalty and retribution, but in and through their mutual destruction the Law prevails.

We have seen this principle operative in Solon, where the innocent also suffered for others' wrongdoing and crime naturally corrupted the body politic so that all had to pay for one man's transgression. The same law operates in the *Agamemnon* and the

Choephoroi with an even greater elemental force. Under the rule of chthonic justice it is not only impossible to follow any spoor of blood to its individual source; it is also unnecessary. The murderous deed is objectively detestable [16] because it poisons the atmosphere and corrupts the life-blood of the family or group regardless of the doer's intention. The pollution is the same.

To be sure, the protagonists in the *Oresteia* have their own personal reasons, too, for committing their deeds, and for the most part their subjective goals reinforce their "guilty" action. But this is beside the point. Not just because their motives are by and large honorable, or at least excusable and understandable even in terms of Aeschylean psychology, but because guilt is independent of motivation, let alone of freedom of the will. [17] Innocent but necessary, "involuntary but inevitable guilt" [18] rebounds on the doer and destroys him even if subjectively he deserves a better fate. This is the paradox of natural justice, that suffering is at once unmerited (subjectively) and fully deserved (objectively). And this is what makes subjective life an almost unrelieved horror in the *Agamemnon* and the *Choephoroi*.

In many ways Aeschylus' conception of man's fate in these two plays resembles the Heraclitean world-view much more than it does that of Hesiod and Solon. In Heraclitus men were ultimately bearers of the *Logos,* possessed and sustained by something more essential than their individual, "private" characters. Now in Aeschylus, individual protagonists are to a large extent *personae;* masks in the masque of fate, willing-unwilling tools and vehicles of a power infinitely greater than their own autonomous will; helplessly driven playthings of chthonic justice. The *ethos* of man is still the *daimon*.

In Heracleitus the *Logos* was preserved selfsame in and through the war and strife of mutually interacting particulars engendering and destroying each other. So is the balance of the Law preserved in Aeschylus now through individual agents, begetters and slayers at once, exacting and paying the price of blood in turn. In Heracleitus the *Logos* was one, though it appeared diverse and even contradictory from the point of view of "private" men. In the *Agamemnon* and the *Choephoroi* individual action splits the one Law into antinomical fragments. In Heracleitus all opposites coincided; the way up and down, good and evil, night and day were one and the same. So now in Aeschylus all single acts and agents are, as it were, contradictory in themselves, just and unjust, pure and corrupt, active and passive at the same time, and only the Law is wholly pure and without taint. In Heracleitus all things in the world were but "Fire's turnings," ceaselessly transmuting into each other according to measure. This is what they do now in Aeschylus as triumph and disaster, hope and fear, joy and depression rythmically engender each other with a terrible regularity, and each act of penance is but a new crime crying for vengeance.

We can observe this terrible rythm not only in each individual's victory-defeat cycle, but in almost every scene, even every speech in the *Agamemnon* and the *Choephoroi,* where momentary confidence swiftly gives way to depression, shouts of joy unfailingly turn into groans of lamentation, and good tidings merely provoke evil forebodings. The very first scene of the *Agamemnon* sets the stage symbolically for the two plays—or the pattern of human life—as a whole.

The watchman, oppressed by fear, sleepless and restless in the night, prays for release from his weary task as he waits in the dark for the light that is the signal for salvation. The house, shrouded in doom, waits for deliverance. Yet when the sign comes the watchman's relief is as brief as the light's life; it quickly yields to anxiety about the future, the signal of good news becomes an omen of evil, and the jubilant cry ends in fearful silence.[19]

No wonder that the chorus echoes Heracleitus' fragment 32 with an even further diminished confidence in man's insight into the way of things and the nature of Zeus, the ruler of all: "Zeus, whoever he be, if it pleases him to be invoked by this name, thus I will call on him. Having pondered all things, I can liken him to nothing save Zeus if I need to cast vain sorrow truly from my mind"

(*Ag.* 160–66). Zeus' nature is no longer imaginable, comprehensible, or expressible in human terms. As if he were but a Heraclitean "*aion pais paizon*," the god can only be invoked in uncomprehending awe and fear in a vain attempt to save man from fear.[20]

Heracleitus advocated *homologia*, the individual's correspondence to the *Logos*, as the way to salvation. In Aeschylus this correspondence becomes much more problematic. On the one hand men no longer need to be exhorted to "follow the common," for they will do that, in the end, in any case. On the other, obedience to the Law no longer brings individual salvation, and thus man's *homologia* itself acquires a tragic dimension. In the *Agamemnon* and the *Choephorai* Aeschylus affirms the incomprehensible ways of god, yet he neither attempts to justify man's unmerited suffering, nor is he willing to rise above such suffering and contemplate man's fate unfeelingly. Though he might agree with Heracleitus' judgment (fragment 5) that the laws of blood-pollution are just about insane from the point of view of human sanity, he neither denies the law's reality nor relinquishes the human point of view. In consequence *Logos* and *logos* still harmonize in Aeschylus in one respect—inasmuch as his protagonists without exception agree with and live up to their fate and in the end willingly don the yoke of necessity—and yet they fail to harmonize in another: obedience to the divine law brings ruin not health, and men perish precisely because they followed the law. The law still abides unshaken, but there is little joy in this for man. Objective harmony with the law means subjective conflict and doom. "Alas for mortal things. . . ."

*　*　*　*　*　*

Much has been written about "tragic conflict," the inevitable collision of man with an overwhelming necessity in Aeschylus and the other Greek tragedians, but the question why the tragic view of life took the form of drama at the height of its development and was presented in a theater with actor and chorus enacting scenes from Homeric myth before a communal audience is less frequently raised. But since Aeschylus was for all intents and purposes the "creator of tragedy," the man who by extending existing conventions and combining older poetic forms in a new way created a virtually new art form, we might do well to consider this problem now. Did Aeschylus have to create *drama* in order to be able to express what he wanted to say? Is there a correspondence between the conventions of Aeschylean drama and the view of life Aeschylus put on the stage?

We have mentioned before that Aeschylus' view of man and world was, in a sense, theatrical: his individual protagonists were less autonomous agents than play-actors on the stage of life, making their entrances and exits and acting their parts in accordance with their assigned role, the requirements of the situation in which they found themselves, and the rules of the divine plot which they did not quite comprehend. We can follow up and qualify this observation now.

It is generally agreed that Aeschylus' main formal contribution to drama consisted of introducing the second actor and curtailing the choral portion of the play.[21] As to content, his turn or return to Homeric themes was equally significant. Why were these contributions crucial for the development of tragic drama?

We have seen that the dithyramb already had a leader (*exarchon*) at least minimally detached from the chorus, and so did pre-Aeschylean drama have an actor—whether he was called *hypocrites, tragodos,* or something else—who stood in some way outside and at least physically detached from the chorus. Aeschylus certainly built on this model, and yet his introduction of the second actor, soon followed by the third in the later plays, was much more than a merely numerical addition. For the *exarchon* or the first actor had been in all likelihood functionally connected with and in spirit an integral part of the chorus itself; he was a *hypocrites* only in the sense of being the interpreter or spokesman of the chorus rather than the representative of a detached point of view of his own. But the Aeschylean actor is a great deal more than that. He is not just protagonist, deuteragonist, or tritagonist, but is above all antagonist: an individual to some extent essentially detached from and standing over against the chorus. He is the first individual actor in a philosophical sense of the word: [22] an individual agent who for all his involvement is at odds with his moral environment.

This appearance of the self-conscious individual confronting the spokesman of the community on the stage was an important event for two reasons. Man's emergent self-consciousness, whose development we have followed from Hesiod to Heracleitus, finally found a perfect artistic image and expression of itself in the person of the dramatic actor. Furthermore, the explicit opposition of individual actor and communal chorus clearly symbolized for the first time the disruption of a natural harmony between the individual and the accepted, or even ideally postulated, social-political and moral-religious order of things.

It is not so much that a single social standard is now suddenly called into question by an individual opposed to it. Existing and generally accepted norms have been called into question by reform-minded individuals ever since Hesiod. Moreover, in the *Agamemnon* and the *Choephoroi,* all protagonists still operate within the generally accepted order of justice without opposing to it one of their own. As Hesiod and Solon regarded their own ideals—although opposed to those of the ignorant—universally true and binding, so do all the actors as well as the chorus regard retributive justice the one real all-encompassing law of the world in the *Agamemnon* and the *Choephoroi.*

But what is new here is that the individual is out of tune with and alienated from the law he himself accepts as binding; that individual life is now seen, more than ever before, as being in necessary conflict with the whole of reality. The individual actor, separated from the chorus and exposed in isolation, introduces an inevitable note of discord into the whole of which he is part.

It is often observed that in Greek drama the choral song is the

most musical, harmonious element, and that the actors' monologues
and dialogues provide a discordant note against the choral background. The reason for this is not just that the chorus's role is to
transmit the moral religious tradition and thus to sing harmoniously
of the universal, the conventional, the common bonds of all mankind; as we have seen, the actors no less than the chorus accept
these as binding. What allows the chorus to remain in unison with
the whole of things and harmonious with the law is that its members do not stand out, i.e., do not try to act on their own. It is
action that splits the world into discordant, warring parts and disturbs its harmony. That is why the actor's voice is *eo ipso* unmusical
and grating; it is the actor's role to grate against the whole and to
be crushed by it to the accompaniment of the "unmusical song"
of the Erinyes. While the Whole is still affirmed and redeemed in
the drama, the separated individual pays the price of this affirmation
in inevitable, unmusical suffering.

Aeschylus' introduction of the single actor standing on his own
parallels Adam's fall and expulsion from the garden of Eden. Indeed, guilt, fall, and expulsion are one and the same thing here.
Man's guilt consists precisely of being an individual out of tune
with the whole, and his being cast out is not the consequence of his
corruption but is synonymous with it. If, as Latte says, the Greek
words for pollution *"hagos, miasma, mysos,* refer to that state of
being that separates man from his fellow beings,"[23] then pollution
and being an individual separated from others, fallen out of the
security of the universal, are one and the same thing. The individual
with his personal claims and aspirations, that are destructive if not
to the unity of the moral order at least to the individual himself,
is necessarily sick and polluted: he is a discordant, disease-carrying
part of the whole who will perish of his own corruption—that of
being an individual. That is what the creation of the actor symbolizes: the outcastness of man, his ecstatic (standing-out) projection
into a world that is for him no fit place to live in.[24]

Solon warned against blaming the gods for men's misfortunes, and the Aeschylean chorus half-heartedly echoes his warning: it is not the jealousy of the gods but man's own crime that causes his downfall (*Ag.* 750–62). Yet Aeschylus not only cannot help attributing jealousy to the gods on occasion,[25] but in the *Agamemnon* and the *Choephoroi* he makes the operation of "divine jealousy" a natural result of man's crime and crime itself a necessary part of being a man. For whoever stands out, above and apart from the ordinary run of men—as the individual actors do—is automatically crushed here by divine-natural law. It takes no special resolution on the part of the Erinyes to destroy the preeminent; like a storm or other natural force they fall upon and level not the lowly but those who stand out. Nor is standing out a special act of crime on the part of the individuals; it is their natural crime, their ontological hybris of being above and greater than others, it is their natural state of "outrage," of exceeding beyond the indistinguishable mass and common measure. Merely to be a separate, noticeable, active individual is hybris, pollution, excess, and crime. The Aeschylean introduction of the actor on the stage provides a vehicle for expressing this insight.

It is important to note, however, that for all his emphasis on the actor Aeschylus curtails but does not abolish the chorus. The chorus remains as background, context, and contrast to the actor; it is at once that from which the individual actor stands out—by virtue of his action—and that to which he belongs—by virtue of the common bonds individual and society share. Actor and chorus are not just paratactically brought together in Aeschylean drama; they are interdependent. This is what makes the dramatic conflict so grievous, that for all his separateness the individual agent is powerless to break or even deny the bonds that tie him to his fellow men. And this is what makes both actor and chorus in their dramatic, i.e., estranged-involved, confrontation necessary devices for the presentation of Aeschylus' tragic view of human action and life.

Speaking of the common bonds actor and chorus share brings us to a consideration of the other major dramatic "innovation" of

Aeschylus: his turn or return in his mature plays to traditional (Homeric) themes. Although Aeschylus was not altogether innovative in his use of myth material—the dithyramb already had some non-Dionysian myth content and so did perhaps some of Thespis' and Phrynichus' plays—he once again extended and capitalized on former usage. And his concentration on Homeric myth was crucial for the development of tragic drama for a number of closely connected reasons.

Historically, the status of Homeric myth in fifth-century Greece was as ambiguous and full of tension as was the estranged-involved confrontation of actors and chorus on the stage: myth was at once affirmed and contested, alive and threatened, unifying and divisive. To a large extent it still supplied the common ground of belief on which all members of the audience in the communal theater could meet; at the same time the ground was an embattled one on which no untroubled and altogether harmonious meeting of minds could take place. On the one hand myth still defined to a large extent the common man's conception of what it meant to be a man, it still prescribed the all-important parameters within which most people were conscious of living, it was still the sacred, i.e., very real, history that sustained and informed the average Athenian's life. On the other, myth had come under increasingly vehement attack by the poets and thinkers in the course of the last few centuries. Even if these exceptional individuals' explicit criticism of the Homeric view of men and gods did not quite penetrate to the public consciousness and could not quite shake the common man's beliefs, their gradual abandonment of myth as a vehicle for expressing timeless truths obscured these beliefs and made them less and less useful for the guidance of everyday life. By leaving myth behind, the post-Homeric writers left the people behind unguided. By allowing myth to decay without replacing it with something the common man could understand, they relegated the average Athenian to a kind of spiritual limbo, living with blurred insights, deeply felt but dimly understood truths, and a very unclear orientation and precarious foothold in the world.

But this means that historically myth itself was in crisis, or, what is the same, that the Athenians themselves were going through a crisis of belief with respect to traditional myth, and this is what made myth, the ground of this crisis, a natural subject for Aeschylean drama. Aeschylus merely crystallized and brought to the public consciousness what was in fact taking place in Athenian spiritual life. Such is the correspondence between the very structure of Aeschylean drama and the historical situation of myth in fifth-century Greece that it is pointless to try to decide whether Aeschylus created drama in order to dramatize the ongoing historical drama, or having conceived of the new dramatic form found myth the most appropriate subject for it. Greek drama was communal theater, and myth was the communal ground of belief. Drama is a representation of conflict, of crucial turning points in the lives of individuals, families, or nations, and myth was historically in conflict, it was at the most dangerous turning point in its career. What makes drama dramatic is that it deals with critical moments in which all is thrown into the balance, everything is at stake, the whole of the past has to be weighed and the whole of the future is to be decided by some great act or judgment now. And this was precisely the historical situation of the Athenian polis with respect to myth: with myth at stake everything was at stake, with myth saved or overcome the whole nation would be saved and given new directions presumably forever.

But tragic drama not only originates in spiritual transition and conflict; its origin also sets it its task. To be truly functional, it must not only dramatize but also seek to resolve the crisis of belief in which it originates. Therefore Aeschylus could not merely reenact traditional myth; he had to reinterpret and clarify it. He could not merely put on stage the moral-religious disorientation of his audience and leave it at that; he had to provide a new orientation by providing new bearings for conduct and a clearer direction for life. What the oral poet did unconsciously Aeschylus had to perform with deliberate intent: he had to recreate and transform old myths in accordance with present needs, readjust the old paradigms to the new context, and assimilate new experience to old belief. And since he had to perform this task consciously, he was also faced with alternatives: he could either infuse the old myths with new meaning and exhibit the old necessities in a way that would show them still valid in the contemporary situation, or, if he thought the old beliefs past saving and incapable of being updated, he could publicly exhibit their shortcomings and create new paradigms to help people leave the mythical ones behind once and for all.

As we shall see later, Aeschylus attempted to do both of these things at once, blending tradition and reform in the *Oresteia* with somewhat paradoxical results. For the moment we are dealing mainly with the *Agamemnon* and the *Choephoroi,* the two plays in which Aeschylus seems to be more concerned with revitalizing than with overcoming myth, and in this connection it is appropriate to point to one further characteristic of myth that made it peculiarly well-suited to provide content for these plays.

The writing down of myth—that which ultimately imperiled its existence—gave it a fixity and rigidity it never had during its oral transmission. This fixity of myth not only gave the playwright a convenient structure on which to hang his tale, but above all it provided him with a framework of *necessity* within which to place the individual actor. For the purposes of the dramatist Homeric myth was the *given,* that which had been laid down once and for all and was in its basic outline impervious to reform. Though unsupported by reason and obscured by the post-Homeric writers' neglect, myth still stubbornly resisted change, and as such the mythical story itself had the structural characteristic of its peculiarly Aeschylean content, dark fate: that which limited individual effort and yet determined its outcome.

It is not accidental that the myths Greek tragedy drew on were largely stories of adverse fate and inevitable doom. Their content was the only kind that agreed materially with those formal characteristics of myth which made myth especially serviceable to Aeschylus in the *Agamemnon* and the *Choephoroi:* immutability, necessity, and a kind of chthonic resistance to rational explanation and reform by self-conscious individuals. Thus both formally and materially myth supplied, as it were, a sustaining-frustrating element in drama: a type or preëstablished pattern that could be neither understood nor bent to human purpose and yet would carry all to completion; something sacred and untouchable that animated the race yet took no account of the enlightened individual's aspirations. Formally, materially, as well as historically, myth was at once life-giving and constricting, sheltering and imprisoning, guiding and obstructing, and elevating and humbling on stage and in real life.

That is why Aeschylus' seemingly negligible dramatic innovations—his increasing the number of actors and his turn to myth—made him a creator of tragedy. For what we still call "tragic" is irreconcilable conflict between individual aspiration and a limiting power, be that adverse fate, jealous gods, hostile society, historical law, the way of the world, or the immutable order of things. Such conflict is possible only on a stage where we have individual actors subjectively detached from and consciously confronting yet objectively involved in and inescapably driven by inevitable necessity. And Aeschylus gave us that stage.

On this stage we have, for the first time, such a thing as tragic irony. The discrepancy between the actors' and the audience's perspective—the audience's knowledge and the actors' ignorance of what is to happen—makes the actors' pronouncements incongruous with the audience's expectations and gives them an added dimension beyond the actors' own plane of vision. While such a dimensional twist can be achieved in nonmythical drama too, in myth-using drama the clash of incongruous points of view simultaneously entertained is present almost without the playwright's explicit design. Myth as the "foreseen (by the audience)—unforeseen (by the actors)" already sets the stage for tragic irony; all the author needs to do is to exploit the possibilities provided for it by the myth-actor dichotomy.

It would be pointless to try to determine whether Aeschylus' dramatic innnovations influenced the temporal framework of the *Agamemnon* and the *Choephoroi,* or if it was rather Aeschylus' sense of time that made his use of actors proper and of myth-material necessary. It is worth noting, however, that Aeschylus' dramatic innovations and his sense of time are in thorough harmony.

The actor's *ti draso?* (what am I to do?) expresses his sense of the openness of a future that hangs in the balance in the irretrievable moment; it is a teleological question concentrated on the present and directed toward the future. But myth, the story written in a distant past, limits this openness by predetermining the final outcome and excluding anything really novel from the processes slowly unfolding in the play. The teleology of myth is that of a closed future, of a predetermined *telos:* "What is to come will come" (*Ag.* 1240), "doom waits overlong . . . and then it arrives" (*Cho.* 464–5). With the plot fixed it is only a matter of time till "Zeus the Fulfiller fulfills" (*Ag.* 973) what has been long ripening in the womb of time. The combined teleologies of the actor's "what am I to do?" and the myth's "what is to come will come" together provide the two polar elements—consciousness of critical moment and timeless necessity—whose tension is so characteristic of the structure of time in tragic drama. It is these two teleologies in fact which make tragedy tragic: the incongruity between the time-perspective of myth and the time-perspective of the actor is what necessarily frustrates the actor's expectations, disappoints his hopes, and makes his efforts futile. Were there no essential difference and opposition between the two perspectives, the actor either could not act, since he would know in advance the hopelessness of his action, or his action, now harmonious with the whole of things, would be totally wholesome and untragic.

Finley called Aeschylus "the inventor of the idea of meaningful time" [26] and there is much to be said in favor of such appraisal. Drama as a gradually unfolding temporal performance has its very existence in time, and the actor's and the audience's time-perspectives together mirror all our experiences of time: our consciousness of the critical moment as well as our awareness of timeless pattern and of the entanglement of past, present, and future. The combination of the actor's teleology—seeking individual self-determination —and that of myth—predetermining individual action—in fact represents the human agent's historical situaiton: the agent always finds himself in the midst of a historical tradition which has to a large extent formed and informed him and provides direction as well as limits to his action. The actor is always ahead of himself (negates the present and looks forward to a better future) and at the same time always too late for controlling his future (since he is fatefully entangled in his own race's and nation's past). He is conscious of freedom of action, and yet his freedom is to a large extent illusory. Aeschylean drama, with all its temporal ramifications, is successful because its structure reflects that of man's temporal-historical existence.

There is, however, a further consideration that must be mentioned here. While it is true that Aeschylean drama faithfully mirrors "meaningful time," the lived time of the human agent, it is also true that in the *Agamemnon* and the *Choephoroi,* taken out of the context of the trilogy as a whole, the significance of time is underplayed even while the tension between the critical moment and the slow unfolding of predetermined events keeps the plays going.

Consider the peculiarity of Aeschylus' treatment of time-intervals: long periods of time are frequently compressed and presented as if they elapsed in a matter of hours or even minutes, and short periods are often extended to inordinate lengths during which time seems to stand still and no action takes place. The fact is that Aeschylus can disregard the actual duration of time and expand and contract time-intervals at will because the passing of time is of little significance in the *Agamemnon* and the *Choephoroi.* What these plays deal with—blood pollution, or the condition of man governed by chthonic law—is unaffected by time. Time's passing of itself does not dilute, let alone erase, the indelible stain of spilt blood, nor does it alter the human condition in such a way that individuals succeeding each other ever find themselves in situations significantly different from those of their predecessors. Since there is no significant change here, it is of no consequence whether little or much time has actually passed between the events or lives enacted on the stage.

This seems to put the emphasis on the individual actors and acts themselves, since only actual blood deeds—and not time's passing—can purify the atmosphere polluted by blood deeds, and, in any case, regardless of what has passed and what will follow, the individual still has to act and live his ephemeral life now or never. But this is merely the individual actor's fond hope based on his own narrow time-perspective. In effect the single moments of action that punctuate the passing of time are as insignificant as the passing of time itself.

The watchman, weary of his long and painful task, waits for the moment that will bring release. The flaring beacon pierces the night, the long-awaited moment has come—and yet it brings no release; it marks, at best, the beginning of a new period of waiting. The critical moment did not turn out to be so critical after all. Its coming did not lift the darkness that enveloped the house. And the same is true of all crises succeeding one another in these plays. They come and go but they change nothing; pollution remains as before. It is only passed on from one carrier to another, like Clytemnestra's signal flame passing from peak to peak, the selfsame fire burning "both first and last" on Ida and the Argive roof (*Ag.* 281–314). As each protagonist reenacts the selfsame role and has his own critical moment, our sense of having seen it all before merely increases.

It is this devaluation of both the critical moment and the duration and passing of time that gives the *Agamemnon* and the *Choephoroi* that almost nontemporal aspect that we had occasion to note before.[27] Since all acts are repetitions, as it were, of the same act, and all actors almost interchangeable performers of a quasi-ritual deed, their before- and after-relationship is in the end insignificant. As variations on a theme acts and agents are moments that are of importance not in themselves but as rhythmical beats in an ever on-going flow that is vibrant and pulsating but essentially unchanging and without clear beginning or end.

One stylistic feature of Aeschylean drama might be mentioned in this connection: the prevalence of bold metaphors in Aeschylus' plays. Aeschylus' fondness for metaphors is easy to understand if we keep in mind that the metaphor as a poetic device has close structural similarities with the view of man, world, and time that Aeschylus presents in the *Agamemnon* and the *Choephoroi*.

As in a metaphor the interacting elements both lose and retain their individual characteristics and are both impoverished and enriched by their being brought together, so in the *Agamemnon* and the *Choephoroi* the interacting protagonists are both less and more than just the individuals they might be outside the context in which Aeschylus presents them as necessarily involved.

A metaphor, unlike the simile which likens things while keeping them apart, fuses things. Yet its fusion is not simple identification; it is a fusion of what is dissimilar, often even incompatible. Thus a metaphor is a paradoxical fusion of terms, it is a nonliteral transference that introduces tension and conflict even while it unites what is disparate. In this the metaphor mirrors structurally the actor-chorus, individual-race, man-fate, unity-dichotomy that is the subject of the *Agamemnon* and the *Choephoroi*.

A metaphor, fusing disparate things, creates a conceptual, emotional, and sensuous ambiguity of meaning that enriches our response while making it difficult for us to tell what exactly we are responding to. Such fusion, confusion, and entanglement of meaning and response clearly parallels and thus is a means for conveying the fusion and entanglement of acts, agents, race, and doom that Aeschylus puts on the stage in these plays.

The Aristophanic Euripides complained about Aeschylus' obscurity: "Why he is obscure even when he talks about facts" (Aristophanes, *Frogs* 1122). But the point is that Aeschylus never really talks about concrete facts as such; his facts are nonliteral and equivocal; they are symbols for what is never itself a fact and allusions to what is not and cannot be directly brought into the play. Taken as facts on their own they would not express the essential, and that is why their metaphoric-symbolic obscurity is designed to prevent us from taking them at face value, from letting the mask obscure the underlying meaning.

Aeschylus' technique closely resembles that of Heracleitus here and is adopted for much the same reason. "The obscurity of both was that of condensation—a pregnant obscurity. . . . We always feel that Aeschylus thought more than he expressed, that his desperate compounds are never affected or unnecessary." [28] His metaphors combine what is seemingly far apart, his much ridiculed compounds unite what is normally seen as separate; his long, involved sentences and allusive, half-finished lines are stylistic devices for expressing the fusion and entanglement of things and the fragmentary, half-finished nature of all that is isolated out of the whole. His puns, like Heracleitus', serve the same purpose: they prevent one-dimensional, superficial understanding. Compressing several, often contrary, meanings into one word, they reveal the antinomical nature of things. (Helen, the epitome of beauty and desirability, is *helenas, helandros, heleptolis,* the destroyer of ships, men, and cities; Apollo, the healer and savior, is *apollon,* the destroyer). It is, after all, this ambiguous and antinomical aspect of things that inspires the chorus with the holy-unholy fear which is in its turn so well expressed stylistically in Aeschylus' hurried, breathless transitions, half-complete sentences, impatient piling up of adjectives, jarring syntax, wild, harsh, barbarous, grating sounds and at times almost inarticulate articulation.

One last word on metaphor. In considering the Homeric simile we have seen that its function was symbolic fixation: the simile established clear and precise meaning; it separated individual forms even while it brought them together so that we could see each better as a well-defined, almost atomic unity. In contrast to this paratactic definition and delimitation of terms the metaphor has the function of synthetizing, fusing what has been set apart. By employing terms outside and contrary to their customary use, it initially disturbs rather than clarifies our linguistic conventions. A metaphor is a device not of symbolic fixation but of expansion of meaning. It simultaneously presupposes and violates literal connotation in order to infuse the old word with new meaning, open up hitherto unapprehended relations of things for our experience and thus enrich and widen the scope of both our language and world.

In thus widening and revitalizing old fixities the metaphor performs the same function stylistically that Aeschylus' revitalizing and reinterpreting Homeric myth performed in terms of content. As Aeschylus transferred the old myth unto a contemporary stage and infused it with a new meaning, so his metaphors transfer old terms into a new context and thereby deepen them. Reappropriation of myth and reanimation of language are but different aspects of the same thing; parallel tasks undertaken for the same reason. As the old myths had lost most of their power and freshness by being taken for granted and becoming too familiar to be really seen and experienced in a vital way, so the old words had lost much of their vitality and power in and through customary use; both had to be reinterpreted: not because Aeschylus was a self-willed innovator bent on originality at any price, but because the old myths and terms had become so problematic through careless use that it was a question whether they still meant enough to carry the burden they had to bear in the contemporary world. Aeschylus had to re-create, reform, reanimate words because he had to revitalize a whole spiritual tradition that was in danger of disintegrating by virtue of its easy familiarity and its concomitant disuse and abuse. He had to superimpose new meaning on old words because he was attempting to superimpose a new vision on an old and to some extent outworn world-view.

This is not to say, of course, that all these considerations were explicitly taken into account by Aeschylus as he set out to refashion both the language and the moral vision of Athens. Aeschylus was a poet rather than a moral philosopher or aesthetician. Still as a poet, and possibly "without knowing why," [29] he adopted the language suitable to his message and this is all that needs to be emphasized. His metaphors were a linguistic counterpart to his moral-educational design and were thus a thoroughly adequate device for expressing what he wanted to say.

The same parallelism obtains between Aeschylus' message and his use of dominant images in the *Agamemnon* and the *Choephoroi*. Dominant images merely convey, insist on, and continually remind us of the dominant theme. Since one theme is predominant in these two plays, it is the absence rather than presence of a dominant image and ever recurring metaphor that should surprise us.

The dominant image of the *Oresteia* is that of a net, web, or finely woven robe that fatally constricts the person or animal entangled in it. This image appears as a constant reminder of the main theme in all three plays.

In the *Agamemnon,* beside the real net or robe thrown over Agamemnon in his bath, there is the figurative net Night cast over Troy (358) so that no man should escape the metaphoric "net of slavery" (360–61); the fish-net Agamemnon's body pierced through and through resembles if all that rumor says is true (868); the "hunting net of fate" (1048) the chorus sees Cassandra caught in like a captured beast (1063, 1065); the "net of death" Cassandra seems to see (1115); and the "net bedded with" Agamemnon that she calls Clytemnestra (1116). So that Agamemnon could not overleap the "hunting-net of misery" (1375) Clytemnestra "cast around him like an endless net . . . an evil wealth of robes" (1382–83), and finally the chorus beholds him "lying in this spider's web, gasping out his life in obscene death" (1492–93), and Aegisthus rejoices over him as he lies wrapped "in the robe woven by the Erinyes" (1580), caught in the "net of justice" (1611).

In the *Choephoroi* real and figurative nets appear with lesser frequency (492, 494, 506, 980, 1015), for by now the theme is so well established that the lightest touch on the metaphoric chord creates strong, instant, and lasting resonance. That the "murderous web" stands for the web of fate which slowly strangles the protagonists, the iron framework of necessity which frustrates their individual designs, the interwoven lines of guilt which cannot be unravelled, the entanglement of events which cannot be put in a single linear order of causation—all that is too patent by now.

By the time the Erinyes' net makes its final appearances at the beginning of the *Eumenides* (111–113, 147), the image has almost become a net itself thrown over the trilogy to hold its parts together; its interwoven threads have been woven into the fabric of the plays to give them like texture and unity.[30] Then suddenly the net metaphor disappears because the snares of the blood-law itself are cut by Athene and man is released from his tragic bondage. Since at this point the dominant theme itself is abandoned or reversed, the dominant image has to be dropped too. It is time now to deal with this reversal.

* * * * * *

At the end of the *Choephoroi* Orestes exists pursued by the avenging Erinyes, and the chorus, confused—"shall I call him savior or doom?" (1073–74)—and oppressed by what it has witnessed, cries out in despair: "When will it ever end? When will the wrath of destruction, laid to rest, ever cease?" (1075–76). The last play of the trilogy presents Aeschylus' answer to this question.

In the first scene of the *Eumenides* the priestess of Apollo, entering the god's shrine, recoils with horror at the sight of bloodstained Orestes and his loathsome pursuers. This recoils characterizes the whole play which develops into an agon between the Erinyes as representatives of the old law and Apollo and Athene as the new, gentle deities whose ultimate victory signals the dawn of a new order. This recoil expresses, at the same time, Aeschylus' own emotional and intellectual attitude toward chthonic justice. An order that so manifestly leads to ruin must not be affirmed. It has to be replaced by something more humane. Men have to be brought from infernal darkness to light. The law of pollution that is itself a source of pollution must be purified, its curse must finally be lifted from the race of men. This is the program of the *Eumenides,* a program that is, unfortunately, a great deal easier to conceive than to execute.

The first essential step toward the execution of this program in the *Eumenides* is Athene's institution of a law court to deal with matters of blood-pollution. In the *Agamemnon* and the *Choephoroi* blood-guilt was an objective fact, and those polluted were pursued by the Erinyes automatically, without any deliberation or judgment on their part. Now Athene suddenly establishes "a court to endure forever" (*Eum.* 485) to hold "the first trial ever held for bloodshed" (*Eum.* 682). By this act crime and criminal are lifted above the dark sphere of natural retributive justice and become subject to rational deliberative judgment.

From the point of view of the Erinyes, this is an extremely highhanded procedure that prejudges their case which is precisely that no judgment is necessary and no court can have jurisdiction in matters of blood-pollution. Nevertheless, the Erinyes present their case against Orestes and Apollo quite reasonably. Their position is as simple as it is legally unassailable. They stand for ancient *moira* and *dike,* and with them, they claim, *moira* and *dike* stand or fall (*Eum.* 490–565). It is their function to pursue all transgressors of the blood-law, and Apollo, interfering with the execution of their office, is nothing but a criminal himself in terms of the law, a transgressor against them and against *moira,* the inviolable allocation of portions. In shielding the polluted, "he polluted his own sanctuary . . . honoring mortal things above the law of the gods and destroying the ancient apportionment (*moirai*) of power" (*Eum.* 169–72).

The antagonism between the Erinyes and Apollo that develops in the *Eumenides* is something new in the trilogy. In the *Agamemnon* and the *Choephoroi,* Zeus, Apollo, the gods, Fate, and the Erinyes worked hand in hand. They represented one single force and one single set of law—however antinomical this might be in its effect on and execution by men. Now suddenly we are confronted with two opposing forces in the realm of the divine and two sets of law in conflict; instead of mortal antagonists tearing at each other and paying the price of maintaining the balanced operation of the law, the gods themselves are turned against one another and are threatened with grievous loss (of function and power).

The divine conflict is as bitter as were the preceding human ones and it seems to open up an unbridgeable gulf between the chthonic and the Olympian deities. Apollo reviles the Erinyes: "loathsome maidens with whom no god, no man, no beast consorts. Born of evil, inhabiting the evil gloom of hell below the earth, creatures hateful to men and the Olympian gods" (*Eum.* 68–72; also 185–197). In return the Erinyes call him "a son of god no better than a thief" (*Eum.* 149), a youth who has "ridden down the old divinities" (*Eum.* 150), one of the upstart gods "who rule altogether beyond Dike" (*Eum.* 162–63), and ask outraged, "what is there in all this that anyone can call just?" (*Eum.* 154).

This opposition between the old and the new, the chthonic and the Olympian deities, is quite reminiscent of the opposition between fate and the gods in Homer, and the terms in which the Erinyes argue their case make this evident: "Seek not to make an end of our functions (*timas*)" (*Eum.* 227), for this is what has been assigned to us by *moira* to hold forever (*Eum.* 208, 334 ff.). Since our allotted portion, honor, and office (*moira, time, laches*) is to pursue the polluted, i.e., to be *moira's* executors, no god can hinder us, "no immortal lay a hand on us nor share our feasts" (*Eum.* 349–51). "Since Zeus has judged our blood-reeking tribe hateful, unworthy, and outcast" (*Eum.* 365–66) "the gods have no authority over our concerns, nor can we ever come before them for trial" (*Eum.* 361–62). For we are "straight and just" (*Eum.* 312), while the gods, interfering with our work, trample justice underfoot.

Thus the trial begins as an acknowledged contest between the old *moira*—the *Agamemnon*'s and the *Choephoroi*'s blood-law—and the new gods. It ends with the triumph of the new order and the conversion of the Erinyes from outraged guardians of the old law—"now is the house of Justice falling" (*Eum.* 515–16)—into tame spirits blissfully chanting in a Hesiodic-Solonic vein. "May discord, insatiate of ill, never rage in our city, for this I pray; nor ashes drink the black blood of the citizens, nor, through wild passion for revenge and mutual slaughter, may ruin seize the state. Rather may they return joy for joy in a spirit of mutual love, and may they hate with one mind; for that is the cure for many mortal ills" (*Eum.* 976–87). With the conversion of the Erinyes into Eumenides the rift between the gods is healed, and "all-seeing Zeus and Moira have come down together" (1045–46) in support of the same cause, the cause of civil justice.

So far, the Aeschylean program executed in the *Eumenides* is but the culmination of the Hesiodic-Solonic reform. Hesiod was the first to insist on law courts and legal arbitration as the only alternatives to the rule of violence. Now Aeschylus incorporates in his play the founding of the Areopagus and the first court trial that is presided over by Athene, the peaceful, rational counterpart of the *Agamemnon*'s demonic-irrational Peitho. Solon and Heracleitus declared lawfulness to be the savior and laws to be the foundation of the city. Aeschylus now points to civic law as that force which alone can save mankind from the doom exhibited in the *Agamemnon* and the *Choephoroi* and insists on the retention of a holy fear of the divine-rational law as a substitute for the unholy terror inspired by irrational retributive justice. Solon had secularized and humanized the role of Dike. Now, the Aeschylean Athene, instead of judging the case by herself, merely arbitrates and indicates by her foundation of a human court that the salvation of the city must come from man himself, from civic laws and institutions rather than the intervention of the gods above and below. At the same time it is Athene herself who assumes Solon's role of mediator and reconciler and thus lends divine sanction to rational human judgment.

Hesiod, Solon, Xenophanes, and Heracleitus were historically conscious individuals. In this respect, too, Aeschylus follows and even surpasses them in the *Eumenides,* a play that dramatizes the process of historical change by staging an occasion when mankind takes a most important step in the evolution of civilization. This historicity of the trilogy, however, creates great difficulties for Aeschylus as thinker as well as playwright.

It is one thing to dramatize historical change and quite another to justify it. But what is explicitly presented as novel, and thus unsanctioned by tradition and time, requires justification. It is one thing to abandon Homeric myth, the story that gave a framework of necessity to the dramatic events, and attempt to write history. But it is quite another to give events lacking mythical support an appearance of necessity in the play. And Aeschylus' insufficient awareness of these requirements makes him incapable of providing a dramatically and intellectually convincing solution in the *Eumenides* to the problems of the *Agamemnon* and the *Choephoroi.* This leaves the transition from the first two plays to the last abrupt, artificial, and full of difficulties.

At the trial of Orestes the partisans of the new order confront the Erinyes' perfectly good legal case with such trivial, sophistic, and biassed arguments, coupled with bribery and threats, that prima facie the trial which marks the beginning of the new judicial order seems rather a parody of legal proceedings and a travesty of justice. While this does not mean that Aeschylus is insincere in his advocacy of the new order, it is an indication that he is aiming at something he devoutly wishes for but cannot quite justify rationally.

A consideration of the actual arguments Apollo and Athene advance against the Erinyes' claim should reveal the paradoxical position of Aeschylus in the *Eumenides*.

Besides reviling the Erinyes on general grounds, Apollo holds Orestes' murder of his mother excusable on two counts. In the first place, Clytemnestra deserved to die because, though not tied to Agamemnon by blood, she was tied to him by marriage, and this bond she broke. But this bond, "the bed of man and wife, is stronger than an oath and is guarded by justice" (*Eum.* 217–18). In the second place, Orestes' deed creates no new blood-pollution while his failure to avenge Agamemnon would leave the old pollution unpurified, because "the mother is not parent of her so-called child but only the nurse of the new-implanted growth. The parent is he who impregnates, while she, a stranger, merely safeguards a stranger's seed" (*Eum.* 558–61). In witness of the fact that one can become a father even without the cooperation of a mother Apollo cites Athene's case. And Athene, concurring, casts her vote for Orestes. "For no mother gave me birth, and in all things save marriage I am my father's child indeed with all my heart. Therefore I shall not hold of higher worth a woman who killed her husband, the master of her house" (Eum. 736–740).

Contrary to first impressions, this devaluation of the female line relative to the male, and of blood ties relative to civil ones, is neither mere sophistry nor simply an expression of Apollo's and Athene's natural prejudices. Chthonic law—the law of blood, kinship, family, tribe—and the guardians and executors of this law have always been associated in tradition with the female sex. In addition, the female—passionate, emotional, unthinking—has ever been associated with the irrational and the male with the rational principle. Therefore the subordination of woman to man to a large extent symbolizes the passing of the old irrational order and the institution of the new rational one that is the subject of the *Eumenides*. The opposition of Clytemnestra and Agamemnon-Orestes as female and male is not presented for its own sake but is symbolic of the opposition between the deities of the underworld and the gods above, the daughters of the Night and the children of the light, tribal darkness and civic enlightenment, emotional-animalistic-unthinking-natural retribution and intelligent-humane-civilized-spiritual arbitration. The shift in emphasis from the female to the male principle simply parallels the shift from blood ties to civic institutions and is thus both symbolic of and thoroughly in line with Aeschylus' program in the *Eumenides*.

On this point the sincerity of Aeschylus cannot be doubted. Far from being sophistic or satirical, he was convinced of the need for reform, and he carried out his program with such singleminded dedication in the *Eumenides* that the trilogy which began in darkness, tension, and conflict ends in the bright sunshine of amity, harmony, and peace. All-seeing Zeus and Moira are at last reconciled. The old opponents, moira and the gods, join hands. "Let all join our triumphant song" (*Eum.* 1045–47).

Since in the Hesiodic-Solonic-Xenophanean reform the gods have been reduced to little more than symbolic representatives and guardians of the law, this reconciliation is but the continuation of that reform and should, as such, present no problems. Nevertheless it does. For in the *Oresteia* Aeschylus has gone further than either Hesiod or Solon, and, instead of merely affirming the rule of justice and the inevitability of punishment for transgression, he has presented not one but two sets of law, diametrically opposed to each other. Because of this, a simple affirmation of one of them, no matter how sincere, cannot effect a lasting reconciliation, and the sudden and arbitrary shift of emphasis from one to the other creates more problems than it solves.

Given two sets of laws, what guarantees the triumph of one over the other? The *Agamemnon* and the *Choephoroi* made it clear that the old laws do not at all function as men might wish them to; that they bring misery rather than joy, and damn rather than save men. But what warrant has man for thinking that they are therefore unsanctioned and unauthoritative; that because they are objectionable to men they are any less real and inevitable? Aeschylus gives no answer.

We encountered two sets of law in Heracleitus—one divine, the other human—but far from being opposed, the laws of the city were founded on and nourished by the one divine law. Now in Aeschylus the two are in conflict, and, what is more, chthonic justice seems to be sanctioned by nature as well as tradition, which leaves the new laws of civic arbitration seemingly unsanctioned by either nature or tradition. If so, what is the ground of these new laws, what determines their goodness, and how is the opposition between nature and convention to be reconciled?

That this opposition is not merely incidental in the *Oresteia* becomes clear if we consider that even the individual motivating forces which reinforce chthonic law in the *Agamemnon* and the *Choephoroi* are entirely natural. Agamemnon's hunger for power, his greed and pride; Clytemnestra's grief at the death of Iphigenia, her anger at being deserted for ten years for another woman's sake, her resentment of Cassandra; Aegisthus' lust, greed, and thirst for revenge; Orestes' and Electra's hate for their father's murderers, anger at their own mistreatment, and desire for their rightful inheritance—all these are forces in human nature as the Greeks well knew long before Aeschylus. In contrast, the *Eumenides'* deus-ex-machina solution seems not only arbitrary but also one that implies that natural motives, unrestrained emotion, instinct, and desire must be curbed under the new law. Here again, natural and artificial law are opposed without any clear indication as to what governs the artifice. If nature is to be tempered by art, what will temper the art itself? If the new form is cut off from the old substance, what guarantees that it will be anything but unsubstantial and groundless? Aeschylus gives no answer.

A law, if it is to serve as a principle of arbitration, must endure. Solon and Aeschylus, deeply aware of this, warn against change. But if tradition is done away with and nature opposed, if, as the *Eumenides* shows, laws can be changed at will, what will make any law last even for a short time, and what will prevent a change so rapid as to be no better than the state of anarchy our reformers, Aeschylus included, so earnestly warn against? We find no solutions to these problems in the *Oresteia.*

This is not to say, of course, that Aeschylus, the inheritor of Hesiodic-Solonic reform, is not on the right track in his attempt to replace the old, irrational Peitho of the *Agamemnon* and the *Choephoroi* with a new one exemplified in Athene, the embodiment of rational persuasion. The only force that can save man from the rule of the blood-law is undoubtedly the force of critical, reflective reason. But the problem is that in Aeschylus' time this redemptive force, the force of a truly rational argument, had not yet developed to the point where it was equal to this task. This is witnessed not only by the manner in which the defenders of the new order argue against the Erinyes in the *Eumenides*. Even Aeschylus' younger contemporaries, the Sophists, whose argumentative skills far surpassed that of Aeschylus, failed to develop reasoning to the point where it could prevent turning Athene's "holy persuasion" into something quite unholy; a tool that, for all its opposition to brute force, became very much an irrational force itself. Wittingly and unwittingly the later Sophists demonstrated what Aeschylus himself did not clearly see, i.e., that unless human judgment is truly rational, human courts can corrupt the city just as much as the operation of the old law polluted it, and civic laws can be just as perverse and ruinous as was chthonic law.

But Aeschylus was not aware of these dangers, and, had he been, he might still not have known how to counter them any more than the Sophists did. And so the *Eumenides'* solution to the *Agamemnon*'s and the *Choephoroi*'s problem remains not only arbitrary and artificial but also internally incoherent. While Athene blithely innovates, she warns against innovation and wants her own institutions to endure forever (*Eum.* 681–84). While she turns the Erinyes into benevolent spirits and does her best to undermine the age-old fear of the blood-law, she counsels men to fear and reverence the new one; for all her rationalization of justice she still can give it no better support than the old irrational emotions of *sebas* and *phobos*.

Since the intellectual tools for supporting and safeguarding the Aeschylean reform and mediating between nature and convention were not yet available to Aeschylus, he should not be blamed, perhaps, for failing to solve the philosophical problems inherent in his work. That as a man of his time he gave expression to the problems of his time might be achievement enough. Nevertheless one cannot altogether excuse Aeschylus by arguing that as a poet he was not even required to solve these problems by discursive reasoning. For the shortcomings of the *Eumenides* are not merely intellectual, they are also artistic shortcomings. The two are, in the end, inseparable. A brief consideration of the stylistic and dramatic shift from the *Agamemnon* and the *Choephoroi* to the *Eumenides* may help to show this.

With Orestes' arrival in Athens the net metaphor disappears from the *Eumenides*. This disappearance is not incidental; the symbolic net—of fate, blood-law, adverse irrational necessity—for which the metaphor stood is itself abruptly severed by Athene's judgment. But this creates a dramatic problem: Athene's Gordian solution does away with more than a mere recurrent image; it severs that which gave the trilogy continuity and coherence. Cutting the thread of necessity that tied all later developments to what went on before, parting the lifeline that connected the plays organically, it destroys to some extent the artistic unity of the trilogy.

This can be observed in other ways too. In the *Eumenides* the the myth material suddenly disappears and Aeschylus invents more freely than in any of the preceding plays. But since myth had supplied the framework of necessity, the unchangeable given that provided firm structure for the drama in the *Agamemnon* and the *Choephoroi,* Aeschylus' abandonment of myth also results, to a large extent, in relinquishing dramatic necessity. The *Eumenides* contains no more predetermined structure, and events have a character of arbitrariness that is not equalled by anything in the preceeding plays. With myth gone and free invention rampant, things no longer have a soil to grow from organically and events are no longer a process of slow but inevitable unfolding. Nothing now seems to have been nurtured in the womb of time. Freedom from myth creates a freedom from necessity, and Aeschylus does not know how to cope with such freedom dramatically. This leaves the *Eumenides* dramatically as well as intellectually incoherent and unconvincing.

Even Aeschylus' introduction of the actor proper, which is not relinquished in the *Eumenides,* suffers in consequence of the dramatic-intellectual shift. In the first two plays, the actor, playing his myth-decreed role and perishing under the dictates of an alien, incomprehensible necessity, was to a large extent a mere mask on the featureless face of fate: his action and suffering made fate visible to the human eye. Driven by something more powerful than his own individual nature, he stepped into a role all ready and waiting for him, slipped on the mask whose features were fixed as if from eternity and thus constrained his own movement.

Yet for all this, the *Agamemnon*'s and the *Choephoroi*'s protagonist was not a mere mask; he was a mask endowed with a voice of his own, a mask that refused to remain silent when his role was played out and he was about to be discarded. Though conscious that he was helpless, that his suffering was inevitable, and that his role was insignificant in the play of Fate, the protagonist still acted with resolution, still spoke with an unresigned voice, still protested against his unendurable even if necessary fate. Because of this, the Aeschylean individual in the *Agamemnon* and the *Choephoroi* did not altogether lack greatness of spirit, and even when he did not quite command our admiration, he engaged our sympathy. For all her shortcomings Clytemnestra was also great.

But all this disappears in the *Eumenides.* Orestes, the only remaining human protagonist, is hardly even a living individual in this play. He has no character, no life, no passion; he is a burnt-out case, "a corpus delicti," as Wilamowitz put it, something for the gods to deal with and dispose of. No wonder he is dismissed long before the play ends; as an individual he is almost incidental to the action of the play. Nor are the gods, the central protagonists of the *Eumenides,* individual characters with personalities of their own. They are merely spokesmen of abstract rights and wrongs, and so is Man, the subject of their contention, an intellectual abstraction: not this or that living individual put on the stage but humanity at large. Since the play celebrates the triumph of the rational, unemotional element, that which is opposed to the passionate-orgiastic nature of men, it is perhaps inevitable that it should dispense with the living individual moved by passionate, instinctual drives. Nevertheless this development helps to make the *Eumenides* as unconvincing emotionally as it is intellectually.

Perhaps the greatest shortcoming of the *Eumenides* is that this play, ostensibly the crownpiece of Aeschylus' only extant tragic trilogy, in fact subverts tragedy itself.

We have noted that what characterizes great tragedy is the irreconcilable conflict between individual action and an irresistible force that sets limit to and frustrates human purpose. But here this adverse power is eliminated, the Erinyes are turned into benevolent spirits, and the new order is supposedly benign to men. Even more than this was the case in Hesiod and Solon, human-divine justice now guarantees human well-being, and the world has become a safe place for men to inhabit. In such a world man no longer falls prey to uncontrollable forces and is no longer alienated from the way of things; with his personal security guaranteed man is now saved. But what he is saved from is tragedy. The *Eumenides'* theodicy has turned tragedy into a wish-fulfillment dream that is the counterconcept of all tragic vision of life.

Nietzsche accused Socratic intellectualism of bringing about the death of tragedy. Regardless of whether this is true, it seems to me that Aeschylus already began to kill it in the *Eumenides.* His relinquishing of traditional myth material eliminated the framework of necessity, the unchangeable story that limited possibilities, closed off the future, and predetermined what was to come. His treatment of the individual—who was now no longer teleologically alienated from what surrounded him (chorus, fate, and the gods)— made the actor an artificial, unnecessary construct. Since whatever he stood for and said, the chorus too stood for and could say, the actor no longer had much dramatic function in the play.

The direct result of Aeschylus' underemphasizing both actor and myth, or at least vastly diminishing their importance, in the *Eumenides,* was the abandoning of tragic drama. For in the absence of an objectively guilty subject, a necessarily polluted individual out of tune with and separated from the inevitable order of things, human existence could no longer be viewed and presented as tragic. Without the incongruous teleologies—the actor's and that of myth—the actor's expectations are no longer illusory and his actions no longer recoil on himself. Pathos is no longer a necessary part of life; it is at best incidental and it can certainly be overcome. The great reconciliation that is the content of the *Eumenides* has brought about an undramatic fusion of all the elements—individual actors, chorus, gods, and fate—on the stage and marks the end of the conflict that is the essence of both the form and content of tragedy.

It would be easy to say at this point in Aeschylus' defense that what he did in the *Eumenides,* dramatically and intellectually, was but the inevitable outcome and culmination of a long development that Hesiod began and Solon continued. After all, we have seen how Hesiod's emphasis on the intellect rather than the imagination and the senses just about killed poetry in the *Erga* and made the poetic form more an obstacle to than a helpful means for expressing what Hesiod wanted to say. And the same was true for Solon, who wrote an equally unimaginative poetry, and for Xenophanes, who could have said all he said just as easily in prose. Such considerations might lead to the conclusion that thought necessarily undermines poetry and that therefore the development of the intellect could not but lead to the downfall of every form of poetry, drama included.

But this conclusion is not tenable either historically or philosophically. It is untenable as a historical defense of Aeschylus since we find great poetry and great tragedy after Aeschylus, at a time when thought was if anything more highly developed than in Aeschylus' own time. And it is false philosophically because only uncritical thought, the too easy and too thoughtless triumph of thought, kills tragedy. The more critical thought becomes, the more it becomes critical even of its own powers and achievements and thus becomes tragic itself: full of internal conflict, aware of its own inevitable limits and of the dangers that its own achievements represent. Only uncritical, naive thinking makes the world appear untragic, a place where being and seeming completely coincide and human knowledge is fully adequate to reality, a place that is totally safe for man to dwell in. The greatest thinkers' greatness consisted, among other things, in their awareness of the abysses that at its most daring thought itself was capable of opening up to threaten man's too easily won security.

But these reflections take us too far beyond Aeschylus. While they warn us against taking Aeschylus' work as the final outcome of Greek intellectual development, they must not disguise the fact that this work, for all its dramatic and intellectual short-comings, still represented a great step forward in this development. It is true that the problems Aeschylus sought to solve in the *Eumenides,* far from being settled there, remained acute and demanded further treatment, and that the too hastily resolved conflict between chthonic and civic justice, nature and convention, tradition and reform, old and new law, survived both in tragedy—the *Antigone,* for example—and in prosaic thought—the *physis-nomos* controversy in late Sophistry. But it is no less true that Aeschylus advanced the problem of law in human events far beyond the point reached by Hesiod and Solon. He did so by posing, even if not resolving, a new problem, not that of law *vs.* lawlessness, but that of law *vs.* law, justice against justice. This is his great moral accomplishment, that enabling others to become aware of the problem he provided the impetus toward its solution.

His achievements are no less great with respect to his creation of tragic drama. It is true that in the *Eumenides* Aeschylus almost abandoned all that made the *Agamemnon* and the *Choephoroi* great. But it is also true that the overall pattern he created for presenting the self-conscious individual's struggle against his adverse fate proved to be imperishable, and, for all superficial modification, still provides structure for and helps form the substance of modern tragedy. Here, too, the dramatic failure of the *Eumenides* may have helped Aeschylus' successors to become aware of the limits of tragedy just as the dramatic successes of the *Agamemnon* and the *Choephoroi* helped to reveal its potentialities.

To be sure, the solution to all the problems of the *Oresteia* could not come from Aeschylus, the poet whose subject was the race's fate rather than that of the single individual, the city rather than the particular human being, human history at large rather than each man's brief span of life. It had to wait for others who could give authentic human beings a greater role and a new dignity, who could internalize and intellectualize natural law even more than Aeschylus was able to do and give it a new foundation within the reflective, emotional, and active individual, while at the same time not forgetting or trying to minimize the force of necessity. It was these men's task to show that salvation could originate from within the individual and man could triumph not so much over as in spite of adverse fate and death. But the germs of such solution were already contained in Aeschylus' work which thus contributed to their flowering in the work of his successors.

8. Oedipus Tyrannus

"Many are the wonders, yet none more wonderful than man. He makes himself a path across the stormy sea, wears away with his plow the unwearied earth, snares the beasts of air, land, water, and masters all creatures by his art. Speech and wind-swift thought and state-ordering craft he taught himself, and how to find shelter from the elements. He has resource for all; without resource he meets nothing that is to come. From death alone he has procured no escape, though against irresistible diseases he devised remedies. Wise beyond belief in inventive craft he comes now to evil now to good. Honoring the laws of the land and god-sworn justice, he stands high in the state; boldly dwelling with what is not right he is city-less." (*Antigone* 332–371, paraphrased).

Read out of context, the first choral ode of the *Antigone* seems to continue and even reinforce the line of thought with which the *Oresteia* ended. The *Eumenides* glorified the city, extolled rational arbitration, reconciled civic justice with divine law, and promised men safety if they only safeguarded these—the first stasimon seems to do the same. In the *Eumenides* Athene innovated boldly and helped what was new gain victory over what was old—the first

Material in this chapter also appeared in "Oedipus: Tragedy of Self-Knowledge" *Arion* (Autumn 1962) and is republished by permission.

stasimon seems to glorify man's inventive-innovative thought. In the *Eumenides* the foundation of human courts symbolized that henceforth man's salvation must come from man himself—the first stasimon seems to declare man fully equal to the task. Ingenious, skillful, intelligent, all-mastering, all-resourceful, all-devising, self-made, self-taught, self-certain man, the inventor of speech, thought, and state-ordering craft, the wonder of wonders, seems to be exalted here to a degree that even the boldest Sophistic eulogies could hardly surpass.

But such a reading illustrates the dangers of taking a Sophoclean ode out of context and using it thus isolated for interpreting Sophocles' view of man. For in its rightful context the ode begins to say something quite different. Its seemingly clear lines begin to blur and its meaning deepens till the bitter undertones begin to drown out the exultant surface strain.

It is not just that in the *Antigone* Sophocles revives the conflict between chthonic and civic law that the *Eumenides* hoped to have settled once and for all, and that in this conflict he seems to sympathize with the upholder of the unwritten, eternal, and divine law of blood-kinship rather than with the defender of conventional and man-made norm. Although this alone would reverse the Aeschylean solution in the *Eumenides* (which the choral ode seems to support), make it doubtful if anyone could obey both the laws of the land and divine justice at the same time (as the chorus advocates), and diminish the emphasis on human achievement and contrivance (which is so strong in the ode), the obstacles to taking the chorus's pronouncements for Sophocles' own view lie deeper.

In the *Antigone* neither Antigone nor Creon, neither nature nor convention, achieve an unambiguous victory. This is clear whether we consider the actual arguments proposed by the opposing sides or the dramatic outcome of the play as a whole. In terms of the actual arguments there is at least as much justification for Creon's conduct as there is for Antigone's,[1] and Sophocles' admiration for Antigone's personal heroism cannot be converted into a simpleminded advocacy of her cause on his part. Sophocles does not merely revive the nature-convention controversy in the manner of contemporary Sophistry, whose line of thought pervades the *Antigone's* arguments,[2] nor does he merely reverse the Aeschylean solution to the problem. He goes beyond Aeschylus by internalizing and, as it were, depoliticizing the conflict, and above all by rejecting all clear-cut and easy solutions to it.

As for the dramatic outcome of the play, it is as ambiguous as the status of the arguments themselves. Honor the laws, be righteous —the chorus sings—and you will be safe, while lawlessness will leave you without foothold in the city. Yet neither Antigone, who obeys one law, nor Creon, who obeys another, prove the chorus's Hesiodic-Solonic-Aeschylean precepts right. One dies an outcast and the other goes on living in the midst of the ruin of his hopes; both are in the end cut off from all they held dear in the world. To call either of them *hypsipolis* (high, proud, firm, and safe in the city) at the end of the play would be nothing but cruel mockery. And so is, in the final outcome, the chorus's naive apotheosis of man. In the light of the mutual destruction of the *Antigone's* antagonists, the first choral ode's exultant appraisal of human power and accomplishment verges on the bizarre; it is a testimony to the chorus's ignorance rather than an expression of Sophocles' view of life.

Much has been written about Sophoclean irony and the role of the Sophoclean chorus as the representative of the average man desperately trying to hold on to some simple traditional certainties at a time when all certainties threaten to give way.[3] But only infrequently is this insight into the ironical and ambiguous use of the chorus concretely applied to interpreting the *Antigone's* first stasimon.[4] Yet if the Sophoclean attitude to the chorus's anxious hopes is that such simple certainties as it would love to have are not available and that human life is a great deal more ambiguous than the average man could ever envisage let alone accept, then it is time to read the Antigone's ode in all its ambiguity and irony; if not as giving Sophocles' answers to the problems of his contemporaries,

at least as raising questions and introducing "serious and unre-
solved doubts"[5] into the contemporary moral situation.

"Many are the wonders and terrors, yet none more wonderful
and terrible than man." Of all things man is the strangest in the
double sense of the word *deinon:* awful, dangerous, astounding, terrible, outrageous, as well as awesome, mighty, wondrous, clever, and
skillful.[6]

On the positive side of the balance the chorus gives evidence.
Man is great, for he overcomes what seem to be the greatest powers:
the most terrible of the elements, the surging sea, he traverses with
impunity; the oldest and most inexhaustible, the earth, he wearies
and subdues; the most savage and tireless beasts he snares, overpow-
ers, or tames; and his skill makes him impervious to the most inim-
ical forces of nature. Nor is it only the external world that man con-
quers; he has developed spiritual powers that surpass all other living
things' capabilities. Speech and thought he taught himself and also
the most difficult art of getting along with his fellow men in communal life. Truly he seems all-resourceful and to meet without resource nothing.

But this appraisal clashes diametrically with the dramatic evidence of the play which makes it only too clear that man has not
truly mastered the state-ordering craft that would enable him to
live a harmonious communal life and that his arts of speech and
thought are woefully inadequate to the resolution of his gravest
and most urgent problems. For all his conquering the strange and
awful things of the world, the strangest of them, himself, man does
not seem to have mastered. He remains awful and dangerous even
to himself.

Therefore a surface reading of the next key words (*pantoporos-
aporos*) is not enough. Though clearly meant to be unambiguous
by the chorus, we do justice to Sophocles only by reading the line
(*Antigone* 360) in all its ambiguity so that its meaning parallels
the double meaning of *deinon*. *Pantoporos, aporos:* man is both all-
resourceful and without resource; all-conquering and all-contriving

as well as lost, bewildered and perplexed; in every direction on
the way as well as continually derailed and at a dead-end. Though
by sheer power and art he breaks himself a path in a trackless world,
for all his furious activity he gets nowhere: in the end he comes to
nothing (*ep' ouden erchetai to mellon*).[7]

The last key words, (*hypsipolis-apolis*) in the corresponding
line of the antistrophe, demand a parallel reading. In the intention
of the chorus the lines 368–71 explain the immediately preceding
sentence (*Antigone* 365–7). "Wise beyond belief in inventive craft,
man comes now to evil now to good" according to whether he
honors or dishonors the law. Justice makes the city safe, while injustice leaves man without a city. But here too, once justice and
injustice are seen as problematical—as they are indeed in the *Antigone*—and human art and invention as far less powerful than the
chorus claims, the well-defined paths to good or evil begin to disappear and the ironical reading of *hypsipolis-apolis* makes itself
heard. Since man is imperfect in wisdom, and therefore the world
is ineluctably obscure to him, he is both *hypsipolis* and *apolis,* state-
founding and state-destroying, sheltered and homeless at once.
Seemingly securely based in the community, he is without safe
foundation even when he seems to stand most firm. As he makes
himself a path and yet is pathless, so he makes himself a home
and yet is homeless; almost as if he cast himself out in the very
attempt to ensconce himself within the walls cast up for his own
protection. With being and appearance at such variance—as they
are in Sophocles—man is most strange: estranged from himself
when he deems to be most himself, and a stranger in the world he
calls his home. Just as in his ignorance he may destroy the city in
the very act of trying to preserve it, so the city may crush him in
the very attempt to provide him with shelter.

But if man is, in terms of the play as a whole, both *pantoporos*
and *aporos, hypsipolis* and *apolis,* then the rest of the stasimon ought
to be read ironically too. Such a reading would imply that although
"against irresistible diseases he devised remedies" (*Antigone* 364),

real health—spiritual rather than just physical—might still be a problem for man; he might be almost constitutionally sick and incapable of saving himself. Human life might be so paradoxical as to be by its very nature an anomaly, an impure and unwholesome condition for which death alone provides a cure. If so, the one final evil, death, the one last limit which according to the chorus man cannot overcome, might not be such an evil after all but rather a boon: a final solution to all our insoluble problems, a long-sought rest after all our fruitless activity, and a secure shelter after all our homeless wandering.[8]

Although I believe the preceding ironical reading to be necessary for an understanding of the *Antigone's* first stasimon in its own context, it is not for its own sake that I have introduced the ode here. My reason for bringing it in at all was that this ode correctly interpreted provides the best introduction to a discussion of *Oedipus Tyrannus.*

Far from settling anything, the ode raises fundamental questions: what are true wisdom, piety, justice, and injustice? What is the human road to good rather than evil? What is man, this strangest of all strange things in the world? Is it possible for us to resolve the deep moral ambiguity which seems to be a part of our condition? In what way, by what human contrivance can we diminish our homelessness and orient ourselves in our disorientation? For an answer to these questions we must turn to *Oedipus Tyrannus.* Not just because it is the greatest of all Sophoclean tragedies, in which, if anywhere, we are justified to look for Sophocles' answer, but because the *Antigone's* ode in the above reading gives us an almost literal description of the nature of Oedipus himself. The ode is full of doubt, ambiguity, and paradox, and Oedipus is above all an ambiguous, paradoxical hero. The ode speaks of man as *deinon, pantoporos-aporos, hypsipolis-apolis,* and Oedipus is the most wonderful and terrible, resourceful-resourceless, and sheltered-homeless hero in all Greek literature. The key words of the ode are simply the key words for an understanding of Oedipus.

However, they also contain a warning. If Oedipus is as strange and his fate as monstrous as the ode, applied to Oedipus, might imply, then an understanding of Oedipus as a paradigm for all men involves the interpreter himself in a strange and dangerous undertaking. For if Oedipus is this strange, can we ever hope to understand him? And even if we do, would it not be safer to refuse, as some readers do, to regard him a paradigm? Might it not be better for us to look upon Oedipus' fate as an abnormal exception, the product of extraordinary ill-luck, the like of which we need fear no more than being struck by a lightning-bolt? [9] And might it not be better to say that the theme of *Oedipus Tyrannus* is anything but universal, and that "there is no meaning in *Oedipus Tyrannus.* There is merely terrible coincidence . . ."? [10]

Superficially this would indeed be a safer approach, but it would hardly be an adequate approach to the Greeks who were always ready to plumb the depths of human experience no matter how dangerous such an undertaking might prove to be. Nor would it be an approach to Sophocles, who in the *Antigone* declared man— and not just Antigone or Creon or Oedipus—to be *deinon,* and in the *Oedipus Tyrannus* dared to put man in all his awful-awesome character on the stage. In the end, a nonparadigmatic reading of Greek drama is simply self-defeating. If *Oedipus Tyrannus* is a unique, abnormal, and implausible, and therefore largely irrelevant and practically meaningless tale, what is the point of reading it today? Indeed, what was the point of Sophocles' writing it at all?

Even so, the question is what in *Oedipus Tyrannus,* what in the character and fate of Oedipus, is paradigmatic and what mere accident or unessential historical reference? Oedipus was an outcast in infancy and maturity, at home in a strange land and a stranger in his own, a tyrant who was not really a tyrant and a king who did not know he was king; a son, father, husband, and brother who was more than son, father, husband, and brother; a guiltless criminal who innocently committed incest and parricide—what in all this is essential to an understanding of Oedipus' nature and fate as paradigms? Who was Oedipus? What is Sophoclean man?

A comparison with Aeschylus' Oedipus might give us a hint. Although the Aeschylean play itself is lost we know that it formed part of a trilogy, and, on the basis of the *Oresteia* and of what survives from this trilogy, we can surmise that its subject was not so much Oedipus himself as the history of a curse-ridden race's fate. In contrast, Sophocles' *Oedipus Tyrannus* is a single play in which the accent falls heavily upon Oedipus as an individual. There is a great temporal as well as dramatic concentration here. Unlike Aeschylus, Sophocles no longer deals with long-drawn-out courses of events in the life of families in which individual family members are hardly more than play-actors performing parts assigned to them within a much larger fable. He deals with individuals who are large enough to demonstrate in their own fate the universal patterns of destiny, and great enough to be almost isolated bearers of the unfolding of human life. In the *Oresteia,* individuals were mere fragments, masks, episodes, as it were, parts of the overall mechanism of the plays. In *Oedipus Tyrannus* Oedipus occupies the center of the stage.

Such dramatic concentration on the individual, which singles him out almost in isolation for our attention, is not a mere technical device. Rather it is the only appropriate manner of dealing with Sophoclean man who is first and foremost a self-concentrated and solitary individual. It is not necessary that he should be actually abandoned on a desert island (Philoctetes), or in fact entombed alive and physically separated from human companionship (Antigone), or wrapped in madness and thus alienated from human society (Aias), or literally outcast and barred from all social intercourse (Oedipus at Colonos). Such fortunes and circumstances are only symbolic of a deeper, more essential isolation which is characteristic of the Sophoclean hero even in the midst of men and within the sheltering embrace of human society.

Antigone, isolated by her unyielding insistence on her own decision and judgment, condemned by Creon, forsaken by Ismene, unsupported by Haemon—the two never even appear together on the stage—and abandoned by the chorus, receives no comfort from any human being, even before she departs unwed, unwept, unfriended (*Antigone* 876), with "no friend lamenting, none bemoaning my doom" (*Antigone* 881-2) to her living grave to "dwell neither with the living nor with the dead" (*Antigone* 850-1). But Creon fares no better. No less self-willed than Antigone, he is no less opposed by all he cares for, and fully aware of the worthlessness of the submissive support of the chorus he lives out his life befriended by neither men nor gods. Even if not physically deserted, the Sophoclean hero lives and dies in a desert of the soul in the early and middle plays. What he most craves for, human companionship, the kind of sharing of life and fortune with family and state that was so important to all Greeks,[11] that is precisely what is denied to him. By his very nature the Sophoclean hero is singled out for a higher—or lower—but definitely more uncommon fate than the rest of mankind.

This is especially clear in the case of Oedipus. Even before he is actually outcast and separated from men by the depth of his fall, he is isolated from others by the height of his rise and the preeminence of his position among men. "Not as one equal to the gods but as first of men . . . first in the fortunes of life and the visitations of the gods" (*Oedipus Tyrannus* 31-5) the spokesman of the suppliants claims to address him, yet the semireligious tone of his address almost belies his words and accords Oedipus a more-than-human status. And though Oedipus does not explicitly pretend to a status higher than the one due to him as ruler and father of his people,[12] he is fully conscious of his uncommon position. Even while he claims to share the common misfortune, he too feels set apart from the common measure by the greatness of his share: "Well I know that you are all ill, yet while you are ill none of your suffering is equal to mine; for each of you suffers on his own account, no more, but my soul grieves for the city, myself, and you, at once" (*OT* 59–64). Long before Oedipus recognizes his true fate —which "no mortal but myself can bear" (*OT* 1415)—he is fully conscious of the extraordinariness of his own fortune. Long before the self-laid curse to exile the murderer of Laius is fulfilled, Oedipus is already a virtual exile among men.

And that is not all. The isolation of Oedipus is deeper than his external position in the state—the height of his rise or the depth of his fall—would indicate. Oedipus is a solitary hero because even in the midst of human society he is a man virtually enclosed in his own universe, a man who has to do with no one but himself, a man fighting a lonely, self-imposed and self-destroying agon for and against himself.[13] In the *Antigone,* the opponents were carefully separated, and opposing arguments were allotted to different antagonists struggling against each other. In *Oedipus Tyrannus* this is no longer the case. There are no real antagonists here; the agon is concentrated in and carried out just about singlehandedly by Oedipus himself—Oedipus, the only true subject and object, the foremost actor and sufferer of the whole tragedy.

He is the real plague of the city (polluted Oedipus) as well as the healer Thebes turns to (wise Oedipus) and the remedy devised (outcast Oedipus); the strongest bulwark of the state and its weakest link; the problem, the problem-solver, and the solution; the measurer, the measure, and the thing measured and found wanting; the accurser, the curse, and the accursed. "It is not for far-off friends but in my own cause that I shall expel this pollution" (*OT* 137–8), and indeed he does; "for whoever the murderer be might easily turn against me with murderous hands" (*OT* 139–40), and indeed he does; and it is only meet "that I who holds his (Laius') power . . . his bed, his wife, and, had he but children, would be even closer bound to him, . . . that I shall uphold his cause even as that of my own father" (*OT* 258 ff)—and ironically he is, he does. The utter self-involvement and self-concentration of Oedipus is fully revealed only at the end of the play. But from beginning to end

Oedipus' action is ironically self-directed. ". . . he is both actor and patient, the thing sought, the finder and the thing found, the revealer and the thing revealed." [14] What greater isolation is there, than to encounter nothing but oneself?

Superficially, there is more involvement with others, more dialogue, more encounter between actor and actor in *Oedipus Tyrannus* than in any other Sophoclean, let alone Aeschylean, play. Yet in reality Oedipus is conducting an interminable dialogue with himself. Others he hardly seems to hear, let alone comprehend; listening to them it is not their advice but his own hopes and fears that he reacts to. The discrepancy between his nature and understanding and theirs—that which isolates him in the first place—is such that it almost insulates him against his interlocutors' voices and makes them mere catalysts for his own self-concentrated vision and action.

It is important to note that all the people Oedipus meets in the play mean to serve and protect him, as indeed they have done most of his life. They are not his real antagonists; on the contrary they try to shield him even from himself. But hardly do they meet and Oedipus turns against them with scorn, and turning against them, of course, only turns against himself. The *Antigone* presented an agon between two main antagonists. The *Oedipus Tyrannus* is the agon of one. In the *Antigone* judge and criminal, though akin and in many ways alike, were at least nominally distinct. In *Oedipus Tyrannus* all is one: Oedipus is his own investigator, prosecutor, judge, executioner, and victim. He is, ironically, duty-bound to be all that, for according to Greek law it devolved on the closest relatives of the murdered man to avenge his slaying by bringing the murderer to trial. And Oedipus is both the closest relative and the murderer as well as highest judge by virtue of his birth, his former actions, and his legal position as ruler. He is doubly *hypsipolis,* by inheritance as well as his own achievement, as well as doubly *apolis,* at birth and as a result of his own action.

We had occasion to note the fore- and aft-entanglement of all actors and events in the *Agamemnon* and the *Choephoroi*. In *Oedipus Tyrannus* this is enhanced to the point where it becomes the self-entanglement of Oedipus with himself. Thinking himself rootless, an apparent stranger to Thebes, unrelated to all, Oedipus manages to lay down roots and to establish himself firmly in the city. But since unknown to himself he is already too firmly bound up with family and city, his attempt to involve himself and lay down roots confounds all his previous legal and natural ties by superimposing on them new ones which are incongruous with the ones already existing. By his own misguided effort Oedipus creates a monstrous double relationship to his blood relatives and the city as well as to himself (the tyrant's relation to the king, the husband's to the child, the father's to the brother) which in the end uproots him from his native and also self-laid, self-cultivated soil. (The tyrant replaces the rightful heir and the coincidence of the two destroys both, etc.)

Because of this self-entanglement, the internecine struggle of the Aeschylean family becomes one man's suicidal self-embrace in *Oedipus Tyrannus*. Oedipus is *autocheir*—a favorite Sophoclean term—in every sense of the word; he is self-propelled, deadly, and self-destructive. It is not a family curse that dooms him but his own (*OT* 819-20). It is not the family's pollution he has to cleanse but his own. It is not other members of his family that perform the cleansing and bring about his doom but he himself. It is not Apollo that deals him the final blow but his own hand (*OT* 1329-31). It is not even his progenitors' acts, not his family's past that he reenacts; rather, step by step he descends into his own past until he arrives at his own beginning and reenacts what he was at birth: by his own act he reassumes the position of an outcast that others once saved him from. The Aeschylean actor was caught in a web not of his own making. Oedipus tracks, snares himself. The Aeschylean actor could protest "not mine the deed" and could rightly point to the gods' commands and his progenitors' fate as the forces impelling his action. For Oedipus there is no such excuse, his deeds are his and his alone.[15] They are altogether *autocheir*, doubly self-directed: directed by and against himself.

It is almost as if Oedipus moved in a world of mirrors: on every path (*pantoporos*) he comes up perplexed-unknowing (*aporos*) against himself. *Hypsipolis-apolis*: he is the ruler of a realm that offers no shelter, for the enemy is enclosed within, i.e., the ruler is his own—and his family's and city's—unwitting foe. With all conflict internalized, transposed from the familial battleground into Oedipus' own soul,[16] the Sophoclean hero has become a living contradiction in *Oedipus Tyrannus*. Divided against himself he is torn within, almost torn apart by himself. This is what makes his life *deinon*: the awful contention of evenly matched adversaries (Oedipus against Oedipus), the fell battle in which all victory (of Oedipus) is necessarily defeat (of Oedipus) and thus all achievement threatens to come to nothing (*ep' ouden erchetai*). Aristotelian *peripeteia* is not just an accidental feature of the play, it is the nature of Oedipus *peripetes*: of Oedipus fallen in with, surrounded and confonted by, turned upon and against, himself.

In the *Antigone,* the mutual incomprehension of the antagonists is the result of their incomprehension of the positions they oppose. In *Oedipus Tyrannus* it is no longer an external—civic or religious—position the hero fails to comprehend; it is his own position and nature. The cause of his alienation from others is, ultimately, his alienation from himself. And, while others might not be bothered by such self-estrangement, it is Oedipus' nature not to rest till it has been overcome.

What motivates all Oedipus' acts, is his restless, probing critical intelligence, his uncompromising, relentless demand for the truth. All through the play we find the same refrain returning with demonic insistence: I must find out, I must reveal, I *will* know. When first approached by the suppliants Oedipus answers their plea with an emphatic and confident 'I already know (*gnota kouk agnota moi, OT* 58), I already thought about your problem, I already found a clue, I already acted on my thought' (*OT* 66–69). Faced with difficulties and with the obscurity of the subject his only answer is "I shall start anew and make all clear" (*OT* 132). Faced with advice he replies, "I already anticipated you and acted" (*OT* 287), or, scornfully, even from the depth of his misery, "do not teach me that what I did was not the best that could be done, do not give me advice, for . . . [he proceeds to give his reasons]" (*OT* 1369 ff). Stung by Tiresias' attack on his most cherished accomplishment—"are you not the best of riddle-solvers?"—he wavers between wrath and contempt: "You taunt me with wherein my greatness lies" (*OT* 441), you who were helpless where I succeeded, you whose bird-omens and divine auguries were of no avail (*OT* 395–6) when "I, know-nothing Oedipus, came and put an end to all by my own insight and not taught by birds" (*OT* 396–8). Even on the dreaded brink of discovery (*OT* 1169) he has but one inflexible, irresistible desire, demand, obsession: "It cannot be . . . that I should fail to reveal" (*OT* 1058–59), "I will not be prevailed upon not to learn the truth" (*OT* 1065). "Break forth what will . . . I am determined to know" (*OT* 1076–77).

The subject of *Oedipus Tyrannus* is not so much divine prophecy as human search: the quest and discovery, ignorance and knowledge of Oedipus. The play is a tragedy not of divine fate but of human knowing. It is not by accident that Oedipus and Tiresias mutually deride each other's knowledge, and that the antithesis, sight/blindness, defines their agon. "You do not see" (*OT* 338), "you live . . not seeing" (*OT* 367), "you taunt me with my blindness, yet you have sight and fail to see" (*OT* 412–3)—thus Tiresias. And Oedipus answers in kind: "You are blind in ear, in mind, in eye" (*OT* 371), "nourished by endless night you cannot harm me or anyone else who sees" (*OT* 374–5), "you are a quack, a charlatan with eyes only for gain but blind in his art" (*OT* 387–9). Nor is it mere accident that Oedipus' self-mutilation takes the form of self-blinding, a self-blinding made necessary by too much sight. "King Oedipus has an eye too many, perhaps," Hoelderlin once said, and he was right. Even putting out his eyes could not shield Oedipus from a too keen, too unendurable vision.

The *Oresteia*'s most pervasive image was that of a web, snare, or net. *Oedipus Tyrannus* has no single predominant image, rather a whole group of literal descriptions, images, and metaphors that mutualy reinforce each other and in the end mean the same. Sight-blindness, light-darkness, insight-erring, wit-stupidity, revelation-hiddenness, knowledge-ignorance—these are the antitheses that define the play. The *Oresteia*'s net image was complemented by that of man as a snared animal and wild beast helpessly trapped. The *Oedipus Tyrannus* images are equally complementary, but they are active rather than passive. Oedipus is hunter, tracker, seeker, pilot, teacher, and guide. Even literally he is investigator and questioner. (By a mechanical count *Oedipus Tyrannus* contains more questions than any other Sophoclean, let alone Aeschylean, play, and of 199 questions in *Oedipus Tyrannus* Oedipus asks 123; he asks more questions than all the characters in any other play put together.[17])

And the questions Oedipus asks have a peculiar focus. Although too much sight, too keen a vision, too searching an inteligence already set Oedipus apart from his fellow men who, in the self-characterization of the chorus, "can neither assert nor deny, do not know what to say, flutter with forebodings, seeing neither the present nor the future" (*OT* 485-7), Oedipus' ultimate isolation comes from the fact that the object of his sight, his search, his discovery, and his knowledge—as well as the primary object of his blindness and ignorance—is nothing but himself. It is an inverted sight and blindness, a self-directed, self-concentrated vision and lack of it, that characterize Oedipus.

At the beginning of the play Oedipus' task is set: find the murderer, i.e., find himself,[18] and Oedipus makes the task his own, claims to fulfill it on his own behalf, in his own defense and for his own safety (*OT* 132-141). To what extent it is really his own task and its execution his fulfillment and doom is what the drama reveals. The unfolding of the play is the unfolding of Oedipus' self-involvement, the self-unfolding and self-revelation of Oedipus. The play is a tragedy of self-knowledge.[19]

It is not surprising that Aristotle, who used *Oedipus Tyrannus* as a paradigm of tragedy, found *anagnorisis* one of the most important elements of the tragic plot. Discovery is the most important element of this play because it is the *daimon* of Oedipus himself. Oedipus' nature and fate are *anagnorisis*. And the other all-important Aristotelian element of the plot, *peripeteia,* is closely bound up with this. Since Oedipus' discovery—as well as his initial ignorance —centers around his own being, his *anagnorisis* is necessarily *peripeteia* too: not just a reversal of Oedipus' state of knowledge (from ignorance to self-awareness) but also a reversal of his state of being. For what makes *anagnorisis* possible is the initial hiddenness of a subject (in this case that of Oedipus to himself), and what makes it necessary is that the subject (in this case Oedipus) cannot live with this hiddenness—"I cannot become other than I am, I cannot give up the search into my origins" (*OT* 1084-5). Given these two factors—that there is a difference in Oedipus' own being between what is apparent and what is real, and that Oedipus cannot accept this difference but must try to bring his two incongruous identities together—his efforts at self-discovery cannot but bring about a reversal of what he has been before.

It seems that Sophocles has not completely abandoned a dramatization of the nature-convention controversy after all, even in *Oedipus Tyrannus*. He merely transformed the *physis-nomos* opposition from an external, social-religious conflict into an internal, personal one and compressed the polar tension between these two forces into a tension within Oedipus himself. It is Oedipus' *physis*—what he truly is though unknown to himself—and *nomos*—what he and others think him to be—that are at odds in *Oedipus Tyrannus,* and it is Oedipus' *physis*—his own critical intelligence—that leads to an overthrow of his *nomos*. And although the incongruity between Oedipus' inner and outer identities, his being and seeming, is no easier to overcome here than other incongruities ever were before,

Oedipus cannot but try to abolish it by equating himself (what he is thought to be) with himself (what he truly is) despite the cost.

Much has been written about Oedipus' *thymos*—excessive passion, ungovernable temper, and reckless pride—as the fatal flaw in his character and the cause of his downfall. Yet if one understands the true nature of Oedipus' ambition—to be himself—and passion—for authenticity—there is nothing reprehensible in Oedipean *thymos*, regardless of its being the cause of his downfall. We can easily undestand why Oedipus meets every appeal to give up his search—*eike*, yield!—with an inflexible *ea*, let me be! [20] To yield would mean to give up not this or that unessential point but his very being, to compromise not just a superficial position but his essential nature. As the man whose primary characteristic, ambition, and passion is to know, he cannot stop the search without becoming untrue to himself. As a man increasingly conscious of not yet knowing and being his true self, he is constrained to try to know and to become himself. Any other alternative would be literally self-defeating: an abandonment of Oedipus' true self. [21]

Since Oedipus has no real alternatives for action, *Oedipus Tyrannus* might well be called a tragedy of fate, provided that we keep in mind that fate here means simply Oedipus' own character and nature. External determination—the traditional complex of *moira*, gods, family, and society—provides merely the setting of the play, the situation in which Oedipus finds himself, but Oedipus' character provides the drama—action—and the tragedy. This does not make *Oedipus Tyrannus* any less a tragedy of fate, for although the source of action no longer lies outside the individual, the new source is no less fateful and compelling. Though Oedipus is constrained by no external force, he is driven just as inevitably and irresistibly by his own nature. Translated from without into man himself, fate appears in a new guise—as the individual *moira*, lot, portion, spirit, *ethos, daimon* of Oedipus—but it has not become any less demonic. [22]

One might say that in *Oedipus Tyrannus* Sophocles drama-

tized the truth of the Heraclitean fragment *"ethos anthropo dai-*
mon" (119). It is important to note, however, that he also gave
Heraclitus' words a definitely sinister twist. For whatever Heracleitus may have meant, in *Oedipus Tyrannus* Sophocles seems to
be saying that man's character is his *daimon* in a double sense: the
irresistible motive force of all his action as well as the source of
his inevitable doom. What motivates Oedipus' action is his nature.
What he refuses to yield and thereby fulfills in the end is his own
nature. But that is also what destroys him, his own nature, *daimon*,
fate: the need to know and be himself. If so, "know thyself" is no
longer the safe and sound precept of the Delphic oracle here, meaning "know your place and stay within it," "do not transgress,"
"nothing in excess." Rather the demand for knowing one's place,
occupying it, and staying within it is itself a demonic obsession that
leads to transgression and excess: a transgression of the natural as
well as the civic order and a fateful excess beyond the boundaries
of the self as defined by both one's public image and initial private
conception. It almost seems that it is not so much exceeding one's
natural station and the traditional limits that define man—the thing
the Delphic oracle warns against—that is fateful here but rather the
contrary: the attempt to be fully what one is by nature. For this is
what in the end almost destroys Oedipus.

The Delphic motto reminded man of his weakness and mortality, of the gulf between him and the gods, of his finitude and
dependence. The Sophoclean *gnothi sauton* still does that, but it
also delivers man from others (men and gods as the motive force
of his action), makes him to a large extent independent (for he
deals mainly with himself) and self-sufficient (to the extent of being both his own savior and doom). There is something profoundly *deinon*, wonderful and terrible, in this new demand that
sets man the task of overcoming, fulfilling, and at the same time almost destroying himself.

What has man done to deserve such wonderful and awful fate?
Is there some "fatal flaw" in Oedipus' make-up that involves him in

his self-concentrated agon? What is Oedipus' *hamartia* that leads to his self-fulfilling self-reversal? In a sense these questions have already been answered. If the tragic action is impelled by Oedipus' own nature, and if this nature can be expressed by the now trans-formed demand to know oneself, then it is this demand for self-knowledge, and man's possession by the demand, that is the "tragic flaw" that leads to Oedipus' downfall. *Hamartia* means not sin or guilt but literally error: erring in the darkness of life, full of ig-norance, yet having to know.

Hamartia is not guilt or sin in the modern sense, for if doing what one could not avoid doing made one guiltless then Oedipus is clearly innocent; he is even less responsible for his action than the Aeschylean hero who at least knew that he was doing something evil. If good intentions and purity of heart could avert evil and pollution, there could be no fatal flaw in Oedipus' nature, and his story would be anything but tragic. But things are not as simple as that. We have seen in the *Agamemnon* and the *Choephoroi* that the same act could be subjectively innocent and yet objectively guilty, and Sophocles not only shares Aeschylus' conviction here but also gives it a rational foundation by explaining it not in terms of blood-pollution but in terms of human ignorance and error. Since no man knows all the circumstances surrounding his action—and Oedipus, the wisest of man, is initially most ignorant of his own circum-stances—human action is bound to have consequences the agent never had in mind. Regardless of the purity of subjective intention the act may disturb the natural balance of things and pollute the body politic as well as the agent. Thus an innocent act may well be objectively awful, reprehensible, and guilty, i.e., subject to inevitable retribution in the course of reestablishing the disturbed balance. (No man is more aware of this than Oedipus who, unlike his Aeschylean counterparts, deliberately visits retribution on himself in full awareness of his subjective innocence.[23])

This is not to say that the subject of human inquiry, delibera-tion and judgment is not ultimately amenable to knowledge. In spite of his initial ignorance about himself and the world he lives in, Oedipus does arrive at full knowledge at the end. But this knowledge comes too late; as a final achievement it merely reverses whatever Oedipus' striving for knowledge has achieved before. Therefore knowledge and the search for it, are themselves something *deinon:* powerful and awful, the bringer of both defeat and victory, and self-assertion through self-knowledge naturally leads to self-destruction. And not just in Oedipus' case. For if human life is essentially a movement from ignorance to knowledge (of self and world), from unauthenticity (not being truly oneself) to authenticity (being what one truly is), then it is not any particular and perhaps avoidable human act but human existence itself that is tragic,[24] and Oedipus' fatal shortcoming (*hamartia*) is not just *his* guilt or personal failing but a flaw inherent in man himself. Man fails and life is tragic because man, "the most wonderful and terrible of all things," is abandoned to his failing, limited, and woefully inadequate devices, because man, for all his self-sufficiency, is in the end insufficient to himself.[25]

This is evident in *Oedipus Tyrannus.* Throughout the play, first unconsciously then consciously, Oedipus tries to know himself, equate himself with himself. But his success reveals that there is something basically wrong with the equation: Oedipus fully equated with himself finds himself unequal to the task of being what he is and what he now knows himself to be. Thus it seems that neither unauthenticity (not knowing and being oneself) nor authenticity are bearable to man. Man the knower cannot live without knowing, yet he cannot live with the truth either. Neither blindness nor sight are conducive to life. Life is an error (*hamartia*): to live is to be out of balance, and every effort on man's part to right this balance merely tips the scale toward his doom.

We have observed something of this process in the *Agamemnon* and the *Choephoroi,* but Sophocles, instead of progressing as Aeschylus did in the *Eumenides* to a more hopeful view of human life and power, seems to regress in *Oedipus Tyrannus* to the lyric poets' insight into man's powerlessness in the face of life. It is almost as if he began with the *Eumenides'* view and then proceeded backwards, beyond the *Agamemnon* and the *Choephoroi,* to a more archaic position. For at the beginning of the play Oedipus, the self-made ruler of Thebes, is fully confident that the civilized intellect, the power that established him as ruler, would be fully sufficient to solve the city's problems and maintain his own power. Then, as the play unfolds, he gradually discovers that no man is quite self-made, that there are awful limits to human action and power; indeed that it is his own ability and power that in the end render him powerless, his own superb control of events that makes him lose control over the state as well as his own destiny. Paradoxically, Sophoclean power and lyric powerlessness seem to be much the same thing.

Even the Sophoclean answer to this discovery is not as different from that of the lyric poet as it first seems. Superficially, the two are diametrically opposed: Archilochus and Sappho, faced with man's inability to control his life, exhorted their contemporaries to endure the unendurable by living in and for the moment without thinking overmuch about the past or the future. In *Oedipus Tyrannus,* however, it is the minor characters and not Oedipus who voice similar precepts. "What should man, who is ruled by chance, with clear foresight of nothing, fear? It is best to live at random, as one may," (*OT* 177–79) Jocasta cries, and her advice that a life without much forethought may be "the easiest to bear" (*OT* 983) seems to be supported by Tiresias: "Alas how dreadful it is to think when wisdom profits nothing" (*OT* 316–7); "most easily you will bear your burden and I mine, if you will agree and let me go" (*OT* 320–21) without inquiring into what is hidden. But Oedipus, however much he might be inclined in the end to agree that wisdom might indeed be a terrible gift for man, a burden rather than a boon, is clearly incapable of following Jocasta's and Tiresias' advice and giving up his fateful urge to think and seek to know.

Nevertheless, this reaction of Oedipus' is in some ways similar to that of the lyric poets. Although Sophoclean man is most active where the lyric individual tends to be passive, both are incapable of relinquishing that (action or passion) which forms the substance of their lives (critical thought for Oedipus, love for the lyric individual). Regardless of how painful a possession such endowment may prove to be, the pain of it must be endured if man is to live at all. The rhythm of life may be as terrible in *Oedipus Tyrannus* as it was in Archilochus' and Sappho's poems, but neither Sophocles nor the lyric poets are therefore inclined to look for something beyond human life as a consolation, and neither seeks for a more-than-human order to redeem man from his intolerable suffering. Rather, both affirm life here and now as the only one which, for all its insufficiency, may also provide man with some moment, however fleeting, of fulfillment.

Before elaborating on this, it might be useful to touch briefly on the subject of Sophoclean piety here. Sophocles is often regarded as a defender of the "validity of the whole traditional religious view," and the *Oedipus Tyrannus* is taken to be "a reassertion of the religious view of a divinely ordered universe" [26] and a "terrifying affirmation of the truth of prophecy." [27] Does Sophocles' attitude toward the gods and their oracles in *Oedipus Tyrannus* justify this appraisal?

As to the oracles, it must be admitted that the play affirms, at least by the way, their validity. But it is important to note that it is not so much religious prophecy as human search that is the subject and motivating force of the play. All that had been prophesied has been fulfilled before the play's action starts and would have been equally fulfilled had no one ever found out, had Oedipus and Jocasta lived happily ever after. And whatever actually takes place in the play has never been predicted before the action begins. Thus the oracles and their fulfillment provide no more than the setting of the drama, they look backward rather than forward; the action itself consists of Oedipus' search for and discovery of what he is and has done. Of course, this is, at least in part, also what the oracles tell us about, but that is precisely the point: the oracles in

Oedipus Tyrannus tell us less of divine will and divinely foreordained fate than about human will and character.[28] Within the play itself the oracle's function (in telling about Oedipus' parricide and incest) is not to prophecy future events but to show that Oedipus has had an intimation of some thoroughly disquieting facts about himself: that there must be something awful and unnatural in his hidden make-up to make him capable of committing the two most detestable crimes the Greeks could ever envisage. Certainly Oedipus' *awareness* of this, and of the fact that his real nature may as yet be hidden from him, *is* an essential factor in the setting as well as the unfolding of the drama.

Even if we ignore the dramatic function of the oracles and emphasize the fact that *Oedipus Tyrannus* does affirm, albeit by the way, the truth of prophecy, Sophocles' attitude toward religious oracles still remains far from unambiguous. For given the fact that whatever the oracles predicted has indeed come to pass, the question is not so much whether oracles are true or false, but rather how we are to behave toward them, what is the right, pious, salutory rather than self-destructive human attitude toward prophecy? And here the only clear answer the play as a whole gives seems to be that, true or not, the oracles are of no earthly use in that they open no saving alternatives [29] and give no real guidance to any man. They are if anything so confusing and misleading that it is just as fateful to try to obey them as it is to disregard them, so that in the end it might be better for men not to have oracles at all. After all, Laius, Jocasta, and Oedipus all believed in and tried to act according to the oracles once, and what did it profit them? Oedipus was exposed in obedience to an oracle, but this awful sacrifice did nothing to avert the predicted catastrophe. On the contrary, like Oedipus' flight from Corinth, also the consequence of an oracle, it only helped to make the prophecy come true. Prophecy may not lie, but what are we to do with its truth? To this no oracle gives answer, and Oedipus' irreverent cry "why should one look to the Pythian hearth or to the birds screaming above" (*OT* 964–66) is not ultimately rebuked by the play; not because the oracles were false but because, even though true, they are of no use to man. Since owing to man's limited insight divine truth only deceives and misleads, man might just as well turn away from prophecy, close his ears to the sinister cries from above, and "live at random," as Jocasta suggests. The fact that Oedipus cannot do this has less to do with the truth of the oracles than with his own nature.

Sophocles' attitude toward the gods is no more orthodox and pious in *Oedipus Tyrannus* than his attitude toward the oracles. From Hesiod to Aeschylus the poets affirmed divine justice and goodness and gradually reduced the gods to being the divine guarantors of human justice. "The good man prospers and evil is punished without fail"—this is what the gods stood for and had to enforce. But we find nothing of this in Sophocles, unless one takes the chorus's ignorant piety for Sophocles' own faith. From the point of view of man, the gods, letting the blameless suffer and the innocent die to no comprehensible purpose, are clearly neither good, nor just, nor merciful, and Hyllus' indictment of them in the *Trachiniae* is not so much an isolated assertion in that play as the expression of an attitude that anyone with the least compassion for man might be inclined to take on observing what actually occurs in Sophoclean tragedy. Certainly Antigone, Oedipus, and Jocasta might justly join in Hyllus' plaint (as Philoctetes does in *Phil.* 446–52): "forgive me friends, seeing that the gods' injustice is great, they do such deeds; begetting children they claim a father's name yet are unmoved by such sorrows as these. The future is unknown but what has come to pass is our misery and their disgrace . . . behold these deaths, so great and new, these many ills and such unheard of grief—it is all Zeus' work" (*Trach.* k264–end). In terms of human justice Sophocles' tragedies amount to more of an indictment of the gods than an apology for divine rule.

What saves the idea of divinity from utter degeneration here is that Sophocles has advanced beyond Aeschylean theodicy as well as Sophistic etiology and criticism. He no longer demands that the gods conform to man's idea of justice and rationality but lets divinity stand as an irreducible element of darkness, mystery, and even absurdity in the human world.[30] He neither denies nor justifies the gods but simply accepts them as real, as belonging to the framework of the world within which man has to live. That in human terms the gods are without purpose, that they are insensible to human values and indifferent to human achievement, that the order they may be enforcing is in many ways incomprehensible to man, and to that extent no better than the rule of senseless chance—all this may be true. But it is also beside the point: it is not divine but human existence and action that we have to clarify and justify, and this is what Sophocles does in *Oedipus Tyrannus*.

There is something Homeric in this treatment of divinity. Although the Sophoclean gods, unlike Homer's, are no longer the visible embodiment of human virtues and failings, and although they, unlike the Homeric deities, hardly ever enter the scene, they still serve as a very real and darkly contrasting background to human action: "Against their pitilessness human pity . . . stands out in a clear, and often ironical, light." [31] And against their injustice human righteousness, against their supreme indifference deep human concern, against their inaction desperate human activity take on a dignity that—for all of Hesiod's, Solon's, and Aeschylus' attempts at religious reform—the gods no longer seem to be capable of attaining and maintaining.[32]

If divine presence—whatever there is of it in Sophocles' early and middle plays—merely serves to bring human doing and suffering into sharper relief but neither explains nor justifies it and neither redeems nor consoles man, then clearly man's doing and suffering must be justified in its own terms. As Whitman notes, "if human action fails to justify life, it remains unjustified, for, in the world of Sophocles, there is no such things as an act of grace, except from within man." [33]

Sophocles does indeed offer such immanent, merely human justification in *Oedipus Tyrannus*. While human life serves no higher purpose and receives no transcendent foundation here, it is therefore neither meaningless nor useless. The immanent purpose of all life is to fulfill itself, its proper end is that it should be lived to the furthest limit of its own potentiality, its rightful use that it should be implemented and perfected in accordance with its inner laws and natural standards of excellence. And this is something Oedipus accomplishes. Measuring himself not so much against the gods as against the greatest adversary any man may encounter—himself—he outwardly fails but inwardly triumphs by recognizing and attaining to his true measure. This attainment of authentic self-identity, the hardest and highest achievement to which a man can aspire, is human excellence.

Sophoclean man is not conspicuously equal to the gods. He is failing, inadequate, limited; a fragile, perishable thing. Within these limits, however, he is capable of growth: a growth beyond the particular confines of what he already achieved, a growth transcending the bounds set by each previous achievement, a growth to fullness of life. Such growth is always a paradoxical achievement; it is victory and defeat at the same time, for when man's measure is full, he perishes. But he perishes of his own accomplishment: through having fulfilled himself, having become all he could. This is greatness. Oedipus' apotheosis takes place not in *Oedipus at Colonus* where a frail old man is exalted by divine grace in reward for all his suffering ("the gods who struck you down now lift you up" *OC* 934), but in the *Oedipus Tyrannus* where man, failing and from a divine point of view insignificant, exalts himself by his own almost superhuman effort and attains an awesome and terrible dignity through self-affirmation, i.e., through the affirmation of his own failing, agonizing, and "ultimately" meaningless destiny. From any point of view but that of man this is a futile gesture, a useless ordeal, a wasted passion. Humanly speaking, it is the greatest thing man is capable of: to become, come what may, what he is.

The absurd courage and paradoxical heroism of Oedipus, the

powerful yet helpless, self-overcoming, self-defeating, yet self-affirming hero, lifts Sophoclean man far above the standard of humanity
implicit in the Aeschylean *Eumenides,* and it also makes tragedy—
the thing Aeschylus almost turned into melodrama at the end of
the *Oresteia*—once again possible. For unlike Aeschylus in the
Eumenides, Sophocles does not avert his eyes from irremediable,
seemingly useless suffering. Rather he transfigures it and makes
it triumphant by letting Oedipus transfigure his own life and
transform himself into his true self at the cost of no matter how
great a suffering. Unlike Aeschylus, Sophocles does not gloss over
the ultimate ambiguity of all human accomplishment; yet he
shows that even in a dark and baneful world man can live without
illusion and for all the ambiguity of human action man can achieve
an unambiguous victory over himself. Nor does Sophocles deny
man's inevitable, as it were congenital, pollution, or try to cleanse
it by a sleight of hand. Instead he changes it from an external to an
internal taint—that of man not yet being essentially himself—and
lets man cleanse himself through his own self-affirming effort, unaided by the Aeschylean Apollo and Athene. It is true that this
process of catharsis remains in some ways as destructive as the
cathartic attempts of the *Agamemnon*'s and *Choephoroi*'s heroes
were. Still purity—pure self-identity—can now be achieved, and,
through the Oedipean demand "that man should cleanse himself
into what he essentially is" [34] Sophocles set before the Greeks a
higher ideal of purity and virtue than they ever beheld before.

Sophocles' intellectual contemporaries, the Sophists, tended to
overestimate or underestimate the power of human intelligence;
Sophocles does neither. While individual Sophists presented man
either as *pantoporos*—an all-devising polymath—or *aporos*—incapable of attaining any true knowledge—Sophocles sees man as both:
grievously limited in insight yet capable of attaining the hardest
type of knowledge, true self-awareness. So the new "know thyself,"
for all its sinister undertones, still turns out to be a saving and
redeeming command. By obeying it man may fall, but his fall is

nothing to be deplored; it is, as it were, natural decline upon maturity, the negligible byproduct of supreme achievement.

The chorus clearly does not understand this as it comments on Oedipus' self-discovery. "Oh generations of men, how I reckon your life as equal to nothing! For who, what man, wins more of bliss than a semblance, and after this semblance decline? Having your paradigm, your fate, oh wretched Oedipus, before my eyes, I will call no mortal blessed" (*OT* 1186–96). In accordance with its own superficial notion of nobility—external excellence and power—this collection of pious, fearful, orthodox, average men only sees the highest brought low and the noblest become base. That there may be such a thing as inward greatness and fulfillment, of this the chorus knows nothing. Here too, Sophocles' use of the chorus is deeply ironical. It not only reveals the chorus' ignorance as opposed to Oedipus' knowledge of what it means to be a man; it also underscores the fact that in the last resort the Sophoclean hero lives in accordance with and up to a purely private standard of excellence. However much Oedipus may have in common with Hector and Achilles, who are also destroyed by their greatness, this separates him from all the Homeric heroes: that the latter, no matter how exalted, could still be understood and admired by their fellow men whose ideals they still embodied. But Oedipus does not. The closer he comes to his goal, the less he cares to shine in others' regard, the less he is willing to measure himself by the conventional norm. He wants to be true to himself even in the sense of wanting honor primarily in his own eyes; he wants self-recognition in the sense not just of full self-knowledge but also of full self-esteem and self-regard. He wants to be himself simply so as to be able to live with himself. That others might find such life horrible beyond endurance and might recoil from the bearer of such destiny simply does not weigh in the balance. To the end Oedipus is a lonely hero. "The attainment of true self-knowledge [is] the most difficult and lonely of all forms of heroism." [35]

"Seek not to master all. For the mastery you once held has not remained with you for life" (*OT* 1522–23). Creon's parting words to Oedipus reveal more about Creon—e.g., that his mentality is akin to that of the chorus, and his relationship to Oedipus is one of incomprehension—than about the truth. For the truth is the opposite of what Creon says. The rule Oedipus once held was but a semblance, based as it was on most insecure foundations. But what he now holds is, all appearances to the contrary, true mastery; he has mastered his own life and, in the very depth of adversity, he has become master of himself. At last he is utterly secure; he has nothing more to fear, not himself, not other men, not even the gods. If human life can ever approach divinity, Oedipus has come as close to it as any man can. The denouement of the play almost disproves the suppliant priest's initial rating of Oedipus as one "not equal to the gods." There is something godlike in Oedipus' purely human victory. Many are the wonders and terrors, yet for all the terrors of human existence nothing is more awesome than man.

That the chorus and the supporting actors do not know the true state of affairs illustrates Sophocles' use of the chorus and the minor actors. On first approaching Oedipus, the ruler whose rule is in fact most questionable, the suppliants, for all their disclaimer—*theoisi men ouk isoumenon*—address him in almost religious tones and pay him almost godlike deference. But now, in the last stasimon, when Oedipus' stature had something truly daimonic in it, the chorus rates him equal to nothing. In both cases Oedipus' interlocutors are mistaken in their appraisal, but their mistaken judgment underscores the truth better than any literally true statement could. And this is precisely the dramatic function of minor actors and chorus alike. As representatives and embodiments of the common measure they counterpoint the uncommon measure, the extraordinary paradigm of humanity, that Oedipus represents.[36] Their very averageness, conventional mentality, and fearful adherence to traditional truths—no matter how questionable these "truths" have become in the light of what transpired in the play—help to enhance Oedipus' exemplary courage in refusing to be satisfied with anything less than the truth as appropriated and established by himself. If these things—oracles, etc.—should prove untrue, the chorus asks, why should I dance, i.e., why should I go on living and worshipping as before, now that the very foundation of my life is gone? This attitude is diametrically opposed to that of Oedipus, who is resolved to search for new foundations when the old ones crumble and is willing and able to endure a life without the comfort and consolation that a transcendent foundation might provide.

Oedipus towers over the other actors in the play no less than he towers over the chorus, and this is something new Sophocles contributes. In the *Oresteia* Aeschylus already used the three-actor format which—if we can trust Aristotle's account—he took over from Sophocles, but his use does not quite explain why increasing the number of actors from two to three was dramatically necessary to him. There is very little interplay between the actors here, and little difference in stature between the protagonist, deuteragonist, and tritagonist. Clytemnestra, Agamemnon, and Cassandra move on much the same level of human excellence, and at the point where Orestes remains the only human actor (not counting the mute jury) on the stage, his stature, far from being increased, almost dwindles to nothing. All this is quite different in Sophocles who obviously knows what to do with his innovation.

The introduction of the third actor enables him to increase the interplay between the individual actors and to illuminate the protagonist's character from many different points of view.[37] Above all, it allows him to detach the protagonist not only from the inactive chorus but also from the other at least nominally active human agents. The Tiresias-Oedipus, Shepherd-Oedipus, and the last Jocasta-Oedipus scenes not only contrast Oedipus' present ignorance with Tiresias' and the Shepherd's actual and Jocasta's finally dawning knowledge, but they also present Oedipus' uncompromising resolve as an antithesis to the others' willingness to compromise the truth by letting it remain hidden. The Creon-

Oedipus, Messenger-Oedipus (as well as the chorus-Oedipus)
dialogues equally reinforce the hero's isolation, faced as he is with
well-meaning interlocutors who share neither his intelligence nor
his standards of judging human excellence. In all these cases the
increased number of actors and the increased interplay between
actors serve Sophocles' dramatic design: that of concentrating our
attention on the protagonist as the central, all-important character
in the play.

It would be too much to say that Sophocles singlehandedly in-
vented the classical and still paradigmatic figure of the tragic hero;
the *Iliad's* Achilles and Hector and the *Agamemnon's* Clytemnestra
certainly prefigure Oedipus. Still in the *Iliad* and in the *Oresteia*
the action is nowhere near as concentrated in the person of one
dominant character as it is in the *Oedipus Tyrannus,* and the hero
is nowhere as effectively isolated as he is here. So even if Sophocles
did not invent the tragic hero out of nothing, he certainly brought
the ideal to perfection by constructing his whole play around one
central figure and sharply focussing all action so as to reveal the
hero's incomparable greatness.

The incomparability of the hero makes his functioning as a
paradigm seemingly paradoxical—for if he is so far removed from
the common man, how can he serve as an example for him to follow? Lesser writers than Sophocles dealt with this paradox of the
paradigm by turning against the heroic image itself or fashioning
heroes of lesser stature and depicting men "more like what they
were than what they ought to be." But Sophocles understood the
problem better than any Greek—with the possible exception of
Homer—had done before. Although his hero is uncommon and exceptional, he is therefore neither bizarre nor inimitable. He is merely
an outstanding example of our common humanity, that humanity
which the common man neglects in his own person. It is precisely
because of this neglect, i.e., because most men forget the essential
and live their lives as if being a man were such a trivial task that
its accomplishment required hardly any effort at all, that it is

necessary to set before men the ideal, the rare example of a self-aware, self-fulfilling agent who dares to demand nothing less than full selfhood, the perfection of his kind.

Sophocles' attitude to and use of traditional myth parallels his concentration on the hero as an ideal type in contrast to and for the guidance of the tradition-minded and conventional community. In *Oedipus Tyrannus* traditional myth is underemphasized and the playwright's creative mythmaking increases with notable results.

All that Sophocles takes from traditional myth forms merely the background of the play. What actually happens in the drama—the plague, the oracle's command to banish Laius' murderer, and Oedipus' subsequent search, self-discovery, self-mutilation, and self-banishment—is Sophocles' own invention in elaboration of and often in contradiction to the traditional story. This use of myth gives Sophocles a much greater freedom than Aeschylus assumed in the *Agamemnon* and the *Choephoroi,* and while Aeschylus took a similar liberty in the *Eumenides,* the difference between the outcome of his new creation and that of Sophocles is striking. Where Aeschylus abandons myth and freely innovates, his drama loses necessity of development and becomes arbitrary and unconvincing.[38] But in *Oedipus Tyrannus* the framework of necessity is never lost; if anything it is all the more compelling for not being supplied by traditional myth. And the reason for this lies in Sophocles' dramatic concentration on the tragic hero.

An instance of Sophoclean deviation from traditional myth might illustrate this. In the *Thebaid,* in Aeschylus' *Septem,* and in Pindar (*Olympian Ode* 2.35ff) we find the traditional story of a family curse, but Sophocles never even mentions a family curse foredooming Laius' house in the *Oedipus Tyrannus.* Oedipus' curse and doom are self-pronounced and self-executed. Yet they are not arbitrary inasmuch as they naturally flow from Oedipus' own character. The point is, that while Aeschylus simultaneously deemphasized both actor and fate in the *Eumenides,*[39] Sophocles retains both by combining the two in the person of the tragic hero. Since the actor is no longer a mere mask, a persona driven largely by external necessity, but a person in his own right whose action is determined from within, the loss of external determination—by the gods, family fate, or other men—is more than compensated for by the increase in internal necessity. One innovation of Sophocles—the emphasis on the tragic hero's self-concentrated agon—supports and justifies the other—the much freer mythopoeia.

When Aeschylus abandoned traditional myth (in the *Eumenides*), he also abandoned nature—the natural, chthonic, blood-law—and tried to base his new myth on convention—insecurely founded and therefore seemingly arbitrary and unexplained civic law and divine-human artifice. But Sophocles' going beyond traditional myth is in fact a return to nature—the given constitution of the individual—and thus a return to that—*moira, daimon,* fated allotment, and portion—which alone is capable of supplying necessity to human events. The *Eumenides'* too hastily effected reconciliation between *moira* and the gods—blind necessity and divine-human foresight—did not work, either dramatically or philosophically. But the Sophoclean reconciliation—of *moira* and man, of fate and human intelligence, volition and action—is dramatically successful because it is philosophically convincing. Sophocles' new drama succeeds where the *Eumenides* failed because Sophocles' new image of man, whose expression the drama is, is truer to the human condition than that of Aeschylus was.

The function of myth has not changed so much, after all, even though the invention of writing put an end to unconscious mythopoeia. Unlike Hesiod, Solon, and Xenophanes, who turned away from myth altogether because the traditional stories no longer seemed to reflect what they held to be true, the tragedians returned to myth because they believed that these stories still had some power to inform our lives, and, where they lost that power, could be revitalized by reinterpretation and new creation. And although this new attitude to myth was one of conscious modification, the vitality and validity of the new myth still depended on the extent to which it visibly embodied the truth about man and world and thus gave men insight into their lives. It is on this level—both ethical and dramatic—that Sophocles' *Oedipus Tyrannus* surpassed the *Eumenides* and brought tragic mythmaking to perfection.

Sophocles' use of that peculiar form of tragic irony most prominent in *Oedipus Tyrannus* reveals another striking connection between Sophoclean dramatic techniques and view of life. Unconscious irony consists in an incongruity between the speaker's opinion and the truth that is manifest to the audience but not to the speaker. That this type of irony should pervade the *Oedipus Tyrannus* [40] is not surprising if we consider that a contrast between opinion and truth, appearance and reality, is not an accidental feature of the play but something inherent in the nature of Oedipus himself. Oedipus is at once the wisest and most ignorant of men; his predominant need is to know, to search, to reveal, and yet the truth, about himself and his own position in the world, is what is most hidden to him. Thus by nature and circumstance Oedipus is plagued by a conflict and incongruity within his own existence, an ironic discrepancy between his own seeming and being, which he is also fated by nature to resolve. Since this resolution is the whole action of the play, "the whole framework of *Oedipus Tyrannus* is dramatic irony" [41] and "irony resides in the mere fact of Oedipus" [42] as Kirkwood justly remarked. We have seen that Sophocles concentrated the tension between *nomos* and *physis* within Oedipus himself and made *hamartia* and *anagnorisis* not just accidental categories but the essential traits of Oedipus. Embodying these seemingly disparate poles in the person of his protagonist, Sophocles necessarily internalized irony too: Oedipus the ironical hero—the incongruous and self-deceived knower—and his overcoming of the irony of his existence—Oedipus' self-overcoming—became the subject of the play. A dramatic technique of irony and the Sophoclean view of man are thus but different aspects of the same thing in *Oedipus Tyrannus*.

Sophocles' language is equally harmonious with the content it expresses. The correspondence between poetic image and the reality it describes is so great here that it is often difficult to distinguish between literal and metaphoric description in the *Oedipus Tyrannus*. And not only do symbol and actuality tend to fuse. As the action is concentrated and is primarily Oedipus' action, and therefore the dominant images are also clustered around the figure of Oedipus himself, the separate images reinforce each other mutually to the point where they begin to blend and become one complex figure expressive of the nature of Oedipus, and, by extension, of all mankind.

Take, for instance, the prominent images of health and disease, sight and blindness. At one time or other, though ironically not at the time employed, they are all literal descriptions of Oedipus' own condition. The medical imagery is literal here, not just because there is a real plague going on—the actual plague is just about forgotten as the play proceeds—but because Oedipus himself is polluted and is the bearer of pollution—to the Greeks actually as well as metaphorically. The sight-blindness imagery is also literally descriptive of Oedipus' condition at the beginning and the end of the play, while it is a figurative description in the reverse order. And the two images—sight-blindness, health-disease—are combined on a deeper level. Oedipus' inner health and disease depend on and are symptoms of his inward sight and blindness, and Oedipus' condition implies that man's true health and self-awareness are infinitely precarious, that pollution and ignorance always lurk beneath apparent purity and knowledge; that real health is not only something to be achieved, rather than something natural and given, but even when achieved—as it is by Oedipus in the end—it looks very like a disease on the surface. Thus health-disease, purity-pollution, sight-blindness, visibility-invisibility, being and seeming are as inseparable images here as they are inseparable from the reality and in the reality—human life—that Oedipus represents.

The same is true of the pilot-ship-harbor, tracking-seeking-finding, hunting-shooting and hitting or missing the mark, equation and puzzle-solving, erring-knowing complexes. Though some of these images are no longer literal—Oedipus does not in fact steer a ship or track or hunt—all of them reinforce each other till they mean just about the same thing. Oedipus is pilot because he seems to *know*—the way and where he is and where to find safe harbor —when others do not. Thus even as helmsman he is path-finder, puzzle-solver, knower, and guide. At the same time he is also an ever wandering mariner, always on the way and never truly at home, finding only harborless harbors and inhospitable, friendless anchorages, because for all his seeming knowledge he does not truly know where he is, where he comes from, and where he goes. Thus knowledge-ignorance, sight-blindness, steering-misguiding, seeking-finding-erring are ironically interrelated images of the being-seeming complex we dealt with above. The harborless harbor— Thebes, his mother's womb—is also the same as the soil which he as ploughman and sower cultivates in ignorance of his place of origin; and that he does so—blind to the truth yet seeking for it— partially causes his pollution and disease which he as healer is almost powerless to cure. Unlike the *Oresteia,* the *Oedipus Tyrannus* has no one predominant image, but all its seemingly diverse images coalesce into a rich and harmonious whole.[43]

They also fuse with the action to the point where not only does a former image (e.g., blindness) become literal description, but the actual event (Oedipus' self-blinding) itself becomes symbolic of a deeper reality. In this fluid interchange between the literal and the actual Sophocles went beyond Aeschylus' practice in the *Eumenides* and almost reversed a trend noticeable there. For Aeschylus' new myth about Athene's foundation of the law courts was in a sense literal reference rather than a symbol. Aeschylus in fact expected man's improvement and society's salvation to come from the civic institutions of Athenian democracy. In contrast to this Sophocles uses not only legal terms and actual law-processes but all concrete events as well as the most concrete person in *Oedipus Tyrannus* as images of a human reality that is not adequately represented by any actual event, person, or institution already existing in the world.

Even Sophocles' mythopoetic activity as such is more coherent, in a purely logical way, with his view of man than is that of Aeschylus in the *Eumenides*. For Aeschylus, in his optimistic appraisal of civilized arbitration, placed, at least by implication, too much faith in human reasonableness and in the power of reason to clarify and order experience. This made his philosophic attitude to some extent antimythical. If reason is such an unambiguously saving and clarifying tool, why resort to myth: a type of storytelling and thinking that is never without ambiguity and is always in need of further interpretation? [44] If the standards of strict verisimilitude are acceptable because they are appropriate to what the poet is trying to say, why resort to the theater, the realm of illusion and mask, the veiled representation of a not immediately representable truth? To write poetically, mythically, and theatrically about an all-powerful human-divine *logos* seems if not altogether self-contradictory at least an unnecessary enterprise.

But Sophocles' mythmaking is not. Even though Sophocles made human intelligence the subject of *Oedipus Tyrannus* much more explicitly than Aeschylus did in the *Eumenides,* he showed it to be a much more limited and ambiguous power and a much less clear-cut and unequivocal blessing for man. And this inherent ambiguity of human knowing, this ironical wedding of error and recognition, illusion and truth, seeming and being, justified his continued use of myth. If the truth, as seen by men, is necessarily ambiguous, then it also requires an appropriate poetic-symbolic rather than purely discursive expression and a mythical embodiment rather than a prosaic-literal description.

There is one last aspect of the correspondence between form and content in Sophoclean tragedy that I would like to discuss. In a purely formal sense, all drama is a temporal representation. As an actual performance before an audience gathered together for the express purpose of viewing it, drama "has its very existence in time." [45] In this it resembles oral epic, but the differences between the two are significant. A monumental oral poem like the *Iliad* is impossible to perform in its entirety at any one time, therefore its performable parts, the episodes, must be complete in themselves without requiring an exact knowledge of what went on before and what follows after each. The episodes being related to each other as a series of unchanging nows, the whole poem is only loosely tied together and permits no significant temporal development. [46] The temporality of drama is quite different.

The play, as Aristotle saw, is a complete, self-contained whole with a beginning, middle, and end. Beginning, middle, and end imply irreversible sequence, i.e., temporal development. They imply organic growth in time, the beginning (potentially) containing the end which, gradually unfolded through the action, actualizes and brings to completion what was contained, potentially though not actually, in the beginning. Such organic growth presupposes something totally alien to the oral epic: hidden potential and depth imperfectly realized and thus at odds with surface actuality; a discrepancy between seeming and being—or already being and not yet being. This incongruity between actuality and potentiality is greatest at the beginning but it persists through and is the motivating force of all the action until it is abolished and the action is necessarily brought to an end.

The temporality of drama is eschatological-teleological, furthermore, not only in the sense in which all organic development is an aim-directed movement from potentiality to actuality. As distinguished from such unconscious natural growth, drama enacts teleology—an understanding of ends and a movement toward ends determined by such understanding of the end as one's own necessary goal —and presupposes a teleological rationality—a consciousness of necessary organic growth—for its effect. Without this consciousness on the part of the audience of a tension between hidden potential and ultimate realization and of the necessity of the movement from one to the other, drama would lack all urgency and tension, all sense of expectancy, anticipation, foreboding, crisis, and doom. It would lack not only what makes tragic irony possible, but also what makes the drama itself effective as a temporal performance.

If we understand the temporality of drama—as involving organic movement plus consciousness of its necessity—it is easy to see that once again there is a perfect correspondence between the form and content of Sophocles' *Oedipus Tyrannus*. For the subject of *Oedipus Tyrannus* is, of course, organic growth. Sophocles does not present men ready-made on the stage; he lets them grow into men before our eyes. The hero's action is not separable from what he is; it makes him be, i.e., become, what he is. Man's character is no longer static and at all times open to sight here—as it was by and large in the oral epic—but it has depth, is capable and in need of development, and the tension between inner core and outer image animates man's life and makes self-unfolding his essence.

Furthermore, Oedipus' development is not only necessary organic growth, not even merely organic growth mediated by consciousness and self-consciousness—a critical attitude toward the present, a dissatisfaction with what is, and a conception of a better future, of further goals to strive for—but it is essentially a growth in self-consciousness. It is not only self-conscious self-unfolding, but a self-unfolding that is nothing but self-discovery. Self-consciousness is both the motive force and the goal of Oedipus' action.

This gives *Oedipus Tyrannus* its peculiar type of temporal structure. Through his action Oedipus moves beyond the present and into the future, but this movement into the future is in fact a movement back into his own past, a discovery of his own origins and true state of being. The play's end and goal is to reveal the beginning of the fateful sequence of events that the end brings to completion.[47] In the *Agamemnon* and the *Choephoroi* each actor reenacted the race's history; the past caught up with the actor and sealed his fate. In *Oedipus Tyrannus* Oedipus catches up with his own past and this discovery seals his fate: now that the past and present, which were hitherto incongruous, are brought together, Oedipus' history, his *historein* (literally: search, inquiry), the only action of the play, is over. Tiresias' prediction "this day shall give you birth and be your grave" (*OT* 438) is fulfilled as beginning and end, the origin and fulfillment of Oedipus, finally coincide.

It is instructive to compare the temporality of *Oedipus Tyrannus* with that of the *Agamemnon* and the *Choephoroi*. In discussing the latter I tried to show [48] that the actor's *ti draso?* implied a sense of the openness of the future, while Aeschylus' use of traditional myth limited this openness by predetermining the final outcome and thus excluding any real novelty. The predetermined telos of myth—"what is to come will come" (*Ag.* 1240)—together with the actor's consciousness of the critical moment provided two types of teleology— a conscious looking forward to an open future on the part of the actor, and the future being in fact determined and closed off by the myth given past—whose tension characterized the time structure of tragedy.

As we have just seen, we find the same double teleology in *Oedipus Tyrannus*. The hero's consciousness of the critical moment, his sense of the future's openness, is accompanied by the hero's past acts and inherent nature in fact closing off and predetermining that future. The action of the play, an action impelled by the hero's illusory sense of freedom, brings about the hero's discovery of how illusory his freedom is and how totally decisive his past. As Driver puts it, "Oedipus has freedom, therefore, only to discover the past . . . he has only the ironical freedom to discover his lack of it." [49]

So far, the temporal structure of *Agamemnon-Choephoroi* and *Oedipus Tyrannus* are similar. In all three plays the past overthrows the present and largely determines the future. Although this process takes time, that is all it takes; the outcome is predetermined whether those involved in the action know it or not. There are, however, important differences between the temporalities of these plays. In the *Agamemnon* and the *Choephoroi* both the critical moments—which in the end do not turn out to have been so critical after all—and the passing of time—which in the end changes nothing essential—seem ultimately of little significance and the importance of time itself is almost denied.[50] Not so in *Oedipus Tyrannus*. Even though Oedipus' future-directed discovery of his own past overthrows his present, and even though it is Oedipus' past acts and inherent nature that determine his future, the process of this discovery and the necessary unfolding of this determination produce significant change. Everything is not as it was before because the hero is not. Having caught up with his past, having equated himself with himself, his outward status with his inner reality, the hero has grown. He has come out of his crisis with an increased realization—increased self-awareness and increased authenticity—of his own being. He has withstood the crisis and passed the test with a real gain: he has become essential. The time that brought him to completion is from the point of view of the hero anything but wasted, it is supremely significant time.

Of course, one does Aeschylus an injustice by considering only the *Agamemnon* and the *Choephoroi* and not the trilogy as a whole. For in the *Oresteia* as a whole there is also real change and development. The subjects of the trilogy, the house, the city, and mankind itself, come out of the crisis, the critical turning point of their history, at a presumably higher, more civilized, and more humane level than they occupied before. But the Aeschylean solution is unconvincing because the change between the temporality of *Agamemnon-Choephoroi*—complete determination and no significant change—and that of the *Eumenides*—significant change but lack of causal determination and justification—makes the temporal structure of the trilogy as a whole inconsistent and the necessity of the development in the trilogy as a whole unexplained. What happens in the *Eumenides* did not lie in the womb of time in the *Agamemnon* and the *Choephoroi*.

Sophocles suceeds where Aeschylus fails because his sense of time is more consistent and allows for temporal determination as well as temporal development. And the reason it does lies in one all-important, though many-faceted, Sophoclean innovation: he compresses the action dramatically, temporally, and materially, from trilogy to single play, from a long period to a single day, from a succession of crises to a single crisis, and from the crisis of a race to that of a single individual. This concentration not only heightens the urgency and seriousness of the crisis but also makes its resolution internally necessary and justified.

To be sure, Agamemnon's, Clytemnestra's, Cassandra's, and Orestes' crises were serious enough for them. But they were not altogether serious dramatically, because they were not the main subject of the trilogy; they were not resolved except by implication;[51] and the final resolution was not brought about by the agents themselves but came from above and beyond their own powers. In contrast, Oedipus' crisis is urgent and serious not only to Oedipus—since it is a crisis of his own identity, a crisis in which his own life hangs in the balance—but also dramatically because it is the exclusive subject of the play. It is not the city's but Oedipus' own past that is being judged here, not the race's but his own present that is being overturned, and not the house's but his own future that is being decided and significantly changed.

And the resolution of the crisis is internally justified because it follows from the subject's—Oedipus'—own nature, because all the judging, overturning, and deciding is done by Oedipus himself. "All-seeing time has found you out against your will" (OT 1213), the chorus sings with its characteristic lack of comprehension. In fact it is not all-seeing time but Oedipus himself who did the finding out, and, no matter how terrible the truth is, it was not against Oedipus' will that the discovery took place. "Come what may, I must know who I am"; it is Oedipus' own nature that brings about the crisis, just as it is his own nature that the crisis concerns and develops to fullness. The temporal involvement of past-present-future, potentiality-actuality, beginning-middle-end that is formally characteristic of all drama becomes Oedipus' self involvement in Oedipus Tyrannus, the temporal unfolding Oedipus' self-unfolding, and the temporal crisis Oedipus' own crisis of identity.

While Sophocles did not create drama out of nothing—not even Aeschylus did that—it is not too much to say that in every respect—and how difficult the diverse aspects of Sophoclean drama are to separate we have just seen—he perfected it and set an imperishable pattern for all drama by establishing a complete correspondence between form and matter in *Oedipus Tyrannus:* the correspondence of the drama's form—crisis, action, growth—and its matter—the crisis of identity, self-cultivation, and self-conscious self-development of man.

One last word: Sophoclean tragedy is not only internally coherent, it is also appropriate externally; its form and content appropriately express the spirit of the time. The second half of the fifth century was a time of unprecedented moral, religious, and intellectual turbulence in Athens. All hitherto taken-for-granted ideas and beliefs, all uncritically accepted customs and conventions were suddenly being questioned, and the very presuppositions of human life that had seemed so firm a foundation suddenly seemed to give way. The critical attitude toward the past that had until now characterized only a few exceptional individuals, poets and philosophers like Hesiod, Solon, Xenophanes, Heracleitus, and Aeschylus, now became general. And it was this public crisis of morality that Sophocles put on the communal stage.

The Greeks were experiencing a crisis of identity, and so was the Sophoclean Oedipus. The Greeks had to scrutinize and reevaluate their past, judge their present, and find new directions for the future, and so had Oedipus in *Oedipus Tyrannus.* The Greeks were disoriented; they had become conscious of the ambiguity of their hitherto clear-cut distinctions and of a possible incongruity between seeming and being, image and reality, apparent status and true excellence, and so had Oedipus. The self-doubt and self-conscious self-reappraisal of a whole nation was concentrated and given a crystallized expression in *Oedipus Tyrannus;* the trial of Athens was put on the stage in the trial of Oedipus.

Tragedy is by its very nature a representation of transition and conflict and is thus a genre appropriate to and flourishing at times of spiritual crisis and transition. This is as true of the Aeschylean *Oresteia* as it is of the Sophoclean plays. But whereas the excessive optimism of the Aeschylean solution in the *Eumenides* just about put an end to tragedy itself, the Sophoclean solution implies that moral ambiguity, crisis, and tragedy itself are something man has to live with. This makes the *Oedipus Tyrannus* not only more co-herent—since as tragedy it affirms tragedy—and more realistic—in that it does not offer illusory solutions but rather shows all final solutions to be themselves illusory—but in the end also more posi-tive and life affirming: crises are not only the stuff of life here, but coping with them and growing through their resolution is the es-sence of life, the function of man. And it is a function that each individual has to fulfill himself. The burden of self-development lies first and foremost on the individual and only secondarily on the community as a whole. Thus in *Oedipus Tyrannus* the individual, for all his weakness, and within the limits that nature and society impose on him, is freer (from others), more responsible (to himself) and more self-sufficient than ever before. What is most essential to him depends primarily on himself. Sophocles' solution to Oedipus' crisis is the best solution not only to the contemporary Athenian crisis but also to the perennial crisis of being a man.

That is why discussing the *Oedipus Tyrannus* provides a fitting conclusion to this study of how Greek self-consciousness grew and developed from Homer to Sophocles. The *Oedipus Tyrannus* puts this subject on the stage as the growth and development of one man's self-consciousness, and represents the historical process of the Greeks' self-critical reflection on their past achievements within and as one man's history. Sophocles not only compresses and crystallizes in Oedipus' person and life the history of a whole culture but he also shows the ideal of human culture to be nothing but human culture: the process of the self-cultivation of man.[52]

Notes

NOTES TO CHAPTER 1

1. *Aletheia* from *a-* (privative) *lanthano* (to escape notice, to be unseen, forgotten).

2. The supposition that the poem was first written down generations after its "composition" we may dismiss out of hand, since we are dealing with our *Iliad,* the written one, which in its fixed form would be necessarily different from earlier oral, and therefore unstable, versions of it. For the purposes of this study "Homer" means simply the last poet who had to do with the shaping of the *Iliad* as we have it and had therefore a close connection with its actual writing.

3. Albert B. Lord, *The Singer of Tales* (Cambridge, Mass., 1960), p. 151.

4. The first line of the poem names the theme, the first book tells us about Achilles' wrath from its origin to its forecasted resolution. But then, from the middle of Book 2 to the beginning of Book 8 just about nothing happens that strictly belongs to this theme. Achilles drops out of the story, and the events that take place are for the most part irrelevant or even contrary to Zeus' announced plan, the defeat of the Achaians in the absence of Achilles.

5. James A. Notopoulos puts it at twenty-seven ("Studies in Early Greek Oral Poetry," *Harvard Studies in Classical Philology* 68 [1964]: 6) but the length of time would vary with individual singers.

6. *"Ton hamothen ge,"* Homer, *Odyssey* 1.10.

7. Wolfgang Schadewaldt, *Von Homers Welt und Werk,* 4th ed. (Stuttgart, 1965), p. 267.

8. Erich Auerbach, *Mimesis* (Princeton, 1954), p. 7.

9. See Hermann F. Fraenkel, *Wege und Formen fruehgriechischen Denkens* (Munich, 1955), p. 1. It is true that in Homer *"chronos"* means duration, much time, but the emphasis here is entirely negative: empty time

when no action takes place, when nothing happens. It has the temporality of the time between two instant locations of Zeno's arrow. Paratactic epic could handle his "time" no better than Zeno's paradox based on atomicity.

10. See Owen Barfield, *Poetic Diction* (London, 1928), p. 151.

11. William B. Stanford, *Greek Metaphor* (Oxford, 1936), p. 126.

12. *Ibid.,* p. 121.

13. *Ibid.,* p. 127.

14. Bruno Snell, *The Discovery of Mind* (Cambridge, Mass., 1953), p. 6. On the subject of the Homeric self read the whole of this chapter, to which I am indebted.

15. *"Alla ti moi tauta dielexato thymos",* another well-worn formula (11.407, 17.97, 21.562, 22.122, 22.385, etc.).

16. Cedric Whitman, *Homer and the Heroic Tradition* (Cambridge, Mass., 1958), p. 221.

17. I am aware of the fact that many readers see real growth in Achilles' character, an inner development gradually taking place in the unfolding of the poem as a whole. But even if there were such growth, it could be perceived and appreciated only by the reader who has an overview of all the books of the *Iliad* and not by the oral audience who are exposed to the poem piecemeal, hearing only a few episodes at most at any one time. Therefore, if we postulated such growth, we would have to say that Homer is already exploiting here the possibilities inherent in written rather than oral composition and transmission. This is not an inherently implausible view; the only reason I cannot agree with it is that I simply fail to see much development in Achilles', let alone anyone else's, character in the *Iliad*. The poem's first line speaks of Achilles' wrath, and wrath is Achilles' dominant characteristic all through the poem. Whether he is actually raging or merely nursing his wounded pride, he is full of anger and is constantly reproached for this even by his best friends; in Book 24 the very gods are offended by the ruthless cruelty, pitilessness, and madness of his heart and order him to desist. To be sure there are moments and episodes in the *Iliad* when Achilles is shown to be almost humane and conscious of his common humanity with other men. But these are moments when his wrath is temporarily suspended awaiting greater fulfillment, or his vengefulness is temporarily sated by recent revenge. And these moments, these aspects of Achilles' personality seem to me simply paratactically arranged rather than hypotactically ordered in an interconnected and irreversible sequence of organic development.

18. For a discussion of stock scenes see Walter Arend, *Die typischen Scenen bei Homer* (Berlin, 1933); also Bernard Fenik, *Typical Battlescenes in the Iliad* (Wiesbaden, 1968).

19. Eric R. Dodds, *The Greeks and the Irrational* (Berkeley, 1951), p. 20, n. 31. The same point is made by Snell, *Discovery,* Chapters I and II.

20. Cf. Werner Jaeger, *Paideia*, vol. 1 (New York, 1945), pp. 8–9.
21. Adam Parry, "The Language of Achilles" *Transactions, American Philological Association* 87 (1956): 3–4.
22. See Adam Parry, "Have We Homer's 'Iliad'?" *Yale Classical Studies* 20 (1966): 192–4.
23. Paolo Vivante, "Homer and the Aesthetic Moment," *Arion* 4 (1965): 422.
24. A piece of pottery is a small, easily overseeable unit, all of whose decorative parts can be seen almost simultaneously, and thus its maker can visualize and its viewer see the total design of the pot all at once. As such its composition is more comparable to that of an episode than that of the monumental oral poem. The latter would be more like an immense frieze that it might take two days' march to view and God knows how long to compose. And even here the analogy is not perfect for the frieze would still have a fixity which the oral poem lacks. Speculating about such a frieze which could be viewed only piecemeal on successive short visits one would have to say that, as long as the whole could never be seen as a whole, a loose episodic unity, like that of the oral poem, would be more functional in its composition than any unitary, large-scale overall design.
25. Whitman, *Homer*, p. 96.
26. Snell, *Discovery*, p. 40.
27. *Ibid.*
28. Erland Ehnmark, *The Idea of God in Homer* (Uppsala, 1935), p. 10.
29. See Francis M. Cornford, *From Religion to Philosophy* (New York, 1912), p. 37; Martin P. Nilsson, *Geschichte der griechischen Religion* (Munich, 1941), p. 166; Vivante, "Homer and the Aesthetic Moment," p. 430.
30. Implicit evidence of this development from natural forces to personal gods in the *Iliad*: nature-powers appear as ancestors of the Olympians; the older gods, including Zeus, bear traces of nature functions while the newer ones do not. Zeus, for example, is still the lord of the skies, clouds, lightning, thunder. He cannot easily subdue Poseidon because his vestigial elemental function gives him little control over the lord of the sea, who has "equal share" with him (15.209; see also the allocation of natural functions to Zeus, Poseidon, and Hades 15.189). Yet elemental function is no longer the source of power or the exclusive domain of operation. Zeus could, if he tried hard enough, subdue Poseidon in this case, while in most others, even though he is still called Ouranios, his power does not seem to be specially connected with or restricted to the skies.
31. Robert Graves, *The Anger of Achilles* (Cassel, 1959), pp. xiv–xvii.
32. Myron J. Luch, *The Homeric Olympus* (Philadelphia, 1925), pp. 222, 225.
33. William E. Gladstone, *Iuventus Mundi* (Boston, 1869), p. 208.
34. Achilles' behavior toward Agamemnon and the Achaians is, incidentally, very like that of Apollo. Countless Greeks have to die to punish Agamemnon and increase Achilles' own glory.

35. Dodds, *The Greeks and the Irrational*, p. 32.
36. It is no change of subject for Achilles to say "and in one honor are held both the coward and the brave" immediately after "like portion receives he who stays home and he who exerts himself in fight" (9.318), for one's portion is equivalent to honor here. This is what Phoenix also points out in his answer: "if without gifts you enter the battle . . . you shall not then be in like honor" (9.604). On the identification of *moira* and *time*, see Leitzke, "Moira und Gottheit" (Ph.D. diss. Gœttingen, 1930), pp. 7–8.
37. "To be a speaker of words and a doer of deeds" (9.443) is at times considered Homer's heroic ideal. What is seldom noticed is how inseparable the two terms are here in both human and divine morality; that deeds unseen, unproclaimed, unheard of, and therefore unremembered, unadmired and uncelebrated by the human-divine community are hardly deeds at all; even the doer cannot be proud of them for pride is a social category in the *Iliad*. Unrecognized and unshared or unenvied it counts for nothing.
38. Cf., for example, Agamemnon's words 1.185–7.
39. See Kurt Latte, "Schuld und Suende in der griechischen Religion" *Archiv fuer Religionswissenschaft* 20 (1920–21): 254–298.
40. See Nilsson, *Geschichte*, p. 339.
41. See, for example, Poseidon's complaint 15.185–95.
42. An exception to this is Agamemnon's apology (19.86–7). To make doubly sure of his own blamelessness, Agamemnon accuses Zeus, *moira*, and *erinys* all in one breath of having put *ate* in his heart.
43. See Nilsson, *Geschichte*, pp. 340–42; Walter Poetscher, "Moira, Themis und *time* im homerischen Denken," *Wiener Studien* 73 (1960): 24.
44. This is far from being just a Homeric problem. The theological difficulties created by the lawlessness of personal gods and the obscurity of their relationship to irreversible order were quite evident to Kierkegaard. Intent on saving faith as a personal relationship to a personal god—not the god of law but the I-am-that-I-am above and beyond the law—and aware of the fact that no personal relationship between god and men was needed in a world where law was absolute, Kierkegaard quite consistently insisted on the teleological suspension of law in faith.
45. See Whitman, *Homer*, p. 241; Hermann F. Fraenkel, *Dichtung und Philosophie* (Munich, 1962), pp. 77–78.
46. Cf. Eric Vegelin, *Order and History*, vol. 2 (Baton Rouge, 1956), pp. 85–6.
47. Cf. *Odyssey*, 24.93–4: "even in death you have not lost your name, but forever there will be glory for you among mankind, Achilles"; *Iliad* 22.304–5, Hector at the brink of death: "Let me not perish without struggle and without glory, but rather doing something great for future men to hear of"; and Achilles' choice (9.410): *kleos aphthiton* (imperishable fame) or long life.

48. The Homeric Hades is a realm of darkness. Whatever remains of the hero is a flitting shade "existing" unseen by men; to the Homeric man who wants to be conspicuous above all this is clearly a state equivalent to death rather than life. That is why the Homeric formula for death is "to be enfolded in darkness," to see and to be seen no more.
49. Whitman, *Homer*, p. 240.
50. On this and the following see Voegelin, *Order*, vol. 2, pp. 86–9.
51. Schadewaldt, *Von Homer's Welt*, p. 351; Nilsson, *Geschichte*, pp. 265–75.
52. Parry, "The Language of Achilles," p. 7.
53. See Hegel's *Phenomenology* on Lordship and Bondage.
54. My reason for omitting a detailed discussion of the *Odyssey* and the *Theogony* is to bring into sharp relief the contrast between the first and the last of the four great poems of Homer and Hesiod. Given the fact that all four works are a mixed form of composition, i.e., that even the *Iliad*, in the form in which we have it, is not the product of an exclusively oral culture (see p. 4), and that even the *Erga* bears some of the marks of the oral tradition which Hesiod gradually overcomes as he develops his new style of writing and thinking (see pp. 64–65), the best strategy seemed to me to concentrate on the first, and therefore presumably most oral, and the last, and presumably most literate, of these works. By contrasting them I hoped to make the differences between the two modes of communication and thought as clear as possible. Once this is done, the reader can apply the thus esablished oral-literate parameters to the intervening epics so as to test the hypothesis and to see where exactly these poems fit into the developmental scheme fixed by the *Iliad* and the *Erga* as the outer limits. For me to do this here would be counter to the purpose of this study which is to deal only with the highlights and most significant turning points in the history of early Greek thought.

NOTES TO CHAPTER 2

1. See below pp. 67–68.
2. Thomas G. Rosenmeyer, "Hesiod and Historiography," *Hermes* 85 (1957): 280.
3. *Ibid.*, p. 265.
4. See Bernard A. van Groningen, *La composition littéraire archaïque grecque* (Amsterdam, 1960), p. 287.

5. See Jaeger, *Paideia,* vol. 1, p. 73.

6. For commentators who emphasize this unity see Paul Friedlaender, "Hypothekai," *Hermes* 48 (1913): 558–572; Wilhelm Schmid, *Geschichte der griechischen Literatur* (Munich, 1934); Friedrich Solmsen, "The 'Days' of the *Works and Days,*" *Transactions, American Philological Association* (hereafter abbreviated *TAPA*) 94 (1963): 293–320; Jula Kerschensteiner, "Zu Aufbau und Gedankenfuehrung von Hesiods Erga," *Hermes* 79 (1944): 149–191; Thomas A. Sinclair, *Hesiod, Works and Days* (Hildesheim, 1966).

7. Cf. Verdenius on word-association rather than thought-connection as the principle of Hesiodic composition: W. J. Verdenius, "Aufbau und Absicht der Erga," in Jan H. Waszink, *Hésiode et son influence* (Vandoeuvres-Genève, 1960) Fondation Hardt Entretiens vol. 7, p. 118. Kurt von Fritz too speaks of "schlechte Disposition, unlogische Gedankenfolge, mangelnde Ueberleitung" in Hesiod (*ibid.,* p. 44) and asserts that strict logical coherence cannot be insisted on as a criterion of what is and what is not Hesiodic in the poem.

8. See Inez Sellschopp, "Stilistische Untersuchungen zu Hesiod" (Ph.D. diss. Hamburg, 1934), p. 85.

9. The stories of Pandora and the five ages, though not strictly enigmatic, are nevertheless enigmas in this sense: it is not their literal truth but the underlying moral that is important in them. Literally, they obviously cannot both be true.

10. See Rosenmeyer, "Hesiod and Historiography," p. 267; Eduard Meyer, *Kleine Schriften* (Halle, 1924), pp. 18–19, 31; van Groningen, *La composition littéraire,* p. 288.

11. Sellschopp, "Stilistische Untersuchungen zu Hesiod," p. 41. See also pp. 35–41 on this.

12. See *ibid.,* pp. 24–27; also John A. Scott, "The Comparative Ages of Homer and Hesiod," *TAPA* 61 (1930): xxvi.

13. Sellschop, "Stilistische Untersuchungen zu Hesiod," p. 118.

14. On Hesiod's etymologies see E. Risch, "Namensdeutungen und Worterklaerungen bei den aeltesten griechischen Dichtern," Eugen Rentsch ed., *Eumusia,* Festgabe fuer Ernst Howald (Zurich, 1947), pp. 72–91.

15. See Fraenkel, *Wege und Formen fruehgriechischen Denkens,* p. 5.

16. See Fritz Krafft, *Vergleichende Untersuchungen zu Homer und Hesiod,* Hypomnemata 6 (Goettingen, 1963), pp. 25–58.

17. Sinclair, *Hesiod, Works and Days,* p. xi.

18. See B. Raphael Sealey, "From Phemios to Ion," *Revue des Etudes Grecques* 70 (1957): 336; Wolfgang Schadewaldt, *Von Homers Welt,* pp. 93–94; Sellschopp, "Stilistische Untersuchungen zu Hesiod," p. 9.

NOTES TO CHAPTER 3

1. See Cedric Whitman, *Aristophanes and the Comic Hero* (Cambridge, Mass., 1964), p. 38; Cecil M. Bowra, *Greek Lyric Poetry from Alcman to Simonides* (Oxford, 1936), pp. 13–14.
2. The numbering of Archilochus', Sappho's, and Solon's poems follows that of Ernst Diehl, *Anthologia Lyrica Graeca* (Leipzig, 1954).
3. See Frederic Will, "Archilochus and his Senses," *Classical Journal* 57 (1962): 295; Max Treu, *Von Homer zu Lyrik*, Zetemata 12 (Munich, 1968), p. 227; Emil Staiger, *Grundbegriffe der Poetik* (Zurich, 1946), pp. 46, 65; Hermann F. Fraenkel, *Dichtung und Philosophie des fruehen Griechentums* (Munich, 1962), p. 151.
4. See Bruno Snell, "Sapphos Gedicht phainetai moi kenos," *Hermes* 66 (1931): 87; Hermann Gundert, "Archilochos und Solon," in Helmut Berve, ed. *Das Neue Bild der Antike*, vol. 1 (Leipzig, 1942), p. 136.
5. Denys Page rightly emphasizes this in *Sappho and Alcaeus* (Oxford, 1955), pp. 18, 26, 86.
6. See Northrop Frye, *Anatomy of Criticism* (Princeton, 1957), pp. 273–78.

NOTES TO CHAPTER 4

1. Although the "laws of nature" were not yet explicitly formulated in Solon's time, to speak of a "natural" order is not anachronistic here. For certain inevitable causal sequences—lightning-thunder, wind-waves, fire-destruction—and unbroken regularities—e.g., the order of the seasons—were well enough known, and their uniformity and regularity was the best illustration for what Solon wanted to say about justice.
2. Friedrich Solmsen, *Hesiod and Aeschylus* (Ithaca, 1949), p. 121.
3. Although Solon does not yet use this term explicitly, he comes close to it in i.72–3 where he speaks of those who have most (*pleiston echousi*) and yet want more. At any rate, the notion of *pleonexia* is implicit in Solon's treatment of the striving for wealth as being essentially insatiable.
4. E.g., Gregory Vlastos, "Solonian Justice," *Classical Philology* 41 (1946): 76ff.

5. Between Jaeger and Ehrenberg.
6. Ivan M. Linforth, *Solon the Athenian* (Berkeley, 1919), p. 124.
7. Cf., Burkhard Gladigow, *Sophia und Kosmos* (Hildesheim, 1965), pp. 9–19.

NOTES TO CHAPTER 5

1. As Wilamowitz-Moellendorf once said. For further discussion of the cult of Dionysus the reader is referred, beyond the works mentioned in the following notes, to Erwin Rohde, *Psyche* (London and New York, 1925); Walter F. Otto, *Dionysus, Myth and Cult* (Bloomington, 1965); Eugen Fink, *Vom Wesen des Enthusiasmos* (Freiburg i. Br., 1947); Otto Kern, "Dionysos" in Georg Wissowa, ed. *Paulys Real-Encyclopaedie der classischen Altertumswissenschaft,* vol. 5 (Stuttgart, 1905), pp. 1010–1046.
2. See Reginald P. Winnington-Ingram, *Euripides and Dionysus* (Cambridge, 1948), p. 1; William K. C. Guthrie, *The Greeks and Their Gods* (London, 1950), p. 179; Eric R. Dodds, *Bacchae* (Oxford, 1944), p. x.
3. Winnington-Ingram, *Euripides and Dionysus,* p. 166. Also Eric R. Dodds, "Maenadism in the Bacchae," *Harvard Theological Review* 33 (1940) and A. Rapp, "Die Maenade im griechischen Cultus, in der Kunst und Poesie," *Rheinisches Museum* 27 (1872) *passim.*
4. William Arrowsmith's translation of *thiaseutai psychan (Bacchae* 75) in David Green, Richard Lattimore eds., *The Complete Greek Tragedies,* vol. 4 (Chicago, 1959).
5. See Ernst Buschor "Ein choregisches Denkmal," *Mitteilungen des deutschen archaeologischen Instituts Athenische Abteilung* 53 (1928): 103–107; Lewis R. Farnell, *Cults of the Greek States,* vol. 5 (Oxford, 1909), pp. 118–20; Nilsson, *Geschichte,* pp. 553, 559; Jane E. Harrison, *Prolegomena to the Study of Greek Religion* (Cambridge, 1908), p. 444; Carl Kerényi, *Der fruehe Dionysos* (Oslo, 1961). The fact that so many Dionysian festivals were trieteric, pentaeteric, and even enneaeteric also argues against this god being a god of the yearly return of vegetation.
6. Friedrich G. Juenger, *Griechische Mythen* (Frankfurt a/M, 1957), p. 175.
7. See Thomas G. Rosenmeyer, "Tragedy and Religion: *The Bacchae*" in Erich W. Segal ed., *Euripides* (Englewood Cliffs, 1968), p. 157.
8. Kerényi, *Der fruehe Dionysos,* pp. 9–11.

9. Heracleitus (15). Besides making fun of Euripides, Aristophanes may be alluding to this aspect of Dionysus in *Frogs* 1082, 1477. At any rate, it is not inappropriate that the god's Thracian worshipers should bemoan the birth and rejoice at the death—the ultimate liberation—of their fellow men (Herodotus 5.4).

10. Gerald F. Else, *The Origin and Early Form of Greek Tragedy* (Cambridge, Mass., 1965), p. 30.

11. Guthrie, *The Greeks and Their Gods*, p. 146.

12. Gilbert Murray, *Ancient Greek Literature* (New York, 1897), p. 272.

13. Winnington-Ingram, *Euripides and Dionysus*, p. 5.

14. See Plutarch *De ei apud Delphos* 9.388F–389C.

15. Cf. for example, Euripides, *Bacchae* 1617, or Aristophanes' take-off on Euripides' Dionysus in *Frogs* 289–91.

16. Plutarch, *De ei,* 9.389B.

17. Sophocles, *Antigone* 1115.

18. Plutarch, *De ei,* 389A.

19. Aeschylus' fragment 341 in August Nauck, *Tragicorum graecorum fragmenta* (Leipzig, 1889).

20. See, for example, Euripides, *Bacchae* 77–79, 125–29.

21. *Hai Bacchai sigosin,* Diogenianus' proverb in Ernst L. Leutsch, Friedrich W. Schneidewin eds. *Corpus Paroemiographorum Graecorum* (Goettingen, 1839–51), p. 222.

22. *Scholia Platonica* to Plato, *Republic* 394C.

23. Aeschylus' fragment 355 in Nauck, *Tragicorum graecorum fragmenta.*

24. *Hesychii Alexandrini Lexicon* on *turbasia;* also Pollux 4.105.

25. Aristotle, *Politics* 1341a21, b33ff.

26. *Ibid.,* 1342b2.

27. On this development see Arthur W. Pickard-Cambridge, *Dithyramb, Tragedy and Comedy* (Oxford 1962), pp. 1–38; Gerald F. Else, *Aristotle's Poetics: The Argument* (Cambridge, Mass., 1963), pp. 155–60; Roy C. Flickinger, *The Greek Theater and Its Drama* (Chicago, 1968), pp. 6–10; Ulrich von Wilamowitz-Moellendorf, *Glaube der Hellenen* (Berlin, 1931–32), pp. 79ff.; Henri Jeanmaire, *Dionysos, Histoire du culte de Bacchus* (Paris, 1951), pp. 232–44.

28. Plato, *Laws* 700B.

29. Whether the saying *ouden pros ton Dionyson* actually referred to the dithyramb and not just to tragedy is unclear. Zenobius 5.40 does apply it to the dithyramb.

30. Pickard-Cambridge, *Dithyramb, Tragedy and Comedy,* p. 97; see also Walther Kranz, *Stasimon* (Berlin, 1933), pp. 4ff.

31. This is what *exarchein* means in the *Iliad* (18.51, 316, 604–5; 24.720), possibly in Archilochus, and as late as Demosthenes *De corona* 259–60, where Aeschines leads the thiasos as *exarchos* and *proegemon* in shouting *euoi saboi.*

32. In Euripides, *Bacchae* 144 Dionysus is called *exarchos;* 115 he "leads the thiasos"; 920 he leads Pentheus as a kind of *kathegemon* (on this see Eric R. Dodds, *Bacchae* [Oxford, 1944] commentary on passage). In Sophocles, *Antigone* Dionysus is *"choragos* of the stars and *episkopos* of the night voices" (1146); in Aristophanes, *Frogs* 351 the chorus of *mystes* invokes Iacchus to lead the way. See also Kranz, *Stasimon,* pp 24, 33; Konrat Ziegler, "Tragoedia" in Georg Wissowa ed., *Paulys Real-Encyclopaedie der classischen Altertumswissenschaft* series 2, vol. 6 (Stuttgart, 1937), pp. 1906–9.

33. Plato, *Ion* 535–6.

34. A purgation of pity and fear, a purification and cleansing of such emotions, or their homeopathic reduction to measure and limit.

35. E.g., as a purification not of the audience's emotion but "of the tragic act by the demonstration that its motive was not *miaron*" (Else, *Aristotle's Poetics: The Argument,* p. 439); a clarification of human experience about pity and fear (Leon Golden, "Catharsis," *TAPA* 93 [1962]); or a cleansing that "removes the conditions that would cause bewilderment and pain and leaves something that is orderly and significant" (H. D. F. Kitto, "Catharsis," in Luitpold Wallach ed., *The Classical Tradition* [Ithaca, 1966], p. 147).

36. Even formally, the irreducible separateness of the actor—the individual who for all his connection with the chorus stands over against the chorus and the world—is never eliminated in tragedy. Far from being absorbed in the chorus as the individual is absorbed in the thiasos and ultimately in the god himself, the actor stands out and his isolation grows rather than diminishes as fifth-century tragedy develops.

NOTES TO CHAPTER 6

1. The numbering of fragments from pre-Socratic philosophers follows Hermann Diels, *Die Fragmente der Vorsokratiker* 9th ed., edited by Walther Kranz (Berlin, 1960). Direct fragments are cited simply by number, indirect evidence by number with prefix A (e.g., A 35) indicating their source in the "Leben und Lehre" section.

2. William K. C. Guthrie argues (*History of Greek Philosophy* vol. 1 [Cambridge, 1962], pp. 376–79) that Xenophanes' god had body rather than being incorporeal. Yet in the only fragments where Xenophanes has

occasion to speak of the *demas*—body, stature, figure, shape—of god he does so negatively. In 14 he chides men's mistaken view that gods have clothes and voices and bodies like their own, and in 23 he says that god is neither in shape like man nor in thought. (Cf. also Clement of Alexandria, *Stromateis* 5.109).

Even if from these fragments we were to conclude that Xenophanes' god had body—and I do not think this conclusion is inescapable—it would have to be emphasized that this body is in no way like any observable body we encounter in the world. It is ungenerated, unmoving, unarticulated, and devoid of perceivable characteristics. It works, as even Guthrie admits, by "intellection alone" (Guthrie, *History of Greek Philosophy,* p. 402; see also Hermann F. Fraenkel, *Dichtung und Philosophie,* p. 378). As such it is at best a metaphysical rather than physical entity, an unimaginable, hardly even conceivable shape or form.

3. See Martin Heidegger, *Vortraege und Aufsaetze* (Pfullingen, 1954), pp. 219–20, 221.

4. See Olof A. Gigon, *Ursprung der griechischen Philosophie* (Basel, 1968), p. 113.

5. Gregory Vlastos, "Equality and Justice in Early Greek Cosmogonies," *Classical Philology* 42 (1947): 156.

6. *Ibid.*

7. Hermann Diels, *Herakleitos von Ephesos* (Berlin, 1909), p. xiii.

8. Bruno Snell, *Discovery of Mind,* p. 220.

9. I am indebted to Snell's and Hoelscher's excellent studies on Heracleitus' language: Bruno Snell, "Die Sprache des Heraklit," *Hermes* 61 (1926): 353–381; and Uvo Hoelscher, "Der Logos bei Heraklit," in *Varia Variorum* Festgabe fuer Karl Reinhardt (Muenster, 1952), pp. 69–81.

10. Robert S. Brumbaugh, *The Philosophers of Greece* (New York 1964), p. 44.

11. "Metaphoric" usage is not quite the word for what Heracleitus attempts here; there are in fact few metaphors in the strict sense in the fragments. It might be more correct to say that Heracleitus goes beyond the metaphor and accomplishes what the metaphor is intended to accomplish with an even greater economy: using one word, instead of combining several, he manages to fuse its diverse and often conflicting connotations together even while keeping them apart and implying each individually as well as stressing all of them together and thereby creating new meaning.

12. Since the preceding notes fail to indicate my indebtedness to a great number of secondary sources, I would like to list in addition a few general works whose study I found rewarding with respect to Heracleitus' thought: William K. C. Guthrie, *History of Greek Philosophy;* Fraenkel, *Dichtung und Philosophie;* Burkhard Gladigow, *Sophia und Kosmos* (Hildesheim, 1965); Georg Misch, *The Dawn of Philosophy* (Cambridge,

Mass., 1951); Geoffrey S. Kirk and John E. Raven, *The Presocratic Philosophers* (Cambridge, 1957).

13. See Alexander P. Mourelatos, *The Route of Parmenides* (New Haven, 1970), pp. 3–4.

14. The causal, syllogistic, argumentative *gar*—for, since, as—is used twenty-one times in the seventy-six lines paraphrased above; *epei,* a similar argumentative conjunction, is used six times. In contrast, Homer uses *gar* four times, *epei* only once in the first seventy-six lines of the *Iliad.*

NOTES TO CHAPTER 7

1. Werner Jaeger, *Paideia* vol. 1 (New York, 1945), p. 252.
2. See Dieter Kaufmann-Buehler, *Begriff und Funktion der Dike in den Tragoedien des Aischylos* (Bonn, 1955), pp. 27ff.; also Leon Golden, "Zeus, whoever he is . . ." *TAPA* 92 (1961): 161–64.
3. William Whallon, "Why is Artemis Angry?" *American Journal of Philology* 82 (1961): 82.
4. As William B. Stanford points out (*Greek Metaphor* [Oxford, 1936], p. 148), *Ag.* 136–8 can and should be read as referring to both eagle and Agamemnon, hare and Iphigeneia at the same time: "sacrificing a helpless hare with her unborn brood" and "sacrificing a poor trembling victim, his own child."
5. Whallon, "Why is Artemis Angry?" p. 80.
6. Albin Lesky, *Geschichte der griechischen Literatur* (Bern, 1957–8) p. 277.
7. Bruno Snell, *Aischylos und das Handeln im Drama,* Philologus Supplementenband 20 (Leipzig, 1928).
8. Eric R. Dodds, "Morals and Politics in the 'Oresteia,' " *Proceedings Cambridge Philological Society* 186 (1960): 30; cf. also Wolfgang Schadewaldt, "Der Kommos in Aischylos' Choephoren," *Hermes* 67 (1932): "Staerker als das Schicksal selber, das den Menschen betroffen hat, trifft ihn dann der Widersinn, der scheinbar in dem Schicksal wirkt" (p. 331).
9. On this see Burkhard Gladigow, *Sophia und Kosmos,* p. 128ff.; Snell, *Aischylos und das Handeln im Drama,* pp. 118–9; Wilhelm Nestle, "Menschliche Existenz und politische Erziehung in den Tragoedien des Aischylos," *Tuebinger Beitraege* 23 (1934): 35–6.
10. With the exception of *Ag.* 750–81, which passage is quite reminiscent of

Hesiod and Solon both in content and in the technique of antithetical description. Yet this passage is unsupported by the events of the play itself and remains, at least in the *Agamemnon* and the *Choephoroi,* a pious hope.

11. See Snell, *Aischylos und das Handeln im Drama,* p. 41; Jacqueline de Romilly, *La crainte et l'angoisse dans la théâtre d'Eschyle* (Paris, 1958).

12. Romilly, *La crainte et l'angoisse,* p. 58.

13. *Ibid.,* p. 91.

14. See Gilbert Murray, *Aeschylus the Creator of Tragedy* (Oxford, 1940), p. 199; Schmid, *Geschichte der griechischen Literatur,* p. 226.

15. Cf. Schadewaldt, "Der Kommos in Aischylos' Choephoren," p. 322; Frye, *Anatomy of Criticism,* p. 209.

16. Kurt von Fritz, *Antike und moderne Tragoedie* (Berlin, 1962), p. 9.

17. Cf. Kurt Latte, "Schuld und Suende in der griechischen Religion," p. 275.

18. Jaeger, *Paideia,* vol. 1, p. 260ff.

19. For an extensive discussion see Karl Reinhardt, *Aischylos als Regisseur und Theologe* (Bern, 1949), Chapter 3; also Snell, *Aischylos und das Handeln im Drama,* pp. 112–3; George D. Thomson, *The Oresteia of Aeschylus* (Amsterdam, 1966), vol. 1, pp. 19–20; Georges Méautis, *Eschyle et la trilogie* (Paris, 1936), p. 124.

20. On particular resemblances of detail between Heracleitus and Aeschylus see Burkhard Gladigow, "Aischylos und Heraklit," *Archiv fuer Geschichte der Philosophie* 44 (1962).

21. Aristotle, *Poetics* 1449a16ff.

22. On the problem of the second and third actor and their genetic connection with true drama, see Gerald F. Else, "The Case of the Third Actor," *TAPA* 76 (1945); "Aristotle and Satyr-Play" *TAPA* 70 (1939): 153; "Hypokrites" *Wiener Studien* 72 (1959); *Origin and Early Form of Greek Tragedy* (Cambridge, Mass., 1965). Also Albin Lesky, *Greek Tragedy* (London, 1965), p. 49; John D. Denniston, Denys Page eds. *Agamemnon* (Oxford, 1957), p. xvii; Arthur W. Pickard-Cambridge, *The Dramatic Festivals of Athens* (London, 1968), pp. 126–32.

23. Latte, "Schuld und Suende in der griechischen Religion," p. 261.

24. Cf. Frye, *Anatomy of Criticism,* pp. 38–41, 213.

25. Latte, "Schuld und Suende," p. 270.

26. John H. Finley, *Pindar and Aeschylus* (Cambridge, Mass., 1955), p. 181.

27. Pp. 168–69 above.

28. John P. Mahaffy, *A History of Classical Greek Literature,* vol. 1, (London and New York, 1890–1), pp. 50–51.

29. Sophocles on Aeschylus in *Vita.*

30. On Aeschylus' use of the net image see Otto Hiltbrunner, *Wiederholungs-ung Motivtechnik bei Aischylos* (Bern, 1950), pp. 61–2.

NOTES TO CHAPTER 8

1. Antigone's position as the defender of chthonic law against civic ordinances is by no means unambiguous. It is true that the laws of kinship demanded the burial of a near relative under pain of pollution, yet the same laws declared the fratricide polluted and made him an outcast whose presence, dead or alive, would bring miasma on the whole city. It is true that the gods below frowned upon all interference with the funeral rites, yet the same gods were equally offended by someone who, like Polynices, "sought to destroy his fathers' land, the shrines of his race's gods, sought to drink kindred blood" (*Antigone* 199) and thus, by intention and by deed (of fratricide) denied and outraged the very blood-ties which Antigone claims to uphold by her act. On the merits of Polynices' case alone, Creon can rightly regard his decree as no less god-fearing than Antigone deems her defiance to be.

   Creon can be accused of attempting to make himself not only the lawful arbiter of civil affairs but the "measure" of the gods, for in the manner of contemporary enlightenment he tries to impose human norms even on the gods, demanding that divinity conform to man's conception of justice (*Antigone* 282–289, 520) and rational purity (*Antigone* 1043–44). But Antigone can be considered as doing no less, for, inflexibly upholding her own individual religious and moral insight against the state and against the advice of all, she makes herself just as much a measure of the gods as does Creon.

   The Hegelian interpretation of the conflict in the *Antigone* as one between two equally, though only partially, valid rights may not do justice to the play as a whole, but there is a great deal in the actual arguments themselves to justify such an interpretation.

2. The *Antigone's* enactment of the *physis-nomos* controversy and its presentation of the arguments on either side of the question are as Sophistic as anything can be. So is the first stasimon's praise of man. Although in the end Sophocles goes beyond Sophistry, the *Antigone* shows that he was not only acquainted with Sophistic theses and techniques, but also perfectly able and willing to use them for his own purposes

3. See, for example, Cedric Whitman, *Sophocles; A Study of Heroic Humanism* (Cambridge, Mass., 1951); Gerhard Mueller, "Chor und Handlung bei den griechischen Tragikern," in Hans Diller, *Sophokles* (Darmstadt, 1967), pp. 220–228.

4. One notable exception is Gerhard Mueller's commentary, *Sophokles: Antigone* (Heidelberg, 1967), pp. 81ff.

5. Gordon M. Kirkwood, *A Study of Sophoclean Drama* (Ithaca, 1958), p. 207.

6. Lesky, Heidegger, Knox, and Mueller rightly emphasize the double connotation of *deinon*.

7. This is where Hoelderlin's and Heidegger's translations do more justice to the deeper sense of *Antigone* 360 than do the straight translations (see Martin Heidegger, *Einfuehrung in die Metaphysik* [Tuebingen, 1953], pp. 112–126). But, as their translation destroys the unconscious irony of the choral ode, the orthodox translation is still preferable, provided it is accompanied by a commentary that brings out the full ambiguity of the passage. Cf. Mueller's commentary (note 4 above) on *Antigone* 360.

8. In line with the deeper meaning of the oracle to Heracles in the *Trachiniae*.

9. As A. J. A. Waldock does in *Sophocles, the Dramatist* (Cambridge, 1966), p. 160.

10. *Ibid.,* p. 168.

11. See Wolfgang Schadewaldt, *Sophokles und das Leid* (Potsdam, 1948), p. 15 ff. "Das Ausgestossensein ist fuer den griechischen Menschen, dessen ganzer Lebensraum die miteinander wirkende Gemeinschaft ist, eine Art Tod, eine Art Hoelle, schlimmer als der Tod" (p. 16).

12. Implicitly he almost does when he takes it upon himself to answer the chorus's prayer to the gods (216ff.).

13. On this see Wolfgang Schadewaldt, *Sophokles und Athen* (Frankfurt/M, 1935), pp. 9–11; Karl Reinhardt, *Sophokles* (Frankfurt/M, 1947), p. 10; Heinrich Weinstock, *Sophokles* (Leipzig, 1931), p. 150.

14. Bernard M. W. Knox, *Oedipus at Thebes* (New Haven, 1957), p. 138.

15. Fate, gods, and oracles merely provide the external situation, the setting of the play, but Oedipus himself provides the drama, the action. See below, pp. 229ff.

16. See Schadewaldt, *Sophokles und das Leid*, p. 12.

17. See John P. Carrol "Some Remarks on the Questions in the *Oedipus Tyrannus*" *Classical Journal* 32 (1937).

18. See Reinhardt, *Sophokles*, p. 108.

19. Cf. Wolfgang Schadewaldt "Der Koenig Oedipos des Sophokles in neuer Deutung," *Schweizerische Monatshefte* 36 (1936): 21–31; Whitman, *Sophokles*, pp. 138–39.

20. This point is well developed in Bernard Knox, *The Heroic Temper* (Berkeley, 1966), pp. 15–18.

21. See Weinstock, *Sophokles*, p. 48; Hans Diller "Ueber das Selbstbewusstsein der sophokleischen Personen," *Wiener Studien* 69 (1956): 78; J. C. Kamerbeek "Individuum und Norm bei Sophokles," in Diller, *Sophokles*.

22. As applied to *Oedipus Tyrannus,* the modern discussion of freedom and necessity as exclusive terms confuses rather than clarifies the issue inasmuch as it imports inappropriate categories into the play. If freedom means, as it did for the fifth-century Greeks, acting in accordance with one's nature—as opposed to being constrained to act against it—and voluntary action is one in accord with one's will, resolve, and inmost desire,

then Oedipus's acts are both free and voluntary. But they are no less determined (from within) and necessary (by nature) for that.

On this see Reginald P. Winnington-Ingram "Tragedy and Greek Archaic Thought," in *Classical Drama and its Influence* ed. by M. J. Anderson (New York, 1965), p. 37; Thomas Gould "The Innocence of Oedipus," *Arion* 4–5 (1965–66): 481ff.; Weinstock, *Sophokles*, p. 231. Even Knox who insists on free will and responsibility as prerequisites of tragedy seems to mean no more by these than that Oedipus' decisions and actions, the causal factors in the tragic plot, are not externally determined but are "the expression of the character of Oedipus" (*Oedipus at Thebes*, p. 14).

23. On the innocence of Oedipus see Reinhardt, *Sophokles*, p. 144: Wilamowitz's introduction (p. 8) to his translation of *Oedipus Tyrannus* (Ullrich von Wilamowitz-Moellendorf, *Griechische Tragoedien Uebersetzt* [Berlin 1899–1929]); Weinstock, *Sophokles*, p. 158; Schmid, *Geschichte der griechischen Literatur*, p. 371; Whitman, *Sophocles*, p. 136.

24. See Frye, *Anatomy of Criticism*, p. 213; Weinstock, *Sophokles*, p. 175; Whitman, *Sophocles*, p. 122.

25. Whitman, *Sophocles*, Ch. VIII.

26. Knox, *Oedipus at Thebes*, p. 46.

27. *Ibid.*, p. 43.

28. See Kirkwood, *A Study*, pp. 72–78.

29. It is often noted that the *Oedipus Tyrannus's* oracles, unlike the Aeschylean ones, are unconditional; they predict with no ifs and buts what will happen.

30. See Kirkwood, *A Study*, pp. 179–85; H. D. F. Kitto, *Poiesis* (Berkeley, 1966), p. 203, 235 and *Greek Tragedy* (New York, 1961), p. 185; and Whitman: "[Sophocles] alone transcended even that form of anthropomorphism which demands that the gods satisfy human moral norms" *Sophocles*, p. 235.

31. Winnington-Ingram in "Tragedy and Greek Archaic Thought," p. 44.

32. On a similar contrast between Homer's gods and men, see above pp. 32–33.

33. Whitman, *Sophocles*, p. 119.

34. Weinstock, *Sophokles*, p. 292: "das der Mensch sich ins Wesentliche reinige. . . ."

35. Whitman, *Sophocles*, p. 139.

36. See Mueller, "Chor und Handlung bei den griechischen Tragikern," pp. 220–28; Whitman, *Sophocles*, p. 135.

37. See Kirkwood, *A Study*, p. 40.

38. See Aeschylus chapter above pp. 202–3.

39. See above pp. 203–5.

40. How pervasive it is is illustrated by the fact that even deliberate irony on Oedipus' part at times contains unconscious irony. Stanford points this

out with respect to Oedipus' intentionally ironic self-characterization (*OT* 392): "So Oedipus describes himself ironically, but—irony within irony—it is, in his present situation, the literal truth" (William B. Stanford, *Ambiguity in Greek Literature* [Oxford, 1939], p. 397). The same is true of Oedipus' deliberately ironic description of "trustworthy Creon, my ancient friend" (*OT* 385). Creon is in fact both trustworthy and friendly to Oedipus here, in spite of the latter's misguided suspicions.

41. Kirkwood, *A Study*, p. 248.
42. *Ibid.*, p. 253.
43. See Herbert Musurillo "Sunken Imagery in Sophocles' Oedipus," *American Journal of Philology* 78 (1957): 51.
44. In the *Erga* Hesiod abandoned mythmaking, and we have seen that the use of poetry as such was to some extent not coherent with his way of thinking, because he had an attitude toward civilized arbitration and rational thought that resembled Aeschylus'.
45. Tom Faw Driver, *The Sense of History in Greek and Shakespearean Drama* (New York, 1960), p. 5.
46. See above pp. 6–8.
47. Cf. Driver, *The Sense of History*, p. 56.
48. See above pp. 186–87.
49. Driver, *The Sense of History*, p. 167; also p. 166: In *Oedipus Tyrannus* "the future is closed . . . the past is dominant. It contains the facts which explain the present and the play, as it moves forward in time through the events of the terrible day, actually moves backward into the completely decisive past."
50. See above pp. 187–89.
51. With the exception of Orestes' crisis. But here too, the accent is not on Orestes; he is as good as forgotten by the time the resolution takes place.
52. This ideal, based on poetic insight and inspiration in Sophocles, is given philosophical foundation and articulation in Socratic thought. But that is a subject I have dealt with in *Socratic Humanism* (New Haven, 1963), a book to which the present study provides introduction and historical background.

Bibliography of
Modern Works Cited

Arend, Walter. *Die Typischen Scenen bei Homer*. Problemata 7. Berlin: Weidmann, 1933.

Auerbach, Erich. *Mimesis*. Princeton: Princeton University Press, 1954.

Barfield, Owen. *Poetic Diction*. London: Faber & Gwuyer, 1928.

Bowra, Cecil M. *Greek Lyric Poetry from Alcman to Simonides*. Oxford: Clarendon, 1936.

Brumbaugh, Robert S. *The Philosophers of Greece*. New York: Crowell, 1964.

Buschor, Ernst. "Ein choregisches Denkmal." *Mitteilungen des deutschen archaeologischen Instituts Athenische Abteilung* 53 (1928): 96–108.

Carrol, John P. "Some Remarks on the Questions in *Oedipus Tyrannus*." *Classical Journal* 32 (1937): 406–16.

Cornford, Francis M. *From Religion to Philosophy*. New York: Longmans, Green, 1912.

Diels, Hermann. *Herakleitos von Ephesos*. Berlin: Weidmann, 1909.

Diller, Hans, *Sophokles*. Darmstadt: Wissenschaftliche Buchgesellschaft, 1967.

——— "Ueber das Selbstbewusstsein der sophokleischen Personen." *Wiener Studien* 69 (1956): 70–85.

Dodds, Eric R. *Euripides, Bacchae*. Oxford: Clarendon, 1944.

——— *The Greeks and the Irrational*. Berkeley: University of California Press, 1951.

——— "Maenadism in the Bacchae." *Harvard Theological Review* 33 (1940): 155–176.

——— "Morals and Politics in the 'Oresteia.'" *Proceedings Cambridge Philological Society* 186 (1960): 19–31.

Driver, Tom Faw. *The Sense of History in Greek and Shakespearean Drama*. New York: Columbia University Press, 1960.

Ehnmark, Erland. *The Idea of God in Homer*. Uppsala: Almqvist & Wiksells, 1935.

Else, Gerald F. "Aristotle and Satyr-Play." *Transactions American Philological Association* 70 (1939): 139–57.

———— *Aristotle's Poetics: The Argument.* Cambridge, Mass.: Harvard University Press, 1963.

———— "The Case of the Third Actor." *Transactions American Philological Association* 76 (1945): 1–11.

———— "Hypokrites." *Wiener Studien* 72 (1959): 75–107.

———— *The Origin and Early Form of Greek Tragedy.* Cambridge, Mass.: Harvard University Press, 1963.

Farnell, Lewis R. *The Cults of the Greek States.* Oxford: Clarendon, 1909.

Fenik, Bernard. *Typical Battlescenes in the Iliad.* Wiesbaden: Steiner, 1968.

Fink, Eugen. *Vom Wesen des Enthusiasmos.* Freiburg i. Br.: Chamier, 1947.

Finley, John H. *Pindar and Aeschylus.* Cambridge, Mass.: Harvard University Press, 1955.

Flickinger, Roy C. *The Greek Theater and Its Drama.* Chicago: University of Chicago Press, 1968.

Fraenkel, Hermann F. *Dichtung und Philosophie des fruehen Griechentums.* Munich: Beck, 1962.

———— *Wege und Formen fruehgriechischen Denkens.* Munich: Beck, 1960.

Friedlaender, Paul. "Hypothekai." *Hermes* 48 (1913): 558–616.

Fritz, Kurt von. *Antike und moderne Tragoedie.* Berlin: de Gruyter, 1962.

Frye, Northrop. *Anatomy of Criticism.* Princeton: Princeton University Press, 1957.

Gigon, Olof A. *Ursprung der griechischen Philosophie.* Basel: Schwabe, 1968.

Gladigow, Burkhard. "Aischylos und Heraklit." *Archiv fuer Geschichte der Philosophie* 44 (1962): 225–239.

———— *Sophia und Kosmos.* Hildesheim: Olms, 1965.

Golden, Leon. "Catharsis." *Transactions American Philological Association* 93 (1962): 51–60.

———— "Zeus, whoever he is . . ." *Transactions American Philological Association* 92 (1961): 156–67.

Gould, Thomas. "The Innocence of Oedipus." *Arion* 4 (1965): 363–86, 582–611; 5 (1966): 478–525.

Groningen, Bernard A. van. *La composition littéraire archaïque grecque.* Amsterdam: Noord-Hollandsche Uitgevers Maatschappij, 1960.

Gundert, Herman. "Archilochos und Solon." in Helmut Berve, ed. *Das neue Bild der Antike.* vol. 1 Leipzig: Koehler & Amelang, 1942.

Guthrie, William K. C. *The Greeks and Their Gods.* London: Methuen, 1950.

———— *History of Greek Philosophy.* vol. 1 Cambridge: The University Press, 1962.

Harrison, Jane E. *Prolegomena to the Study of Greek Religion.* Cambridge: The University Press, 1908.

Heidegger, Martin. *Einfuehrung in die Metaphysik.* Tuebingen: Niemeyer, 1953.

———— *Vortrage und Aufsaetze.* Pfullingen: Neske, 1954.

Hiltbrunner, Otto. *Wiederholungs- und Motivtechnik bei Aischylos.* Bern: Francke, 1950.

Hoelscher, Uvo. "Der Logos bei Heraklit." in *Varia Variorum.* Festgabe fuer Karl Reinhardt. Muenster: Boehlau, 1952.

Jaeger, Werner. *Paideia*. New York: Oxford University Press, 1945.

Jeanmaire, Henri. *Dionysos: histoire de culte de Bacchus*. Paris: Payot, 1951.

Juenger, Friedrich G. *Griechische Mythen*. Frankfurt a/M: Klostermann, 1957.

Kamerbeek, J. C. "Individuum und Norm bei Sophokles." in Hans Diller, ed. *Sophokles*.

Kaufmann-Buehler, Dieter. *Begriff und Funktion der Dike in den Trageodien des Aischylos*. Bonn: Roehrscheid, 1955.

Kerenyi, Karl. *Der fruehe Dionysos*. Oslo: Eitrem, 1961.

Kern, Otto. "Dionysos." in Georg Wissowa, ed. *Paulys Real-Encyclopaedie der classischen Altertumswissenschaft*. vol. 5. Stuttgart: Metzler, 1905.

Kerschensteiner, Jula. "Zu Aufbau und Gedankenfuehrung von Hesiods Erga." *Hermes* 79 (1944): 149–91.

Kirk, Geoffrey S. and Raven, John E. *The Presocratic Philosophers*. Cambridge: The University Press, 1957.

Kirkwood, Gordon M. *A Study of Sophoclean Drama*. Ithaca: Cornell University Press, 1958.

Kitto, H. D. F. "Catharsis." in Luitpold Wallach, ed. *The Classical Tradition*. Ithaca: Cornell University Press, 1966.

——— *Greek Tragedy*. New York: Barnes & Noble, 1961.

——— *Poiesis*. Berkeley: University of California Press, 1966.

Knox, Bernard M. W. *The Heroic Temper*. Berkeley: University of California Press, 1966.

——— *Oedipus at Thebes*. New Haven: Yale University Press, 1957.

Krafft, Fritz. *Vergleichende Untersuchungen zu Homer und Hesiod*. Hypomnemata 6. Goettingen: Vandenhoeck & Ruprecht, 1963.

Kranz, Walther. *Stasimon*. Berlin: Weidmann, 1933.

Latte, Kurt. "Schuld und Suende in der griechischen Religion." *Archiv fuer Religionswissenschaft* 20 (1920–21): 254–98.

Lesky, Albin. *Geschichte der griechischen Literatur*. Bern: Francke, 1957–58.

——— *Greek Tragedy*. London: Benn, 1965.

Linforth, Ivan M. *Solon the Athenian*. Berkeley: University of California Press, 1919.

Lord, Albert B. *The Singer of Tales*. Cambridge, Mass.: Harvard University Press, 1960.

Méautis, Georges. *Eschyle et la trilogie*. Paris: Grasset, 1936.

Meyer, Eduard. *Kleine Schriften*. Halle: Niemeyer, 1924.

Misch, Georg. *The Dawn of Philosophy*. Cambridge, Mass.: Harvard University Press, 1951.

Mourelatos, Alexander P. *The Route of Parmenides*. New Haven: Yale University Press, 1970.

Mueller, Gerhard. "Chor und Handlung bei den griechischen Tragikern." in Hans Diller, ed. *Sophokles*.

——— *Sophokles: Antigone*. Heidelberg: Winter, 1967.

Murray, Gilbert. *Aeschylus the Creator of Tragedy*. Oxford: Clarendon, 1940.

————— *A History of Ancient Greek Literature.* New York: Appleton, 1897.

Musurillo, Herbert. "Sunken Imagery in Sophocles' *Oedipus.*" *American Journal of Philology* 78 (1957): 36–51.

Netsle, Wilhelm. "Menschliche Existenz und politische Erziehung in den Tragoedien des Aischylos." *Tuebinger Beitraege zur Altertumswissenschaft* 23 (1934): 1–99.

Nilsson, Martin P. *Geschichte der griechischen Religion.* Munich: Beck, 1941.

Notopoulos, James A. "Studies in Early Greek Oral Poetry." *Harvard Studies in Classical Philology* 68 (1964): 1–77.

Otto, Walter. *Dionysus, Myth and Cult.* Bloomington: Indiana University Press, 1965.

Page, Denys. *Sappho and Alcaeus.* Oxford: Clarendon, 1962.

————— and Denniston, John D. eds. *Agamemnon.* Oxford: Clarendon, 1957.

Parry, Adam. "Have we Homer's *Iliad?*" *Yale Classical Studies* 20 (1966): 175–216.

————— "The Language of Achilles." *Transactions American Philological Association* 87 (1956): 1–7.

Pickard-Cambridge, Arthur W. *Dithyramb, Tragedy and Comedy.* Oxford: Clarendon, 1962.

Poetscher, Walter. "Moira, Themis und *time* im homerischen Denken." *Wiener Studien* 73 (1960): 5–39.

Rapp, A. "Die Maenade im griechischen Cultus, in der Kunst und Poesie." *Rheinisches Museum* 27 (1872): 1–22; 562–611.

Reinhardt, Karl. *Aischylos als Regisseur und Theologe.* Bern: Francke, 1949.

————— *Sophokles.* Frankfurt a/M: Klostermann, 19

Rhode, Erwin. *Psyche.* 3rd ed. Tuebingen & Leipzig: Mohr, 1903.

Risch, E. "Namensdeutungen und Worterklaerungen bei den aeltesten griechischen Dichtern." *Eumusia.* Festgabe fuer Ernst Howald edited by Eugen Rentsch. Zurich, 1947.

Romilly, Jacqueline de. *La crainte et l'angoisse dans le théâtre d'Eschyle.* Paris: Les Belles Lettres, 1958.

Rosenmeyer, Thomas G. "Hesiod and Historiography." *Hermes* 85 (1957): 257–285.

————— "Tragedy and Religion: the *Bacchae.*" in Erich W. Segal, ed. *Euripides.* Englewood Cliffs: Prentice-Hall, 1968.

Schadewaldt, Wolfgang. "Der *Koenig Oedipus* des Sophokles in neuer Deutung." *Schweizerische Monatshefte* 36 (1936): 21–31.

————— "Der Komos in Aischylos' Choephoren." *Hermes* 67 (1932): 312–54.

————— *Sophokles und Athen.* Frankfurt a/M: Klostermann, 1935.

————— *Sophokles und das Leid.* Potsdam: Stichnote, 1948.

————— *Von Homers Welt und Werk.* 4th ed. Stuttgart: Koehler, 1965.

Schmid, Wilhelm. *Geschichte der griechischen Literatur.* Handbuch der Altertumswissenschaft section 7, part 1, vol. 4. Munich: Beck, 1934.

Sealey, Raphael B. "From Phemios to Ion." *Revue des Etudes Grecques* 70 (1957): 312–355.

Sellschopp, Inez. "Stillistische Untersuchungen zu Hesiod." Ph.D. diss. Hamburg, 1934.

Sinclair, Thomas A. *Hesiod, Works and Days.* Hildesheim: Olms, 1966.

Snell, Bruno. *Aischylos und das Handeln im Drama.* Philologus Supplement 20. Leipzig: Dieterich, 1928.

———— *The Discovery of the Mind.* Cambridge, Mass.: Harvard University Press, 1953.

———— 'Sapphos Gedicht phainetai moi kenos." *Hermes* 66 (1931): 71–90.

———— "Die Sprache des Heraklit." *Hermes* 61 (1926): 353–381.

Solmsen, Friedrich. "The 'Days' of the *Works and Days.*" *Transactions American Philological Association* 94 (1963): 293–320.

———— *Hesiod and Aeschylus.* Ithaca: Cornell University Press, 1949.

Staiger, Emil. *Grundbegriffe der Poetik.* Zurich: Atlantis, 1946.

Stanford, William B. *Ambiguity in Greek Literature.* Oxford: Blackwell, 1939.

———— *Greek Metaphor.* Oxford: Blackwell, 1936.

Thomson, George D. *The Oresteia of Aeschylus.* Amsterdam: Hakkert, 1966.

Treu, Max. *Von Homer zu Lyrik.* Zetemata 12. Munich: Beck, 1968.

Vivante, Paolo. "Homer and the Aesthetic Moment." *Arion* 4 (1965): 415–438.

Vlastos, Gregory. "Equality and Justice in Early Greek Cosmogonies." *Classical Philology* 42 (1947): 156–178.

———— "Solonian Justice." *Classical Philology* 41 (1946): 65–83.

Voegelin, Eric. *Order and History.* Baton Rouge: Louisiana State University Press, 1956.

Waszink, Jan H. ed. *Hésiode et son influence.* Fondation Hardt Entretiens vol. 7. Vandoeuvres-Genève, 1960.

Weinstock, Heinrich. *Sophokles.* Leipzig: Teubner, 1931.

Whallon, William. "Why is Artemis Angry?" *American Journal of Philology* 82 (1961): 78–88.

Whitman, Cedric. *Aristophanes and the Comic Hero.* Cambridge, Mass.: Harvard University Press, 1964.

———— *Homer and the Heroic Tradition.* Cambridge, Mass.: Harvard University Press, 1958.

———— *Sophocles; A Study of Heroic Humanism.* Cambridge, Mass.: Harvard University Press, 1951.

Wilamowitz-Moellendorf, Ulrich von. *Glaube der Hellenen.* Berlin: Weidmann, 1931.

———— *Griechische Tragoedien Uebersetzt.* Berlin: Wiedmann, 1899–1929.

Will, Frederick. "Archilochus and His Senses." *Classical Journal* 57 (1962): 289–296.

Winnington-Ingram, Reginald P. *Euripides and Dionysus.* Cambridge: The University Press, 1948.

———— "Tragedy and Greek Archaic Thought." in M. J. Anderson, ed. *Classical Drama and its Influence.* New York: Barnes & Noble, 1965.

Ziegler, Konrat. "Tragoedia." in Georg Wissowa, ed. *Paulys Real-Encyclopaedie der classischen Altertumswissenschaft.* series 2, vol. 6. Stuttgart: Metzler, 1937.